TACKLING DISAFFECTION AND SOCIAL EXCLUSION

TACKLING DISAFFECTION AND SOCIAL EXCLUSION

EDUCATION PERSPECTIVES AND POLICIES

Edited by
Annette Hayton

Kogan Page Limited
120 Pentonville Road
London N1 9JN

British Library Cataloguing in Publication Data

A CIP record for this book is available from the British Library.

ISBN 0 7494 2889 9

Typeset by Saxon Graphics Ltd, Derby
Printed and bound by Clays Ltd, St Ives plc

Contents

Contents

Series Editors' Preface

The issue of social exclusion has been a major preoccupation of the New Labour Government since it came into power in May 1997, as it tries to deal with the legacy inherited from a long period of Conservative administration. One aspect of this legacy is the increase in disadvantage resulting from the pursuit of market-led policies. As this book points out, these policies have not only affected education, but also health, housing and the wider economy.

Tackling Disaffection and Social Exclusion: Education perspectives and policies has been included in the *Future of Education from 14+* series because the problem of social exclusion is critical for those involved in education policy and practice. Education has been seen by New Labour as a major tool for tackling the issue of social exclusion. What this book argues, however, is that the underlying factors involved are much broader and deeper than is often understood by policy-makers and that one area of social policy is unlikely, by itself, to be able to address the problem.

The book stresses the complexity of the issue of social exclusion and tries to confront this in at least three ways. First, it provides a number of different perspectives on the concept itself, including an examination of the concept of social exclusion in a European context. Second, the book discusses interpretations of what is still a very ill-defined, loosely used and contested term. Third, it opens up a debate about the underlying factors behind social exclusion and, in many chapters, draws out broad messages for education policy-makers.

In doing this, the book takes a wider view across the whole education and training system and is not, therefore, confined to the 14+ boundary associated with this series. As Series Editors, we see this as both necessary, because of the complexity of the issues involved, and beneficial, because it builds up a more comprehensive picture of the problem and its implications for the education and training system as a whole.

In stepping back from the immediate policy issues related to social exclusion, the book is able to take a longer perspective. It is tempting to see the issue in narrow political terms precisely because of its current policy prominence. However, the theoretical perspectives provided by many chapters in this book open up the analysis and suggest that the struggle for social inclusion is deep-rooted and historical. The implications of this analysis for policy-makers, therefore, are that the issue of social exclusion will need to be high on the governmental policy agenda for more than one term of office and that education measures will have to be reinforced by wider social and economic reforms if social exclusion is to be seriously addressed.

Ann Hodgson and Ken Spours
Institute of Education
University of London

Introduction

Annette Hayton

At the time of writing this introduction the New Labour government has been in power for nearly two years. New Labour's election victory was highly significant as it appeared to be the concrete expression of a nation-wide reaction against the materialistic and individualistic values of the 1980s and early 1990s that had kept the Conservatives in power. Certainly a concern with the plight of the homeless, the mentally ill and other vulnerable sections of society is no longer considered 'wet'. Rather there appears to be a general recognition that 'eighties' values are ultimately unable to meet the deeper needs of individuals and society as a whole. Of course this change may well have a material base in that, except for the very rich and very fortunate, most people have been adversely affected by the materialistic and individualistic policies they once supported. After 18 years the divisions between rich and poor are greater than ever and extreme poverty in some sections of society is a serious issue. Redundancy, unemployment, homelessness and housing problems, reductions in public transport and a decline in health services have affected most of the population in one way or another. Also, of course, there have been radical changes in the education and training system including the introduction of the National Curriculum, local management of schools and league tables, as well as changes in the qualification and funding systems for post-compulsory education. These policies were all based on a belief in the virtue of individual and institutional competition and the need for greater accountability through direct government control of the system.

Before the general election of 1997 New Labour made a brave attempt to formulate policies which reflected the concerns of the population and took account of changes in the economy and society as a whole – they were successful in that they won the election. Much was made of a 'Third Way' which would find new solutions to social and economic problems. Indeed, a return to 'Old Labour' or even old socialist policies for alleviating poverty and discrimination does not appear to be an option – cultural and economic changes would not even make these strategies desirable. For example, however much schools and colleges might, quite rightly, bemoan wasteful competition between institutions and call for a greater degree of collaboration and joint planning, it would be hard to find a school or college which would wish to return to the bureaucratic control of an old-style education authority. If we are to go forward in any meaningful sense new solutions have to be found. Since the election the concept of a 'Third Way' has been developed further and the ways in which it could form a basis for policy innovation to tackle social exclusion have also been expanded. However, after two years in office the way forward remains unclear.

Our particular concern in this book is to consider how far education can reduce inequality and social exclusion and to consider whether New Labour policies are adequate for the task. However, developing an education policy that combats social exclusion is not a task which lends itself to 'quick fix' solutions, as the contributions in this volume demonstrate. The authors have taken the opportunity to reflect on and reconsider some of the underlying issues in the light of broader social and economic changes that have taken place over recent years. This reassessment is particularly important at a time when we are searching for new ways of dealing with old problems.

Part 1: Social exclusion, education and training

Ann Hodgson sets the context for the debate by outlining some of the major policy initiatives of the last 30 years that were designed to tackle educational disadvantage. The final sections of her chapter consider some of New Labour's initiatives for tackling social exclusion. She also begins to unravel the ways in which the terms social exclusion, non-participation and disaffection are being used, often indiscriminately, in the current debate about educational underachievement. She offers working definitions of the three terms as they could be applied to education policy and demonstrates how they can be used to describe and define some specific educational problems and thus point to practical solutions. For example, she argues that the term 'non-participation' has a different meaning depending on whether it is applied to adults or young people under 16 in compulsory schooling. However, she also points to the danger of considering disaffection, non-participation and social exclusion separately when we are attempting to analyse the underlying causes of educational underachievement and disadvantage. The problem is that this separation could imply a simplistic 'cause and effect' perspective which is unable to offer an adequate analysis of the extremely complex relationship between education and wider society.

The problem of language and definitions bedevils the debate about social exclusion in the UK. The Social Exclusion Unit's definition is as follows:

> Social exclusion is a shorthand label for what can happen when individuals or areas suffer from a combination of linked problems, such as unemployment, poor skills, low incomes, poor housing, high crime environments, bad health and family breakdown.

> (SEU, 1999)

Until recently we were more likely to use terms such as discrimination, disadvantage, equal rights and perhaps even poverty, sexism and racism.

Tom Leney points out that this is not the case in Europe and quotes Lynne Chisholm who says that, in France at least, the term *L'Exclusion Sociale* has a long history. However, he also describes how the European Commission had a lengthy debate about whether its policies to tackle social exclusion should continue to be based only on the alleviation of poverty and unemployment or whether it should extend its policies to include a wider range of social measures. The latter course of action was decided upon but there remains a diversity of approach within the European Union that belies a clear definition.

In their chapter Eva Gamarnikow and Tony Green consider the limitations and possibilities for developing social capital in relation to education. In contrast to Margaret Thatcher's complete rejection of the term 'society' (*Woman's Own*, 31 October 1987) there is a recognition by New Labour that 'society' does exist and therefore solutions to social problems can at least be considered by government. One of the 'new' features of New Labour policy is the recognition that the development of social capital is an important aspect in tackling social disadvantage and should be welcomed. However, as Gamarnikow and Green point out, the concept of social capital is not unproblematic. There are a number of competing theoretical definitions stemming from differing economic and political perspectives that have very different policy implications. One interpretation of building social capital is the development of progressive notions of co-operation, empowerment and community action that, they argue, would support dynamic and sensitive state policy implementation. Alternatively, building social capital could be regarded as a solution to the perceived 'deficits' of inadequate individuals and groups who fail to live up to the accepted norms and values of society. This latter interpretation does not question how these accepted norms come about or which groups in society define them but it does imply that sanctions should be brought to bear against those who fail to 'conform'. As such the development of social capital would become just part of the rhetoric for social control rather than part of a strategy for social change.

Gamarnikow and Green then ask us to consider the concepts of economic, social and cultural capital developed by Bourdieu and Passeron that link the possession of cultural capital with class privilege. In this way the power relations of social structures are not obscured but solutions can be considered within the social and cultural arena. The concept of cultural capital has also been developed to describe how the power relations involved in gender and race inequalities can operate and therefore can be used to analyse these aspects of social exclusion as well as those associated with class. Gamarnikow and Green provide a framework within which to assess whether New Labour education policy is sufficiently focused to deal with the underlying causes of social inequality and use the example of Education Action Zones as a case study to explore the issue. They conclude that current policy appears to be more concerned with endorsing conventional 'success' within global capitalism than with exploring the critical possibilities of developing cultural capital.

Part 2: Developing education policy to tackle social exclusion

In their chapter Geoff Whitty and colleagues consider the connections between wider social and economic disadvantage and educational disadvantage. Sir Donald Acheson's recent report for Secretary of State for Health Frank Dobson demonstrated the depths of poverty amongst some sections of the population, finding it to be the main cause of health inequality in the UK today. Whitty *et al* point out that while poverty should not be used as an excuse for underachievement in education, this should not obscure the fact that it can be an explanation. They quote Robinson (1997) who argues that 'a serious programme to alleviate child poverty might do far more for boosting attainment . . . than any modest intervention in schooling'. However, they go on to show that education can have a positive impact on health and well-being through building social and cultural capital, and discuss some of the specific problems caused by health inequalities and homelessness. They conclude by emphasizing the importance of developing a multi-agency approach to tackling multiple disadvantages and welcome the government's talk of 'joined-up' policies to do so. However, they do stress that there are a number of lessons to be learnt from other initiatives that have set out with similar good intentions in the past.

Peter Mortimore and Geoff Whitty consider the limitations of the 'school improvement' approach in dealing with educational underachievement. The main criticism of this approach has been that it does not allow for critical thinking about curriculum content, the culture of schooling, or indeed what counts as legitimate knowledge in schools. If school improvement strategies ignore these structuring elements of the system, efforts to raise achievement and improve the way that schools run can, too easily, slip into strategies directed at 'deficient' individuals and institutions. An additional problem for the 'school improvement' approach has been the competitive context within which it has developed, which is exemplified by the introduction of league tables and more recently the 'naming and shaming' of failing schools. Although we all wish to see schools 'improve', it is extremely problematic if the measure of improvement is solely based on performance in the league tables. As Plewis (1998) has argued, within this framework overall improvement may result in an *increase* in the differences in performance between the most disadvantaged groups and other pupils. However, as Mortimore and Whitty point out, in a different context dynamic 'school improvement' initiatives could be developed as part of broader social policy to tackle educational disadvantage.

Gareth Parry and Heather Fry use their chapter to consider the potential of the recommendations in *The Learning Age,* the Government's Green Paper on post-compulsory education. Parry and Fry point out that *The Learning Age* appears to signal a significant shift away from the discourse of 'education and training' to promote national and individual competitiveness towards a more holistic notion of 'learning' that is concerned with personal well-being and social cohesion as well as economic success. *The Learning Age* was an ambitious attempt to draw together the various strands of thinking about post-compulsory education, the most notable being the reports of the Kennedy Commission on further education and the Dearing Inquiry into higher education. Parry and Fry consider the very different concerns and approaches of the two reports towards widening participation and creating a 'learning society'. They conclude by arguing that if government really is concerned with promoting a more inclusive and holistic concept of lifelong learning, a more radical overhaul of the current system, in particular the boundaries between the sectors, is required.

Norman Lucas and John Mace consider how current approaches to funding affect the capacity of colleges to widen the participation of groups currently excluded from education and training. They point out that the present system was designed to increase accountability and foster competition between colleges rather than tackle social exclusion. They begin by considering economists' critiques of marketization as a strategy for organizing education. They find that it is rejected on the grounds that it leads to inequity, is no guarantee of efficiency and is not the correct mechanism for promoting a policy of social inclusion. They go on to explore the effect on FE provision of the FEFC funding mechanism. They conclude that while some improvements have been made in participation and retention rates and provision for adults, the new funding mechanism has led to significant problems in other areas: for example, reductions in teaching hours and increased rigidity in course design. They recommend a complete overhaul of the funding mechanism in order to encourage strategies that would recruit and retain excluded groups.

Part 3: Perspectives on social exclusion

The next three contributions consider the issues of 'race', gender and special needs but approach them in very different ways. Dave Gillborn reviews policy on 'race' and education in Britain over the last 50 years and charts the different approaches that have developed over that time. He welcomes the contrast between New Labour's recognition that racism is a serious issue in Britain today with the colour-blind approach of the last administration. However, in considering two recent government initiatives, the White Paper *Excellence in Schools* and the Social Exclusion Unit's report *Truancy and School Exclusions* Gillborn argues that New Labour's approach is naïve and superficial and denies the deeper issues of inequity and racism. As he points out, the equal opportunity approach which New Labour appears to have adopted slips too easily into a deficit model of 'race' which sees black children as the problem rather than the education system that fails them. If we return once again to the conditions for building social and cultural capital we can see how this approach to 'race' is unable to promote the positive action around collective concerns that is required.

In my piece on male and female participation and achievement in education and training I set out to address some of the issues around 'boys' underachievement' which have been causing concern over the last few years. I chose to do this alongside a consideration of girls' and women's educational performance in order to unpick the implicit, and often explicit, polarization of male and female achievement that has been a feature of the debate. However, it is not my intention to minimize the very real problems faced by young men who leave school without qualifications and with little hope of employment as this is a serious issue, both for them as individuals and for society as a whole. It is my intention that the comparisons I make between male and female performance, as well as reminding us of the disadvantages that confront girls and women, should also highlight the complexity of the relationship between class and gender. If we were to include a full consideration of issues related to 'race' and ethnicity as called for by Dave Gillborn the problem would become even more complex and therefore the need for a broader critical debate around educational policy becomes even more evident.

Jenny Corbett begins her chapter by pointing out how the tensions between the use of a medical model to define special needs and a more progressive social model have been heightened by the marketization of education and training. She goes on to give some positive examples of how schools can develop an inclusive curriculum and school culture and stresses the commitment and effort required to promote such a culture. She then considers the issues for further education and finds, like Mace and Lucas, that competition between institutions and the funding system have reduced the range of flexible options that offered a wider scope for participation. In higher education the conditions for individuals receiving extra support are clearly based on a medical model, which requires lengthy assessments. Corbett concludes by suggesting that, while the market ideology is still in place, we should follow the examples she gives within this chapter of 'brave headteachers who are using their market astuteness to support inclusion'.

Alison Kirton uses the example of Access education to consider policy formation. She argues that although Access education is often presented as a top-down policy it was in fact a 'bottom-up' initiative based on the innovative curriculum development of teachers responding to the needs of students' returning to study. In its initial phase Access education was extremely successful in recruiting and retaining students from ethnic minorities and working-class backgrounds with no family experience of higher education. It appears that the main reason for this early success was that the flexible nature of the courses allowed the students' own knowledge and experience to become part of the curriculum and therefore began the process of building social and cultural capital. However, once Access courses were incorporated into the qualifications system in order to receive funding, the reduced flexibility resulted in fewer students from 'hard to recruit' groups. Kirton suggests that there are two main lessons to be learnt from the history of Access education. Firstly, it demonstrates that rigid funding and assessment methodologies, as we have seen above, are not effective for systems concerned with promoting social inclusion. Secondly, Access education from the earlier era provides an excellent example of a strategy for developing an inclusive curriculum.

Michael Young concludes this volume by offering an extremely timely analysis of *The Third Way* by Anthony Giddens. *The Third Way* was published in October 1998 some time after the election of the New Labour Government and suggests that a new strategy for tackling social exclusion should be developed which avoids the redistributive approach of Old Labour. As Young points out, although this may well be politically expedient, it is clear that previous approaches to reducing inequality have failed and that an alternative strategy must certainly be developed. Giddens describes social exclusion as a mechanism for the detachment of certain groups from society, including those at the 'top' as well as those at the 'bottom'. Young draws our attention to the importance of this dual notion of exclusion, pointing out that, if the issue is to be addressed without creating further marginalization, then public provision must be able to encompass both groups. However, it appears that the many Government strategies do not take this dual process into account and therefore run the considerable risk of developing old-style compensatory strategies based on a 'deficit' model of the excluded. Young regards this as stemming from a failure in the analysis to recognize the power relations involved in the process, as the rich exclude themselves whereas the disadvantaged often do not have a real choice. Young suggests that the concept of reflexive modernization, which Giddens developed with Ulrich Beck and Scott Lash, could form the basis for analysing social exclusion as a 'manufactured risk' of modern society. Young sees this approach as optimistic for a number of reasons; it reminds us that social exclusion is socially produced; it highlights the interdependence of 'exclusion at the top' and 'exclusion at the bottom'; and finally, it emphasizes the importance of multi-dimensional strategies to tackle social exclusion.

Conclusion

The contributors to this volume have approached the issue of social exclusion from a diversity of perspectives and are often critical of Government policy. However it is not their intention to undermine change and innovation as such (Whitty, 1998). Rather, they are concerned that the long-awaited reforms in education and training should be as successful as possible in reducing inequalities. In order to contribute to this process their aim is to initiate a critical debate about the processes involved in 'manufacturing' social exclusion and to explore the possibilities for creative and collective solutions.

References

Giddens, A (1998) *The Third Way: The renewal of social democracy,* Polity Press, Cambridge

Plewis, I (1998) Inequalities, targets and zone, *New Economy*, **5** (2), pp 104–08

Robinson, P (1997) *Literacy, Numeracy and Economic Performance*, CEP, School of Economics and Political Science, London

SEU (1999) *Social Exclusion Unit: What's it all about?*, www.cabinet-office.gov.uk/seu 2 March 1999

Whitty, G (1998) New Labour, Education and Disadvantage, *Education and Social Justice*, **1** (1)

Part 1

Social Exclusion, Education and Training

1

Analysing Education and Training Policies for Tackling Social Exclusion

Ann Hodgson

The problem of social exclusion is not new, but the common use of this term by policy makers in the UK is. Social exclusion has also emerged as a major focus of the current administration, as evidenced by the setting up of a Social Exclusion Unit based in the Cabinet Office and reporting directly to the Prime Minister. Among educationalists the term social exclusion has often been linked to two other terms – disaffection and non-participation – and it is all three terms which will form the subject of discussion here.

This chapter begins by discussing the usefulness of the terms disaffection, non-participation and social exclusion for examining and analysing education policy initiatives. The chapter goes on to outline the major education policy responses to the changing political, social and economic context in this country over the last 30 years, in order to provide a historical framework within which to set the current educational debates on social exclusion. What emerges from this discussion is that there are different perceptions of the problems of disaffection, non-participation and social exclusion, which often lead to different and potentially conflicting policy proposals for tackling them. In the final part of the chapter, New Labour's policies for addressing the problems of disaffection, non-participation and social exclusion are analysed. The chapter concludes by arguing that despite this Government's evident commitment to tackling these problems, their policies, while innovative and, in many cases, well funded, currently appear to take the form of individual remedial initiatives rather than forming part of a clear long-term strategy for addressing the underlying causes of disaffection, non-participation and social exclusion.

Definitions and terminology

Different labels are used to describe those groups of people who are 'either impeded in gaining access to, or are unable to maintain themselves within, mainstream education and training' (Education and Employment Committee, 1998) or, more generally, who are 'detached from the organisations and communities of which the society is composed and from the rights and obligations that they embody' (Room, 1995). Three terms are in common usage:

- *Disaffected* – here the focus is on the individual who does not support societal norms and is thus seen as potentially deviant, or, at the least, has negative feelings about social institutions (including the education and training system) and therefore either participates reluctantly or does not participate at all in education and training (and possibly other aspects of conventional social or community activities);
- *Non-participating* – this is a technical term for describing behaviour in relation to the education and training system. The term only becomes value-laden when associated with the idea of participation as the responsibility of, or even the norm for, all individuals;
- *Socially excluded* – here the focus has moved away from the individual towards an emphasis on what society is doing to individuals, either within the education system or more widely in relation to society as a whole.

There is little consensus about which term to use, because each tends to reflect a different perspective or value. The term disaffected, for example, implies something about individual attitude and therefore individual responsibility, whereas the term socially excluded suggests that there should be a focus on society and its impact on individuals rather than on the behaviour and attitudes of individuals themselves.

A recent IPPR report, *Wasted Youth: Raising achievement and tackling social exclusion* (Pearce and Hillman, 1998), chooses to use the concept of 'disaffection' as an umbrella term to cover young people in compulsory education, whether they are non-attenders and disenchanted pupils or those exhibiting behavioural difficulties or anti-social behaviour. The term 'non-participation' is used in relation to those beyond compulsory school age. This is helpful because it distinguishes between the problems associated with those for whom participation in education is not a choice and those for whom it is voluntary.

However, even this distinction leaves us with difficulties with a working definition – there may, for example, be pupils who have behavioural difficulties but who might not be classified as disaffected. Similarly, in post-16 education, there needs to be a distinction made between those who are not participating in full-time education, but who are employed in a job that provides the type of training which allows them to pursue qualifications or to progress, and those who are in a job that provides no such opportunity to participate in training of any kind, whether or not they have the motivation to do so. Moreover, as we have seen above, the notion of disaffection is complicated when used as an umbrella term because it confuses the attitude of individuals with what society (or the state) is doing to the individual.

I would argue that there is a need, therefore, to make use of all three terms – disaffection, non-participation and social exclusion – in conjunction with one another when discussing education policy, particularly since this is the more inclusive or holistic approach which is favoured by recent policies in this area. Each of these three terms is useful in its own right, because it attempts to describe a particular problem or set of problems, but each is also limited in its focus and can be misleading on its own.

These three related concepts – disaffection, non-participation and social exclusion – may affect different age groups, for example, those in compulsory education (pre-16), young adults (16–25 years) and adults (25+) in different ways. This idea can be explored by way of a matrix (see Figure 1.1) which attempts to locate different aspects of the phenomenon of disaffection/non-participation/social exclusion in terms of different dimensions and different age groups.

The matrix in Figure 1.1 suggests that the problems of disaffection, non-participation and social exclusion may become more serious with the passage of time: moving from rejection of school, through non-participation in education and training, to exclusion from the economy and norms expected of family life. That is 'disconnection' from mainstream society and a process of 'ghettoization'. The critical factor for both disaffection and non-participation appears to be the role of labour markets and employment, but the process of social exclusion appears to be more multi-dimensional. I will return to this point later in the chapter when I look at the dimensions of a framework for analysing problems and policy solutions related to disaffection, non-participation and social exclusion.

Dimensions of a framework for analysing disaffection, non-participation and social exclusion

The changing economic and social context since the 1970s: the education policy response

Over the last 30 years a range of socio-economic issues has raised the profile of the problems of disaffection, non-participation and social exclusion of sections of the population. Society and the economy have changed dramatically over this period (Oppenheim, 1998). The stability of manufacturing jobs and close-knit communities has declined, social and ethnic diversity has increased and there have been significant changes in the labour market (particularly the youth labour market). These changes have resulted in a new relationship between education and work (Glennerster, 1998); an increase in 'individualization' and consumerism (Field, 1996); a moral panic about the direction of society and particularly the plight and behaviour of young people and a deepening of social divisions linked to neo-liberal economic policies (Robinson, 1998). At the same time, education policy makers and researchers have used international skill comparisons to

	disaffection	non-participation in education and training	social exclusion
learners in compulsory schooling	• lack of engagement with the curriculum; • disruptive behaviour; • prioritization of alternative activities	• truancy; • persistent lateness; • off-task; • low production levels and achievement	exclusion from: • school; • the curriculum or aspects of the curriculum; • achievement; and • positive relationships or role models
young adults (16–25)	• anti-social or criminal activity; • addiction; • unemployment or casualized employment	• 'Status 0';[1] • early course drop-out; • poor or non-progression; • low value-added achievement	• homelessness; • lack of employment and training opportunities; • lack of progression opportunities; • lack of advice and guidance; • lack of inter-agency collaboration and support; • lack of financial support
adults	*as carers* • non-positive parenting; • collusion in children's negative behaviour and attitude to education; • abandonment of children *as learners:* • anti-social or criminal behaviour; • welfare dependency; • non-involvement in community or use of democratic rights	• long-term unemployed; • 'Status 0'	lack of access to: • housing, employment, child care, education and training opportunities; • adequate benefits or financial support for study

1. 'Status 0' was a term coined by Howard Williamson when he was undertaking fieldwork analysis of those not participating in education, training or employment in mid-Glamorgan (Istance and Williamson, 1996).

Figure 1.1: *The relationship between different dimensions of disaffection/non-participation/social exclusion and different age groups*

argue the case for increasing educational participation and achievement in this country to meet the needs of both work and society in the 21st century (Green, 1997).

During this period, not only have debates and perceptions of the problem of disaffection, non-participation and social exclusion differed, so too have the education policy initiatives designed to tackle the problem. New Labour's distinctive approach in this area will be discussed in more depth towards the end of this chapter, but first it might be helpful to set this in the context of earlier approaches. Each of the last three decades has arguably seen a different emphasis on policies in this area.

1970s – tackling the effects of economic crisis and the changing labour market

At a time of growing economic crisis, the end of the 'long-boom' and the beginnings of rising youth unemployment, there were criticisms by employers that young people were ill-equipped for working life. They led to the raising of the school leaving age, discussions on the vocationalization of the curriculum and the introduction of a number of work-based initiatives such as the Youth Opportunities Programme and Unified Vocational Programme. The major focus of education policy in this period was on young people, because of fears about the potential danger to society of large numbers of unemployed and disaffected adolescents (especially male adolescents). However, there was also an attempt to tackle the problems of adult basic skills deficits through the launch of the national Adult Literacy Campaign in 1973 and adult unemployment through the Training Opportunities Programme (TOPs) courses.

1980s – increasing the effectiveness and efficiency of the education system through expansion and marketization

During the 1980s, in the context of Thatcherite policies, there was an emphasis on individual responsibility, upskilling of the workforce through expansion of the education and training system and the role of markets in increasing the effectiveness of this system. In the early part of the eighties, before the introduction of the National Curriculum, there was a move to support pedagogy, curriculum development and accreditation designed to motivate disaffected young people (eg modularization and flexible learning, TVEI, records of achievement). However, this move, although in some cases nationally funded, was largely locally determined and was thus uneven in impact. Towards the end of the 1980s, 'trickle-down' theory was used to justify policies which focused on increasing participation and achievement in full-time education, while leaving behind a significant minority of lower achievers and marginalizing those who dropped out of education and training. Alongside this there was a continuing focus on skill development for adults both inside and outside the workforce and a push to increase the number of adults participating in higher education with the rapid expansion of Access course provision. In addition, a number of short-term initiatives

(Youth Training, Youth Training Scheme, Employment Training) were put into place to try to reduce the effects of unemployment. However, a voluntarist approach to the labour market and employers failed to ensure that either young people or adults were being adequately trained to meet the demands of the modern workplace.

1990s – identifying and dealing with the effects of marginalization

In the early part of the 1990s, there was an increasing focus on market-led approaches to education and training policy (eg league tables, FE incorporation). However, there was a gradual realization in the mid-1990s that these policies on their own were proving insufficient to push participation and achievement levels beyond a certain level and that, in many cases, they were exacerbating the problem of disaffection, non-participation and social exclusion. Government reports (Audit Commission/Ofsted, 1993; Dearing, 1996), as well as academics and policy analysts, were increasingly highlighting the worrying proportion of young people failing to achieve qualifications, dropping out of the education system and displaying disruptive or anti-social behaviour. Similarly, there was pressure from a number of sources to address the problems of low basic and other skills in the population as a whole (Bynner and Parsons, 1997) and to widen participation in lifelong learning (Kennedy, 1997; NCIHE, 1997) in order to build the kind of learning society that was beginning to attract cross-party support (DfEE, 1995, 1996; Labour Party, 1996d). This has led in the late 1990s to the beginnings of a shift away from apportioning blame to individuals and marginal groups and towards seeing a greater connection between individuals and society as a whole. What potentially follows from this shifting emphasis is a more interventionist, whole-system and multi-dimensional approach to addressing the issues of disaffection, non-participation and social exclusion. This approach will be examined in more depth later in the chapter after a discussion of the current debates, definitions and perceptions of the problem which provide the context for such policies.

Education has always been seen as one of the mechanisms the state can use to address particular socio-economic issues because of its universal application. There have been a number of major secondary and post-16 education policy initiatives over the last 30 years that could be seen as responses to the changing socio-economic context described above. These include:

- the raising of the school-leaving age;
- the introduction of comprehensive schools, but within the context of continuing selective and private education;
- the development of a common and inclusive but subject-based national curriculum with a common examination at 16 — GCSE;
- changes to the qualifications system (eg CPVE, NVQs, GNVQs) to meet the needs of the expansion in full-time provision post-16 for a wider range of the cohort unable to enter the labour market;

- attempts to link the workplace and education more closely (eg New Vocationalism, TVEI, work experience, Youth Training, Modern Apprenticeships, education–business partnerships);
- the introduction of market-led policies designed to increase efficiency or 'value for money' from the education system – eg incorporation of colleges, league tables, training vouchers;
- massification and marketization of the further and higher education sectors;
- the loss of large areas of traditional adult and community education but the increase in access to certificated and formal learning for adults;
- a focus on the diversification of pedagogy to deal with increased social diversity.

Issues affecting younger and older learners

Over this 30-year period, the changing social and economic context and the education policy responses to that context have together given rise to a number of issues related to disaffection with, and non-participation in education and training. For some people, seriously disadvantaged by both context and policy responses, these have caused social exclusion from mainstream society. For the purposes of this chapter, I will focus on those issues that relate most closely to the education and training system and I will attempt to distinguish between those that affect younger learners more acutely and those that pertain more specifically to older learners.

For younger learners (ie those under 25 years) the following issues have emerged during the last two decades:

- literacy and numeracy deficits and low levels of achievement at 16+ in relation to international competitors (Bynner and Parsons, 1997; Green and Steedman, 1997);
- polarization of achievement with strongly differentiated performance for boys/girls, specific ethnic or socio-economic groups (Glennerster, 1998; Murphy and Elwood, 1997; Gillborn and Gipps, 1996);
- high exclusion rates (Parsons and Castle, 1998);
- poor discipline at school (DES, 1989 – Elton report);
- disaffection with the current education and training system, particularly from 14+ (Dearing, 1996; Pearce and Hillman, 1998);
- persistent non-attendance at school (Education and Employment Committee, 1998);
- low levels of participation post-16 and particularly at 17 and 18+ (Green and Steedman, 1997; Pearce and Hillman, 1998).

The issues affecting older learners include:

- long-term unemployment which exacerbates the problem of finding future employment (OECD, 1996);

- basic skills deficits (Bynner and Parsons, 1997);
- negative attitudes towards participation in education and training (Kennedy, 1997);
- financial and other barriers preventing access to learning, eg childcare, transport, despite increasing moves in the direction of opening up formal educational institutions to adults (McGivney, 1993);
- differential economic rates of return from education (NCIHE, 1997).

Current debates

As a result of the changing economic and social context and the recent political and education policy responses to that context, a number of debates has arisen around the problems of disaffection, non-participation and social exclusion and around the range of strategic approaches required to tackle these problems. Some have focused on the role of the individual in society (eg Home Office, 1988; Audit Commission, 1996), others on the problems of specific socio-economic groups (eg Armstrong *et al,* 1997; Garnett, 1992) and others more generally on the role of social class in society (Gillborn and Gipps, 1996). Furthermore, in many cases, these problems have been located in a particular policy area – housing, health, the criminal justice system, social services, education. This may be the result of these problems being analysed from a particular academic standpoint, but also represents their complexity. However, more recently, with the focus on policy rather than on analysis of the problems themselves, there has been a tendency to try to see the connections between the different causes of these problems and their potential policy solutions (Howarth and Kenway, 1998; Mulgan, 1998; Halpern, 1998).

As we have seen above, definitions of disaffection, non-participation and social exclusion are related to different perceptions of the underlying causes of these problems. Recent literature includes mention of a large number of factors that contribute to these problems (see Table 1.1). These factors would appear to divide into four broad major dimensions: the individual's position within society (social class, race and gender); the role of the labour market (levels of employment and unemployment for different age groups, wage/salary levels and differentials, employer skill demands); structural features of the education and training system (this includes the role of the state, the nature of the education and training system, institutional culture and delivery); and the culture and values of the individual (this includes attitudes, relationships, self-image and role models). It is arguable, therefore, that an analysis of the problems of disaffection, non-participation and social exclusion and proposals for its solution should not only focus on each of the factors listed above, but should also consider the dynamic interrelationship between these four underlying major dimensions of factors.

Figure 1.2 attempts to illustrate this interrelationship by demonstrating how each of the four dimensions of factors – the individual's position within society; the culture and values of the individual; the structural features of

Table 1.1: *Factors contributing to problems of disaffection, non-participation and social exclusion*

- *socio-economic position,* particularly the relationship between socio-economic group, underachievement and low levels of post-16 participation (Smithers and Robinson, 1986; Spours, 1995; Gillborn and Gipps, 1996; Metcalf, 1997);

- *ethnicity* – e.g. Afro-Caribbean pupils suffer disproportionately high rates of exclusion from school; white working-class boys are least likely to participate post-16 (Gillborn and Gipps, 1996; Parsons and Castle, 1998);

- *gender* – e.g. the majority of those excluded and gaining the lowest levels of GCSE attainment are boys (Murphy and Elwood, 1997);

- *family and area effects* – e.g. concentration of families without work and on benefit placed in certain geographical areas, compounded by lack of services to outlying estates (West and McCormick, 1998)

- *attitudes of disaffected* – e.g. welfare dependency, lured to casualized labour market, engaging in alternative negative behaviour, family collusion with children's negative behaviour (Audit Commission, 1996);

- *school selection procedures* which have benefited higher achievers but have disadvantaged lower achievers (Glennerster, 1998);

- *increasing gap between educational attainment* of high achievers and low achievers, with long and persistent tail of underachievement (Glennerster, 1998; Pearce and Hillman, 1998);

- *school/college ethos and effectiveness* – eg some schools exclude more students than others and a lack of discipline and direction in some schools feeds disaffection (Ofsted, 1996). Research on student retention by the Further Education Development Agency (Martinez, 1995) suggests some colleges do not have strategies to tackle this problem effectively;

- *curriculum and qualifications* – eg Key Stage 4 curriculum breadth is seen as potentially demotivating to some students; GCSE grade thresholds reduce prospects of progression; and the post-16 curriculum is seen as exclusive and divisive (Cockett and Callaghan, 1996; Hodgson and Spours, 1997; Pearce and Hillman, 1998);

- *funding* – eg output-related funding tends to inhibit the recruitment of those least likely to succeed; inequity of funding for post-16 education and training (Rathbone, CI, CSV, NACRO and TEN 1997; Leney, Lucas and Taubman, 1998);

- *sharp decline in relative youth wages* without improvement in relative youth employment rates (Blanchflower and Freeman, 1997);

- *significant increases in wage inequality* between the late 1970s and mid-1990s which have resulted in the exacerbation of the divide between rich and poor (Robinson, 1998);

- *benefit and welfare system* – eg benefit and welfare system interacts negatively with low wage labour market to discourage some groups, such as lone parents, from seeking work (McLaughlin, 1998).

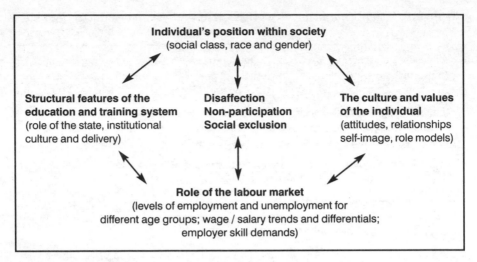

Figure 1.2: *A framework for analysing problems and policy solutions related to disaffection, non-participation and social exclusion*

the education and training system and the role of the labour market – has a direct impact on the problems of disaffection, non-participation and social exclusion. At the same time, each dimension is also related to each of the other three in a dynamic way. Although for different age groups and at different times one of the dimensions might be more important than the other three, it is likely that all four dimensions will have some effect all of the time. As indicated in Figure 1.1, the picture in relation to education and training is likely to be more complex for adults because of the dual role they play as both carer and learner.

This dynamic interrelationship between the complex set of dimensions underlying the problems of disaffection, non-participation and social exclusion indicates the necessity of taking a multi-dimensional and multi-agency approach to their solution. At both national and local levels this is likely to mean policies which cross traditional departmental and ministerial boundaries and responsibilities. It is, therefore, likely to mean quite radically new ways of working that confront both precedent and, potentially, jealously guarded territory. This is no mean feat at either local or national government level. The extent to which New Labour is prepared to tackle this issue is discussed below in the context of their policies for tackling disaffection, non-participation and social exclusion.

New Labour's approach to the problem of disaffection, non-participation and social exclusion

In this section I examine some of the recent major policy initiatives designed to address the problems of disaffection, non-participation and social exclusion in this country. I then refer back to the four-point model outlined in Figure 1.2 above to analyse their likely effects. I start by making a distinction between the approach of recent Conservative administrations and the approach of New Labour. This is followed by a discussion of New Labour's strategies for those in compulsory education – with a particular focus on the 14–16 age group where much attention has been concentrated to date – for 16–25-year-olds and finally for adults.

Conservative policy in this area was characterized by a belief in the power of wealth creation and the trickle-down effect, the culture of entrepreneurialism, individualism and competitiveness, the notion of a minimal welfare state (in practice a welfare state biased towards the middle classes), demand-led participation in education and training, and a divided education and training system to suit different levels of ability and segmented labour markets. This approach did initially lead to increased levels of participation and achievement in education and training in the late 1980s and early 1990s (Spours, 1995). However, by the mid-1990s this trend began to plateau, leaving a 'hard to get' cohort increasingly detached from the system (Hodgson and Spours, 1997a). During this period, the overall effects of the Conservative approach to education and training policy were, therefore, to accentuate social divisions in society, to highlight individual responsibility and blame and to downplay the role of society and citizenship. This resulted in the growth of a so-called underclass and to stigmatization of the poor and unemployed (Pearce and Hillman, 1998; Oppenheim, 1998).

New Labour's approach, since the formation of its policies on education and training from 1994 onwards, has been to focus on the economically inactive and to try to break the cycle of welfare dependency and poverty through its 'Welfare to Work' and New Deal strategies (Labour Party 1996a, 1996b and 1996c). This is a three-way approach linking policies related to employment, education and training and benefit reform. Since New Labour has eschewed macro-economic management, which was a feature of Old Labour policy, it has put its primary emphasis on the role of education and training in supporting and promoting employability and the majority of its policies in this area can be described as supply-side rather than demand-side.

New Labour's approach to the problem of disaffection, non-participation and social exclusion in the compulsory education system up to the age of 14 could be characterized as 'standards driven' and has, to date, focused largely on raising levels of achievement (particularly in the basic skills of literacy and numeracy), on improving school effectiveness, on combating behaviour issues, truancy and exclusion and on creating better school–community links. This is part of an approach that is designed to promote equality of opportunity and inclusiveness, while at the same time emphasizing individual responsibility for participation and achievement in education and training.

New Labour's approach in relation to the 14–19 curriculum, on the other hand, can be characterized as 'divisive flexibility' and includes reducing the compulsory element of the Key Stage 4 curriculum, retaining unreformed

GCSEs and A levels and promoting vocational qualifications and work-based and college-based activities for younger disaffected learners.

The way New Labour addresses the issue of involving employers in the post-compulsory education and training system is voluntaristic, but its approach to disaffected young people is not. Through its New Deal initiative for 18–25-year-olds (and now for 25-year-olds and over) and its New Start initiatives for disaffected 14–16-year-olds, New Labour appears to be promoting a combination of an enabling framework and a degree of compulsion. The element of compulsion is focused on the younger age group and is seen as a way of tackling the problems associated with disaffection and social exclusion, while there is a strong strand of voluntarism plus an enabling framework to combat the problems of non-participating adults. These policies are not underpinned by a desire to stimulate entrepreneurialism and competition – two key watchwords of the previous administration – rather they are designed to promote the work ethic and individual responsibility at the learner level and collaboration at the provider level, through exhortation combined with a range of financial incentives.

Earlier in this chapter, I used Figure 1.1 to examine the relationship between different dimensions of disaffection, non-participation and social exclusion and different age groups. I will use these same age categories here to examine New Labour's strategies in this area in more detail before going on to analyse new Labour's overall approach.

Strategies for those in compulsory education (with a particular focus on 14–16-year-olds)

Excellence in Schools (DfEE, 1997), New Labour's first major education policy document after its election to power, although focusing strongly on basic skills and schools standards, also has a chapter entitled 'Helping pupils achieve' which sets out a number of initiatives designed specifically to tackle disaffection and non-participation. These include LEA behaviour support plans, advice on assertive discipline and behaviour policies within schools, on ways of tackling truancy and on establishing better family, community and business links to support learners through, for example, study support and mentoring and suggestions of a more flexible Key Stage 4 curriculum. The White Paper's approach to social exclusion is to set up remedial Education Action Zones in areas of particular deprivation, to focus on the specific issues faced by ethnic minority groups in schools and by those children excluded from school. For the rest of the population, the approach is to consider the introduction of parenting and citizenship education as part of the secondary school curriculum.

This White Paper has been followed up by a number of policies which take the ideas in the document further. Since April 1998, for example, LEAs have been required by the Education Act 1997 (DfEE, 1998a) to draw up Behaviour Support Plans which set out arrangements for strategic planning of provision for pupils with behavioural difficulties both inside and outside mainstream education. Excluded pupils will have to be tracked so that they can be reintegrated into mainstream education. As mentioned earlier, a Social Exclusion Unit has been set up and has laid out a range of proposals aimed at reducing the amount of time lost to truancy and the numbers of both permanent and fixed-term exclusions by a third by the year 2002 (Social Exclusion Unit, 1998). Sir Bernard Crick has been given the task of setting up a committee to advise the government on citizenship education, a Ministerial Working Group on Personal Social and Health Education has been formed and the Qualifications and Curriculum Authority has begun the task of reviewing the National Curriculum. The DfEE has written to schools informing them about the terms surrounding relaxation of the National Curriculum at Key Stage 4 and encouraging them to make available work-related learning opportunities for disaffected 14–16-year-olds. Ten million pounds has been allocated to strategic partnerships in 17 areas of the country to set up New Start initiatives focused on disaffected 14–17-year-olds and pilot Education Action Zones have been set up in 25 areas of the country. It appears that New Labour has been convinced by the arguments in reports from this country (eg Kennedy, 1997) and further afield (eg OECD, 1996) about the importance of achievement in foundation education for successful participation and achievement later in life.

Strategies for 16–25-year-olds

Although, as stated earlier, the majority of New Labour's initiatives for tackling disaffection, non-participation and social exclusion in the post-compulsory education and training sector are supply-side and rely on financial incentives to make them successful, New Deal can be seen as an exception to this rule. New Deal has dominated New Labour's agenda for tackling the issues of disaffection, non-participation and social exclusion related to younger adults. With its focus on the links between employment, education and training and welfare reform, it has been characterized as a typical example of New Labour's 'Third Way' approach to economic and social policy. New Deal relies on the idea that tackling the causes as well as the effects of unemployment on young people will help to eradicate disaffection, non-participation and social exclusion (see Hodgson and Spours, 1999 for a more detailed discussion and analysis of New Deal). According to DfEE officials (in an interview in September 1998), it is not, however, seen as a long-term strategy, but rather as an intensive and costly way of remedying a deep-rooted problem related to a particular cohort.

The other three interrelated themes on which New Labour is focusing in this area are changes to the funding of post-16 provision and learner support, strategies specifically aimed at increasing the participation of 16–19-year-olds in education and training, and reform of post-16 qualifications. Taken together, these policies are intended to create an enabling infrastructure that will promote progression, retention and achievement in initial post-compulsory education and training.

The government is examining quite fundamental, and sometimes contro-versial questions in relation to the funding of both post-16 provision and individual learners. There is an emphasis on widening participation in education and training, with money for further and higher education being targeted at learners traditionally excluded or under-represented (DfEE, 1998b; DFEE, 1998c; DfEE, 1998d). This is underpinned by discussions about using common funding principles across all post-16 provision, which would be likely to result in a redistribution of funding in this area. As far as support for individuals is concerned, under the terms of the 1998 FHE Act (DfEE, 1998e), students in higher education are being required to fund a greater proportion of their study – with safeguards for those who are unable to pay – so that the cap on numbers entering higher education can be lifted. At the same time, financial support for 16–19-year-olds in full-time educa-tion is currently under consideration as an alternative to child benefit for this age group. All of these policies are designed to reach out to disaffected, non-participating and socially excluded learners, although there is consid-erable concern at present about some of the measures and little consensus on whether they will be successful in achieving this goal.

The second major policy thrust in this area is the Investing in Young People Strategy, which was outlined in New Labour's second major educa-tion policy document since coming to power – *The Learning Age* (DfEE, 1998b). This strategy focuses on a number of initiatives which, as a package, are designed to encourage 16–19-year-olds to participate and achieve in post-compulsory education and training: New Start for 14–17-year-olds, legislation to ensure that all 16 and 17-year-olds in employ-ment are able to undertake education and training; the provision of a reformulated National Record of Achievement, additional funding for careers education and guidance focused at 16-year-olds and over not in education; training or work and putting the Youth Service on a statutory footing.

Allied to both of the above is New Labour's strategy for reform of post-16 qualifications. The Dearing Report (Dearing, 1996), which was commis-sioned by the previous administration to look into some of the problems of the existing 16–19 qualifications framework, made a strong case for reform of the 16–19 qualifications system to address the problems of disaffection, non-participation and social exclusion. Sir Ron Dearing's arguments and those of researchers who specialize in post-16 qualifications reform (eg Hodgson and Spours, 1997b) are strongly supported by the recent IPPR Report *Wasted Youth* (Pearce and Hillman, 1998). This report suggests that a unified system of 14–19 qualifications could help to raise achievement, particularly for the non-participating, the disaffected and the socially excluded by providing a more flexible, broader and more relevant curriculum framework for 14–19-year-olds.

Currently, however, despite its own policy position outlined in *Aiming Higher* (Labour Party, 1996d) and considerable practitioner support for reform of the 14+ qualifications framework (AOC *et al,* 1997), New Labour appears to be moving very cautiously in this area. The tentative and incremental reforms emerging from the recent *Qualifying for Success* process (DfEE, 1998f) can be seen either as a first step in the direction of more radical changes to the 14+ qualifications system (Hodgson, Spours and Young, 1998) or as reneging on previous Party policy (*Times Educational Supplement*, 1998). In either case, there is certainly more work to be done before the qualifications system in this country is sufficiently sensitive to the needs of the disaffected, the non-participating and the socially excluded.

Strategies for adults

New Labour has been made fully aware of the inequalities of access to and benefits from the current post-compulsory education and training system for adult learners and the particular problems of the disaffected, non-participating and socially excluded (Kennedy, 1997; NCIHE, 1997; Fryer, 1997). *The Learning Age* (DfEE, 1998b) recognizes this problem and sees it as a major barrier to attaining its goal of promoting lifelong learning for all. Its answer lies in five separate but strongly interrelated strategies: raising the skills base and employability of the adult population; encouraging the development of more flexible provision and delivery mechanisms; putting into place a framework for recognizing the outcomes of adult learning; providing financial incentives for adults to participate in learning; and creating a local and regional infrastructure for planning coherent post-compulsory education and training opportunities.

Just as New Labour sees the fundamental importance of tackling low levels of literacy and numeracy among schoolchildren in this country (DfEE, 1997), it also recognizes the necessity of raising the low level of basic skills among adults. There is a pledge in *The Learning Age* (DfEE, 1998b) that all adult basic skills provision will be free. There will be £4 million per year given to the Basic Skills Agency for innovatory projects in this area and there will be support for family literacy schemes and the work of the University for Industry (UfI). The allocation of the first Individual Learning Accounts (ILAs) is likely to be targeted initially towards adults with basic skills needs. In addition, a Working Group on Post-school Basic Skills, under the chairmanship of Sir Claus Moser, has recently laid out a national strategy for basic skills (Moser, 1999). This focus on basic skills appears to be a recognition not only of the economic necessity of improving the skill levels of the adult population in this country, but also a strong commitment to equity.

The extension of New Deal to those beyond the age of 25 is the other significant step New Labour has taken to increase the employability of the adult workforce and to ensure that all adults, particularly the long-term unemployed, have greater access to work and training, thereby possibly avoiding some of the complex problems of social exclusion described earlier in the chapter.

Encouraging the development of more flexible adult-friendly education and training provision to facilitate lifelong learning can be seen as the second of New Labour's major policy thrusts designed to tackle the problems of disaffection, non-participation and social exclusion. Here it relies largely on a mix of initiatives – the UfI and ILAs – and funding mechanisms, mentioned earlier in relation to widening participation, which are designed to change institutional behaviour.

The UfI, which is one of the most widely publicized but least understood of New Labour's initiatives for increasing adult participation in education and training, is still in its infancy. Now that its Chief Executive has been appointed, there is likely to be further elaboration of the way it will work. At present, according to the Secretary of State for Education and Employment, David Blunkett, the UfI is seen as a mechanism that will '. . . offer access to a learning network to help people deepen their knowledge, update their skills and gain new ones' (DfEE, 1998g: 8).

It is essentially intended to act as a broker between learners and learning opportunities, whether these are delivered in a specific educational setting or via information and communications technologies directly into the home or the workplace. The UfI will, therefore, provide a front-line service of advice and guidance about learning opportunities and learning providers to learners and employers through its telephone line, Learning Direct. It will co-ordinate the setting up of a network of learning centres in accessible locations around the country; publicize the importance of learning; identify gaps in provision; commission specific learning packages or provision to satisfy learners' demand; and quality assure the products and services to which it provides access (DfEE, 1998g). Central to the UfI project is a belief in the power of new information and communications technologies (ICT) to widen participation in education and training by taking learning to the learner in his or her own context.

Allied to the development of more flexible and accessible adult provision is the idea of a national credit accumulation and transfer system to accredit smaller steps of learning and to allow adults to build up credits towards larger qualifications over time. This idea, which was outlined in the Kennedy Report (1997) and picked up again in *The Learning Age* (DfEE, 1998b), has not been elaborated on as yet, but could provide a useful enabling framework for recognizing and rewarding adult learning of all types.

The fourth set of policy proposals put forward by New Labour to tackle disaffection, non-participation and social exclusion in relation to adults revolves around providing financial incentives for adults to participate in learning. The major proposal here is the development of ILAs. ILAs, which were highlighted in New Labour's policy documents prior to the election, are given pride of place in *The Learning Age*. They are seen as a mechanism for encouraging individuals to invest in their own education and training with support from the government and, in some cases, from their employers. There is an indication too that ILAs could be used 'to make providers more responsive to learners' needs' (DfEE, 1998b: 26).

The details of how ILAs will be organized, what form they will take and whether eventually they will be provided on a universal or on a targeted basis are not spelt out in *The Learning Age*. There is, however, a clear commitment to their future development as a means of encouraging people to participate in learning. The Green Paper announced a £150 million pilot project to test out how ILAs might work in practice.

Alongside the proposal for the piloting of ILAs, which is clearly seen as one of the most important potential mechanisms for funding lifelong learning, *The Learning Age* also includes a number of proposals for supporting individuals to participate in learning. These are designed not only to support those on low incomes, but also to make it more attractive for those on benefits to undertake education and training to improve their employability skills. Proposals include an increase in the size of the access fund for students in further education and a £36 million access package for part-time students and those facing financial hardship in higher education. There is an amendment to the Jobseeker's Allowance, so that those who are unemployed can study for up to a year full-time and only need to be available for work outside term time; and there are changes in the benefit rules for those on Workskill pilot projects.

The final area where New Labour is tackling the problem of disaffection, non-participation and social exclusion in relation to adults is the development of a local and regional infrastructure for planning coherent post-compulsory education and training opportunities. The problems for learners created by market-led policies and competition between education and training providers – promoted by the previous administration – and the consequent need for coherent local and regional planning are well documented (Hodgson and Spours, 1997a; Kennedy, 1997; Pearce and Hillman, 1998; Oppenheim, 1998). Traditionally-excluded learners are particularly vulnerable in a competitive education and training marketplace. New Labour's plans for greater collaborative and strategic oversight of post-16 provision and for the setting up of Regional Development Agencies (DfEE, 1998b) therefore, potentially constitute an important longer-term approach to the problem of disaffection, non-participation and social exclusion.

The challenge for New Labour

Earlier in this chapter, I argued that it might be useful to use the four-point framework in Figure 1.2 as a way of understanding the problem of disaffection, non-participation and social exclusion. I also suggested that it might be helpful to look at the interrelationship between the four points of the framework (the individual's position within society; the individual's cultural and value system; the role of the labour market and the structural features of the education and training system) when discussing policy solutions designed to address this problem. This was likely to suggest the need for multi-dimensional and multi-agency approaches. There is no shortage of support for this position (eg Coles, 1996; Mulgan, 1998; Halpern, 1998; Pearce and Hillman, 1998), although there is less consensus on what the precise balance of dimensions and agencies should be.

It could be argued that New Labour appears to have understood the need for multi-dimensional and multi-agency approaches to the problem of disaffection, non-participation and social exclusion. Some of its policy proposals, such as the New Deal initiatives, the setting up of the Social Exclusion Unit – particularly its recent work on disadvantaged neighbourhoods – and the development of Regional Development Agencies, exemplify this approach. However, there are also, I would suggest, three major concerns with New Labour's current policies.

First, there may well be tensions between different initiatives in different policy areas and even within one policy area, which give rise to 'perverse policy outcomes'. If one takes education, for example, it is not difficult to see that there is likely to be a tension between the desire to raise educational standards through policies such as the use of league tables, target setting, early benchmarking and a heavy reliance on external testing in national qualifications for 16–19-year-olds, and the desire to encourage greater access, participation and achievement in education and training. Some of these policies, although intended to set high standards and open up opportunities for all, may well instil an early sense of failure in some, which is reinforced over time. Similarly, there is likely to be tension between the desire to create diversity and choice for learners through, for example, the creation of specialist schools and the retention of sixth forms, and the need to provide a comprehensive and inclusive education system which is accessible to all learners. In both these cases one set of policies encourages exclusivity while the other demands inclusivity.

Second, there is a very strong reliance on certain key initiatives, such as ILAs, New Deal and the UfI, to increase the volume of lifelong learning and to tackle the problems of long-term unemployment and poverty. These initiatives require, at the very least, strong employer and labour market support and possibly, if recession bites, intervention in the labour market. Yet New Labour is currently relying solely on exhortation and a voluntarist approach to employers and the labour market and does not seem prepared to consider more interventionist policies in this area at present.

Third, even the Social Exclusion Unit, while accepting the principle that the problems of disaffection, non-participation and social exclusion are multi-dimensional and that a 'joined up' multi-agency approach to solutions is likely to be the most effective one, is still working in a piecemeal project-based way. The Unit is small (approximately 30 staff), consists almost exclusively of secondees, limits its work to discrete project areas and has an initial lifespan of two years. For this reason, the work of the Unit, while innovative and challenging to the *status quo*, still has a somewhat remedial focus and cannot substitute for the development of a long-term strategy for tackling the problems of disaffection, non-participation and social exclusion. A similar criticism might be levelled at many of New Labour's other policies for tackling disaffection, non-participation and social exclusion described above. That is, that several of them still appear to be isolated initiatives or experiments, albeit often well funded, rather than forming part of a more coherent long-term strategy for addressing these problems over time.

However, there can be no doubt that New Labour has a strong commitment to social justice and believes that the state has an active role to play in creating opportunities for individuals to become part of a more inclusive society. It is still early days for many of the policy proposals outlined in this chapter and the full impact of their individual and combined effect remains to be evaluated. At this stage, as several of the authors contributing to *An Inclusive Society* (Oppenheim, 1998) point out, it may well be helpful to develop some form of social exclusion indicators so that we can move beyond speculation about the effects of New Labour's policies and can attempt to measure to what extent they are actually being successful in addressing the complex problems of disaffection, non-participation and social exclusion. The Social Exclusion Unit now appears to be turning its attention to developing such indicators (Robinson and Oppenheim, 1998), although there has been no public announcement to date.

Acknowledgement

I would like to acknowledge the invaluable help Ken Spours gave me with framing the initial draft of this chapter.

References

AOC, ATL, GSA, HMC, NAHT, NASUWT, NATFHE, NUT, PAT, SHA, SHMIS (1997) *Key Principles for Curriculum and Qualifications Reform from 14+*, Post-16 Education Centre, Institute of Education, University of London

Armstrong, D et al (1997) *Status 0: A socio-economic study of young people on the margin*, NIERC, London

Audit Commission/Ofsted (1993) *Unfinished Business: Full-time education courses for 16–19-year-olds*, HMSO, London

Audit Commission (1996) *Misspent Youth: Young people and crime*, HMSO, London

Blanchflower, D and Freeman, R (1997) Creating jobs for youth, *New Economy*, **4** (2), pp 68–73, Summer 1997

Bynner, J and Parsons, S (1997) *It Doesn't Get Any Better: The impact of poor basic skills on the lives of 37–year-olds*, Basic Skills Agency, London

Cockett, M and Callaghan, J (1996) Caught in the middle – transition at 16+, in *Education and Training 14–19: Chaos or coherence*, ed R Halsall and M Cockett, David Fulton, London

Coles, B (1996) *Youth Transitions and Youth Policy: The need for co-ordination,* Institute for Employment Research, University of Warwick

Dearing, R (1996) *Review of Qualifications for 16–19-year-olds: Full Report*, School Curriculum and Assessment Authority, London

DfEE (1995*) Lifetime Learning: A consultation document*, Department for Education and Employment, Crown Copyright, London

DfEE (1996) *Lifetime Learning: A policy framework*, Department for Education and Employment, Crown Copyright, London

DfEE (1997) *Excellence in Schools,* Cm 3681, The Stationery Office, London

DfEE (1998a) *LEA Behaviour Support Plans,* Department for Education and Employment Circular No 1/98, Department for Education and Employment, London

DfEE (1998b) *The Learning Age: A renaissance for a new Britain,* Cm 3790, Department for Education and Employment, London

DfEE (1998c) *Higher Education for the 21st Century: Response to the Dearing Report,* Department for Education and Employment, London

DfEE (1998d) *Further Education for the New Millennium: Response to the Kennedy Report,* Department for Education and Employment, London

DfEE (1998e) *The Teaching and Higher Education Act 1998* (Commencement No 2, Transitional Provisions), Order 1998, Department for Education and Employment, London

DFEE (1998f) *Qualifying for Success: Outcomes and next steps,* Letter from Rob Hull to Heads of Secondary Schools in England and Principals of all Colleges in the Further Education Sector in England and other organizations on the attached list, 3 April 1998

DfEE (1998g) *University for Industry: Engaging people in learning for life: Pathfinder Prospectus*, Department for Education and Employment, London

DES (1989) *Discipline in Schools (The Elton Report)*, HMSO, London

Education and Employment Committee (1998) *Disaffected Children*, vol 1: Report and Proceedings of the Committee Department for Education and Employment, The Stationery Office, London

Field, J (1996) Open learning and consumer culture, in *The Learning Society: Challenges and trends*, ed P Raggatt, N Small, Routledge, London

Fryer, R (1997) *Learning for the 21st Century: First Report of the National Advisory Group for Continuing Education and Lifelong Learning*, DfEE, London

Garnett, L (1992) *Leaving Care and After*, National Children's Bureau, London

Gillborn, D and Gipps, C (1996*) Recent Research on the Achievements of Ethnic Minority Pupils*, Ofsted, London

Glennerster, H (1998) Tackling poverty at its roots? in *An Inclusive Society: Strategies for tackling poverty*, ed C Oppenheim, Institute for Public Policy Research, London

Green, A (1997) *Education, Globalization and the Nation State*, Macmillan, Basingstoke

Green, A and Steedman, H (1997) *Into the Twenty-first Century: An assessment of British skills, profiles and prospects*, Centre for Economic Performance, London

Halpern, D (1998) Poverty, social exclusion and the policy-making process: the road from theory to practice, in *An Inclusive Society: Strategies for tackling poverty*, ed C Oppenheim, Institute for Public Policy Research, London

Hodgson, A and Spours K (1997a) From the 1991 White Paper to the Dearing Report: a conceptual and historical framework for the 1990s, in *Dearing and Beyond: 14–19 Qualifications, Frameworks and Systems,* ed A Hodgson and K Spours, Kogan Page, London

Hodgson, A and Spours, K (1997b) *Dearing and Beyond: 14–19 Qualifications, Frameworks and Systems*, Kogan Page, London

Hodgson, A, Spours, K and Young, M (1998) Broader and broader still in post-16 education, *Times Educational Supplement*, 16 May 1998

Hodgson, A and Spours, K (1999) *New Labour's Educational Agenda: Issues and policies for education and training from 14+*, Kogan Page, London

Home Office (1988) *Behaviour and Delinquency: A review of research*, HMSO, London

Howarth, C and Kenway, P (1998) A multi-dimensional approach to social exclusion indicators, in *An Inclusive Society: Strategies for tackling poverty*, ed C Oppenheim, Institute for Public Policy Research, London

Istance, D and Williamson, H (1996) *16 and 17-year-olds in Mid-Glamorgan Not in Education, Training or Employment (Status 0)*, TEC, Mid-Glamorgan

Kennedy, H (1997) *Learning Works: Widening participation in further education*, FEFC, Coventry

Labour Party (1996a) *Lifelong Learning*, Labour Party, Coventry

Labour Party (1996b) *Labour's Plans for a Skills Revolution*, Labour Party, London

Labour Party (1996c) *Getting Welfare to Work*, Labour Party, London

Labour Party (1996d) *Aiming Higher*, Labour Party, London

Leney, T, Lucas, N and Taubman, D (1998) *Learning Funding: The impact of FEFC funding, evidence from twelve FE colleges*, Institute of Education/NATFHE, London

McGivney, V (1993) Participation and non-participation: a review of the literature, in *Adult Learners, Education and Training*, ed R Edwards, S Sieminski and D Zeldin, Routledge, London

McLaughlin, E (1998) Taxes, benefits and paid work, in *An Inclusive Society: Strategies for tackling poverty*, ed C Oppenheim, Institute for Public Policy Research, London

Martinez, P (1995) *Student Retention in Further and Adult Education: The evidence*, Mendip Paper 084, FEDA, Blagdon

Metcalf, H (1997) *Class and Higher Education: The participation of young people from lower social classes*, Council for Industry and Higher Education, London

Moser, Sir C (1999) *Improving Literacy and Numeracy: A fresh start*, Crown Copyright, London

Mulgan, G (1998) Social exclusion: joined up solutions to joined up problems, in *An Inclusive Society: Strategies for tackling poverty*, ed C Oppenheim, Institute for Public Policy Research, London

Murphy, P and Elwood, J (1997) Gendered experiences, choices and achievement – exploring the links, *International Journal of Inclusive Education 1998*, **2**, pp 95–118

National Commission of Inquiry into Higher Education (1997) *Higher Education in the Learning Society*, NCIHE, London

OECD (1996) *Lifelong Learning for All*, OECD, London

Ofsted (1996) *Exclusions from Secondary Schools 1995/6*, HMSO, London

Oppenheim, C (1998) Poverty and social exclusion: an overview, in *An Inclusive Society: Strategies for tackling poverty*, ed C Oppenheim, Institute for Public Policy Research, London

Parsons, C and Castle, F (1998) Trends in exclusions from school – New Labour, new approaches, *Forum for Promoting 3–19 Comprehensive Education,* **40** (1), Spring 1998

Pearce, N and Hillman, J (1998) *Wasted Youth: Raising achievement and tackling social exclusion*, Institute for Public Policy Research, London

Rathbone CI, CSV, NACRO and TEN (1997) *Learning and Earning: Education, training and employment for all in the 21st century*, Rathbone CI, CSV, NACRO and TEN, London

Robinson, P (1998) Employment and social inclusion, in *An Inclusive Society: Strategies for tackling poverty*, ed C Oppenheim, Institute for Public Policy Research, London

Robinson, P and Oppenheim, C (1998) *Social Exclusion Indicators: A submission to the social exclusion unit*, IPPR, London

Room, G (1995) *Beyond the Threshold: The measurement and analysis of social exclusion*, The Policy Press, London

Smithers, A and Robinson, P (1986) *Trends in Higher Education*, Council for Industry and Higher Education, London

Social Exclusion Unit (1998) *Truancy and Social Exclusion*, The Stationery Office, London

Spours, K (1995) *Post-Compulsory Education and Training: Statistical trends*, Learning for the Future Working Paper 7, London Institute of Education/Centre for Education and Industry, University of Warwick

Times Educational Supplement (1998) Heads condemn sixth-form plans, 10 April 1998

West, A and McCormick, J (1998) Three steps and beyond: micro-economies for social inclusion, in *An Inclusive Society: Strategies for tackling poverty*, ed C Oppenheim, Institute for Public Policy Research, London

2

European Approaches to Social Exclusion

Tom Leney

Introduction

Recently, a growing number of researchers and policy makers in the UK have enthusiastically taken up the term social exclusion. Proponents maintain that a social exclusion approach offers a dynamic form of analysis and policy development that could potentially tackle more effectively at least some problems and challenges that previous approaches were unable to resolve. They see a social exclusion/social inclusion approach as appropriate to analysing and tackling issues of poverty and disadvantage in a society such as Britain at the end of the 20th century.

The concept of social exclusion has its origin in French intellectual and political debates. Furthermore, the agencies of the European Commission have been successful in promoting the combating of social exclusion as an important element in the European Union's economic, employment and social policies. This latter development is bringing about a certain convergence in the policy debate – though not necessarily in established practice or in institutional arrangements – across the EU member states. Thus, it seems wholly appropriate to survey the European dimension as part of an exploration of research and policy associated with social exclusion in the UK.

This chapter will begin by exploring briefly how the concept of social exclusion came into use in the research and policy debate in the UK. Then the social exclusion perspectives will be compared with other approaches to analysing and tackling issues such as poverty, disadvantage and the development of an underclass. Next, I will outline how the European Commission has developed its approach to tackling social exclusion as an important part of its economic and social policies, and draw attention to some of the strengths and weaknesses of the position the Commission has been able to adopt. Finally I will draw attention to some of the main policy areas in education and training in which different European countries are attempting to tackle inequality and, explicitly or implicitly, social exclusion.

The UK context in which the term 'social exclusion' came into use

Once the new sociology of the education (see, for example, Young, 1971 and Bernstein, 1975) had opened up fresh perspectives on the relationship between the structuring of knowledge and the structures of society, and while a number of research traditions continued to develop, the approach exemplified by the cultural studies movement associated with the Centre for Contemporary Cultural Studies in Birmingham became the dominant influence in education research in Britain. *Learning to Labour* (Willis, 1977) was an influential study that emerged from CCCS. Willis attempted to develop a theory that would provide a sophisticated link between social class, culture and the reproduction of the division between mental and manual labour. Through a series of interviews with a group of 'lads', the study relied on cultural explanations of reproduction and resistance to attempt to explain why working-class children got working-class jobs.

At the same time, the publication of *Fifteen Thousand Hours* (Rutter *et al*, 1979) helped to create an intellectual climate in which both the differential impact of particular schools on the experience and, particularly, on the achievements of young people became prominent.

The cultural reproduction theorists seemed unable to make an effective link between patterns of social or cultural reproduction and individual processes of conformity and resistance, and tended to revert to an over-reliance on structural notions of reproduction. Meanwhile, the 'school improvement' research, whatever its weaknesses, challenged the prevailing theoretical formulation to take account of the particular impacts of particular learning environments on young people in transition in a more dynamic and, simultaneously, a more policy-oriented way. One outcome of these tensions (together with other developments, whose analysis lies outside the scope of this chapter) was that, by the end of the 1980s, many researchers in the fields of education and youth were looking for more encompassing and less narrowly restrictive conceptual frameworks to work within.[1]

It was on to this ground that the concepts of social exclusion, social inclusion and tackling social exclusion found their way into UK research, then policy and debates in the 1990s. As Lynne Chisholm has put it:

> The term social exclusion is a recent entrant into British research and [even more so] policy discourse on disadvantage and poverty. . . . [Yet] *L'exclusion sociale* has become an almost banally familiar term of political, policy and public debate in France since the mid-1980s. Social exclusion now serves as a fundamental paradigm for the analysis of contemporary French society and its discontents.

> (Bynner, Chisholm and Furlong, 1998: 4–5)

That the new Labour government set up a cross-departmental Social Exclusion Unit in 1997, and that the Institute for Public Policy Research has now produced a report on tackling social exclusion (Oppenheim, 1998), indicates the status that this recent entrant has achieved in a short time.

Tackling social exclusion, compared to other approaches to poverty and disadvantage

The IPPR Report just referred to attempts to create a multi-dimensional framework to link a social exclusion approach to the analysis of problems associated with poverty with the lived experience of individuals and groups of people, including feelings of anomie and being – perhaps only in some respects – an outsider. At the same time a social exclusion/inclusion perspective attempts to recognize the dynamics of the networks and trajectories of both individuals and groups over a time-scale. Thus, contributors to the IPPR Report maintain that social exclusion is a more dynamic and relevant concept than earlier approaches to tackling poverty, disadvantage and disaffection (Oppenheim, 1998).

Oppenheim argues that the framework for policies relating to poverty and disadvantage has changed over the past two decades. She cites the globalization of the economy, changes in the labour market and the organization of work, patterns of income and wealth distribution, changes in patterns of family formation and a shift in how individuals now see their place in society. She goes on to argue that these trends mean that we need to unpick the differences between poverty and social exclusion, in order to clarify what the goals of policy in social, education and related areas should be. Oppenheim makes the following distinctions:

Poverty is defined as an absolute or relative lack of material resources, particularly income, and the policy solution usually proposed is the provision of an adequate minimum income, whether through employment or benefit;

Deprivation is defined as a lack of material standards, services and amenities, and the policy solution envisaged in this scenario is usually to provide adequate minimum standards of living that include income, services (including education and training) and amenities;

Social exclusion is given a more complex definition: the process of being detached from the organizations and communities that compose society, and from the rights and obligations (which are economic, social, political, cultural and educational) of mainstream society. Policy solutions include both providing access to employment, income, adequate housing and education, training and other resources and developing processes that create and reinforce forms of social inclusion, such as family support and common citizenship, social capital (hence the emphasis on education and training) and regenerating local communities.

Thus, social exclusion attempts to take full account of the processes of marginalization from the mainstream of society, which can include the labour market, family and informal networks, and from effective access to the local and national facilities of the state. It concerns institutional processes, a range of factors and the individual's own experience at different moments in the life cycle. And policies to address social exclusion involve, at least, access to employment that can be sustained, access to education, training and skills, changes in the housing sector, improved standards of living – including for those locked outside the labour market – and an enhancement of social capital through improved social networks.

In summary, the particular emphasis of the social exclusion approach is to place importance on both access to income and other services and on the relational aspect of access. Its proponents maintain that the multi-dimensional approach to exclusion and the relational aspect of the analysis allow a more dynamic approach than did earlier analyses of poverty and deprivation, in terms of both research and policy.

Clearly, the social exclusion/social inclusion perspective is a defining element of New Labour's innovations across the field of education and training, for example in the New Deal for unemployed young people, and in the proposed Education Action Zones. It is worth remembering that both set out to tackle problems that have persisted in the UK through successive reforms, both place emphasis on the role of education and training in tackling other problems and both, however innovatory, are still pretty well untested.

It may also be worthwhile to examine the concept of social exclusion with reference to another theory that appeared to be gaining currency a few years ago – the idea that a new underclass was developing in advanced capitalist societies.

The article (Bynner *et al*, 1998) referred to above suggests that researchers and policy makers concerned with the transitions and trajectories of young people who are vulnerable should consider the social exclusion approach, but should also reflect on 'underclass' theories. The latter, which derive originally from the work of Myrdal (underclass is the translation into English of a Swedish term) was given impetus by the strategies adopted to combat poverty in the United States in the 1960s, and seemed poised in the 1980s to become an important conceptual framework for analysis. An underclass approach to analysing poverty sees the tendency for economic and social polarization, combined with a credentialism in education and the labour market, and both impacting on particular communities intensely, as creating almost impenetrable barriers for the unemployed and groups with low skills. This is associated with particular geographical communities as well as with particular groups, such as the unemployed, people with low skill levels and ethnic minorities. The earlier variant of underclass theory explained growing inequality and polarization in affluent societies as the key factors that bring an underclass into existence. The 1980s variant of underclass analysis in Britain, according to Bynner *et al*, placed less emphasis on the impact of social structures on young people with multiple disadvantages as they lived through the Thatcherist era of politics and economics. Instead it tended to categorize disadvantaged young people as 'somehow directly or indirectly responsible for their plight' (Bynner *et al*, 1998: 3).

Not surprisingly, Chisholm observes, an account of disadvantage that individualizes the problem of vulnerable young people found little longer-term support among youth researchers. Nevertheless, she argues, a social exclusion approach needs to take full account of the earlier, robust insights of Myrdel's underclass theory.

Clearly, it is quite possible that social exclusion theories and policies run a risk of becoming reductionist – either by falling back into a version of reproduction theory or by pathologizing individuals or specific social groups. The challenge is to develop an analysis that links the changing social structures of advantage/disadvantage with the mechanisms and networks that operate in Britain as we reach the end of the century, and which can also engage with the trajectories and feelings of the individuals or groups involved.

In the field of policy, numerous proponents of the social exclusion approach in the UK have begun the attempt to map out the links between structural aspects of disadvantage and the relational aspect of developing networks, and access to them (see, for example: Whelan and Whelan, 1995; Walker, 1995; and Mulgan, 1998). The IPPR Report (Glennerster, 1998) attempts an assessment of how education can assist in tackling poverty. Glennerster points out that there is a clear correlation between poor educational achievement and unemployment or low income, and, furthermore, that this is linked to the wide dispersion of levels of education attainment in the UK, and the impact of globalization and technology on the patterns and organization of work. He emphasizes that whatever the causal relationship, poverty and deprivation in children's families and neighbourhood tend to correlate with their school performance. More cautiously, he goes on to recognize that research is inconclusive as to how far investing more in education improves individuals' earning capacity. He indicates, too, that while education and training programmes for the unemployed have produced some gains in the UK, success is patchy and varied, and can be costly. Oddly – and adding a note of perhaps unintended pessimism in a collection of essays on tackling social exclusion – Glennerster states that virtually all the evidence suggests that spending more money on schools and on reducing class size beyond their present levels is a waste of money. After a brief, and perhaps necessarily superficial, survey of some of the curriculum, school management and wider community factors that are most often components of successful schooling, Glennerster concludes on the following cautious note: 'We should be extremely careful about offering easy solutions or suggesting that education can solve the problems of poverty. But carefully thought out quality interventions, targeted at low performers, both adults and children, especially in poor areas, could, over the long haul, make a difference' (p 140).

This introduction has attempted to show that the growing number of proponents of the social inclusion/social exclusion perspective believe that it can add a dynamic dimension to research and policy debates. The perspective offers the possibility of making meaningful links between: social structures with their related inequalities of poverty and deprivation; social relationships and networks; and the experience of people as they experience a range of transitions. Later chapters will explore this contention in a range of educational and training contexts.

The development of the European Commission's policy

It may now be helpful to turn back to the European level, firstly by tracing the emphasis that the European Commission places on combating social exclusion as an important part of its social and economic policies. Since the early years of the decade, the policy of the European Commission (EC) has increasingly come to emphasize the importance of combating social exclusion as a multi-dimensional phenomenon. For this reason, the Commission has certainly broadened out its more traditional approach to addressing issues of poverty and unemployment. It may be helpful to trace both how and in what context the policy has developed.[2]

An early step was taken in 1990, with the establishment of a European Observatory[3] on Policies to Combat Social Exclusion. Influenced substantially by Jacques Delors and Francophone currents of thought within the Commission, discussions were held and data gathered to decide whether the Commission should keep to the well-established parameters of policy on poverty, or whether the time was right to extend the analysis and the policies to take up a social exclusion perspective.[4] Over the course of three years or so, the second of these views prevailed, and the European Commission's policy became to integrate the earlier distributional approaches to poverty with a broader approach that emphasized the relational aspects of social exclusion. It should be noted that even at this early stage, the main policy emphasis of the Commission was on combating unemployment and promoting employability, as part of a package of policies geared to improving competitiveness and growth (Room, 1995).

Thus, in 1995, when the European Commission published its White Paper on education and training (European Commission, 1995), it proposed the need for an inclusive learning society. In doing so, it took as its starting point an analysis of the upheavals that had occurred in European economic activity, which had resulted in the phenomenon of youth unemployment. The White Paper states unambiguously that these upheavals constitute 'a trend which has increased uncertainty all-round and for some has led to intolerable situations of exclusion' (p 5).

The stated objective of the Commission's White Paper was to help find ways that member states could develop for all their citizens the broad-based knowledge and the skills and aptitudes needed for employability. Among the other components of the approach that the White Paper developed, lifelong access to education and training and measures to combat social exclusion have an important role. The Commission expresses the view that so far as the organization of education and training is concerned, there is now common agreement across the EU that:

- a broad and increasingly comprehensive knowledge base for all young people, and training for employment are prerequisites, and are no longer seen as in conflict with one another;
- bridges need to be built between schools and the business sector;
- equal rights in education are increasingly recognized and applied by member states, and this involves combating exclusion through forms of positive discrimination for those with disadvantages;
- the development of an information society, whilst making more demands, has also facilitated innovation.

The actions proposed by the Commission specifically in the field of education to combat social exclusion have, until now, been quite limited. Certainly, the approach of the Commission, under its structural programmes, is to encourage and fund training in the member states designed to counter unemployment and to improve the employability of marginalized groups. Also, the research and dissemination activities of the Commission and its agencies (such as the Leonardo Project, and the work of the European Centre for the Development of Vocational Training – CEDEFOP) are making a notable contribution to the internationalization of debate and research on the issue. The Commission's programme, which is outlined in the White Paper, places emphasis on inclusive elements – encouraging the acquisition of new knowledge and the recognition of skills gained other than through formal qualifications, extending vocational education and training, and encouraging apprenticeship, traineeships and new forms of 'alternance'. However, as implied above, the only specific actions that the White Paper on the learning society adopts with reference to combating social exclusion are second chance schools and the concept of European voluntary service. The former is now established as a small pilot in the member states, while the latter appears to be less prominent an initiative than might have been anticipated.

In this regard, it is important to bear in mind that the terms of successive treaties define a position in which the European Commission can take a leading role on certain policy issues, while on other issues it must observe a subsidiarity, which member states guard carefully and jealously. The principle of subsidiarity applies across the fields of education and training. This limits the interventions that the Commission can make in education and training policies, and the allocation of its budget reflects this position.

However, the main thrust of the Commission's policy on combating social exclusion has come through the EU's employment policies, which reached a key point of development in the autumn of 1997. In July 1997 the Commission had published its Agenda 2000 (European Commission, 1997a), which set a broad agenda for the Commission itself and for member states. It set objectives of achieving sustainable economic growth alongside a strategic approach to improving employment and skill levels, and for combating unemployment. Strong emphasis was placed on both economic and social cohesion. The perspectives contained in this policy blueprint were taken forward to the negotiations that formed part of the Amsterdam Treaty (European Commission, 1997b) that was signed in October 1997, and which, in turn, led to the calling of an inter-government conference on unemployment during the Luxembourg presidency.

The Luxembourg conference, held late in 1997, attempted for the first time to produce agreement between the member states that they would co-ordinate their employment policies. On the basis that a sound macro-economic framework could be developed, and that a sustained upturn in European economies and a genuine internal market were prerequisites for tackling unemployment, the Conference decided that the European Commission should attempt to negotiate the member states' agreement to co-ordinate their employment policies, in order to both improve competitiveness and combat unemployment (European Commission, 1997c). The main emphasis was to be on small business (SMEs), information technologies, new economic and employment sectors, trans-European networks (including research) and the creation of sustainable jobs. The report of the conference placed particular emphasis on education, initial and continuing training and the development of appropriate research networks. It appears that the Commission was attempting to develop an approach that was not dirigiste, but which set general policy goals and provided a framework in which some convergence of the national employment policies could occur, without negating the particular circumstances, structures and traditions of particular member states.

The Commission's particular role after the Luxembourg Conference was to set up and co-ordinate discussions through which each member state could produce its policy guidelines according to agreed criteria, which would then become the subject of action plans. Emphasis was to be placed on the strategies needed to reduce youth unemployment and on developing and funding activity that involves developing employability, rather than passive support for the unemployed.

The Commission's Communication on the national action plans for unemployment was published in June 1998 (European Commission, 1998). At this point, the Commission is clearly relieved and pleased that each member state has followed through its commitment to produce an action plan, and reports that this marks a move towards a more comprehensive and inclusive employment strategy across the European Union. The Commission believes that this may open the way towards a more strongly community level approach to competitiveness and to combating exclusion. However, the Commission is also clearly conscious that some of the plans are vague or merely list a number of initiatives that were already taking place. It is also clear that member states are finding it difficult to develop policies that achieve an appropriate balance between reinserting the excluded into employment, and preventing the new groups in the population from drifting into long-term unemployment. The emphasis in most of the plans is on the former.

In conclusion, it is demonstrably the case that the European Commission has been influential in promoting both research and policies within a social exclusion framework, although it is required to keep its role of subsidiarity in education and training matters clearly in mind.

Emphases across the EU member states

Up to this point, this introduction to the European context has concentrated on developing aspects of the research and policy debates. It will perhaps be helpful to conclude with a brief overview of the range of specific areas of education and training policy in which the different European Union member states are – against the background of their own varying histories, traditions, structural arrangements and political processes – attempting to tackle disadvantage. This may have a direct relevance to tackling social exclusion.[5] Several aspects are worth emphasizing.

Providing access for all to pre-school education

This has been a marked priority across the member states of the European Union, in part to counter the effects of social disadvantage at an early, formative stage of a child's development. However, the kinds of provision made and the proportion of the pre-school cohort receiving pre-school education both vary from country to country (see Eurostat and Eurydice, 1997, Chapter C).

Providing common opportunities for access to a wide range of knowledge and a growing range of skills during the phases of compulsory education

Primary education has been divided into phases or stages in most EU member states, to provide greater coherence in the child's learning experience. Arrangements for secondary transfer vary, with some systems remaining selective and others comprehensive. Generally, there may be some trend towards comprehensivization, but many of the systems operate selection of one kind or another at secondary transfer. Nevertheless, specialization has been delayed over the past few years in all systems and emphasis is placed on the acquisition of basic skills and broad knowledge, with a growing emphasis on new kinds of skills and knowledge, such as ICT (Eurydice, 1997), meeting the challenge of increasingly diverse cohorts of young people (including issues of language, gender and ethnicity), and a wide range of special needs. No member state of the EU has been successful in educating all of its young people to what it would see as a satisfactory basic level. Ways of grouping pupils vary, with some states remaining committed to 'repeats' for pupils who do not successfully complete a year or grade. Approaches to teaching young people with special learning needs also vary from one country to another, as do, for example, the proportion of young people who have a physical disability and who are educated separately. In most member states, patterns of geographical mobility mean that teaching more hetero-geneous cohorts of young people has increasingly become an issue of pedagogical concern (Green, Leney and Wolf, 1997; Chapter 3).

'Making provision for a high proportion of each cohort to continue into post-compulsory education and training, which means that the end of compulsory education marks the end of schooling for fewer and fewer young people. . .'

Although rates of participation and qualification in post-compulsory edu-cation and VET vary considerably between one country and another in the European Union, the clear trend has been towards high levels of participa-tion in each member state. The rapid increase in participation by 16-year-olds did not take off in the UK until the mid- to late-1980s, and participation and qualification rates for 17 and 18-year-olds in this country are still considerably lower than is the case in most comparable EU member states. Providing appropriate general and vocational courses for the whole range of the cohort and avoiding educational 'dead ends' and 'parking lots' has been a challenge for each European system.

Opening up constructive opportunities for the 10 to 20 per cent of young people who leave formal education or training with few or no qualifications

Some 10 to 20 per cent of each age cohort are defined across the member states as particularly disadvantaged or excluded in that the young people concerned leave formal education or training with few or no qualifications. These groups are identified as containing many young people who are disaf-fected. Each member state, including the UK, has attempted a number of policy solutions to the issues posed, but the problem appears to remain obdurate. A number of the new Labour Government's initiatives aimed to tackle this issue, notably, the New Deal.

Improving the quality and raising the status of vocational education and training (VET) and tackling the status differential between general education and VET (including apprenticeships)

While the high status of general education ensures that in most member states, though not all, the proportion of the age cohort that takes a general education qualification in the post-compulsory phase has remained static or grown, governments have relied substantially on the growth of vocational courses and qualifications to enable a higher percentage than used to be the case to progress through the post-compulsory phase. Different countries are trying different approaches to tackling the educational and status divides that mostly exist between academic and vocational courses (Lasonen and

Young, 1998). This has also been one of the factors that have led to a renewed interest in apprenticeship and other forms of training such as 'alternance'. As well as the kinds of provision and qualification available, most member states are seeking ways of opening up more flexible pathways between different kinds of education and training.

Recognizing skills gained through other means than formal qualification, and establishing ways of achieving more flexible access to both higher education and lifelong learning

The growing emphasis on access to continuing education and training and the importance attached to the development of lifelong learning have led to an examination of the limits of traditional methods of access to and qualification in both higher and continuing education and training. Several European systems, including, of course, much of higher education in the UK, have explored the possibilities of modularized or unitized qualifications. Developments such as credit accumulation and transfer are attracting interest as a more inclusive method for the individual to acquire a portfolio of recognized qualifications. Furthermore, several member states, as well as the European Commission, are turning attention to the issue of how skills gained other than through formal qualifications can be recognized and validated.

Conclusion

Necessarily, this chapter has covered wide ground in surveying the European context. In doing so, it has been possible to explore the possibilities opened up by a social exclusion perspective, and to indicate where some of the difficulties in the approach may lie.

The European Commission has been influential in encouraging the member states' research and policy communities to explore and give serious attention to a social exclusion/social inclusion approach. This is, in turn, indicative of the increasing importance of collaborative policy and research networks that cross the boundaries of EU member states.

Each member state is, of course, seeking to find solutions that may meet the needs of its own particular structures, processes and traditions. But it does appear that – across the range of issues that this book explores – the different countries of the EU face some similar problems, and have similar policy and research priorities. In this context, tackling social exclusion is a perspective that has grown increasingly influential over the last decade.

Notes

1. Sociological approaches to youth and schooling in a number of EU states are explored in some detail in a report titled *Les Approches Sociologiques de la Jeunesse Scolarisee en Europe* (Boyer *et al*, 1997). The UK contribution was prepared by Andy Green and Tom Leney.

2. Of course, the previous UK government favoured the maximum influence of market factors in social policy and, in any case, opposed the Commission's more interventionist social policies, such as the Social Chapter of the Maastricht Treaty. Whilst continuing to adopt a significantly market approach to many issues of education and training, the new Labour government has quickly adopted the 'social exclusion' frame of reference for some key aspects of its social policy.
3. As with a number of terms introduced in this chapter, the concept of an observatory derives from French policy-making traditions. An Observatoire is somewhat like a think-tank in that it assembles data, creates scenarios and analyses policy options. The difference is that the forum may actually take decisions, and the participants at this level are the social partners involved in whatever the process. The European Commission uses observatories, in this sense, quite frequently. The author is currently participating in a feasibility study for the European Commission's DG22, with colleagues from France, Belgium, Germany and Spain (together with Michael Young, Head of the Post-16 Education Centre), to establish whether a European Observatory on innovation in vocational education and training could have a useful role.
4. A clear account of the work of the observatory is given by Jos Berghman (1995) in his contribution to *Beyond the Threshold*.
5. A detailed descriptive analysis of all the EU member states' education systems is available on the Internet through the European Commission's Eurydice Web pages, which give easy access to the Eurydice Database on Education Systems. Two further publications give an overview of European education systems (Eurostat and Eurydice, 1997) and of European VET systems (Eurostat and CEDEFOP, 1997). The Institute of Education has conducted a detailed analysis of trends in education and training across the EU member states (Green, Leney and Wolf, 1997).

References

Berghman, J (1995) Social exclusion in Europe: policy context and analytical framework, in *Beyond The Threshold: The measurement and analysis of social exclusion*, ed G Room, The Policy Press, Bristol

Bernstein, B (1975) *Class, Knowledge and Control,* vol 2, Routledge and Kegan Paul, London

Boyer, R *et al* (1997) *Les Approches Sociologiques de la Jeunesse Scolarisee en Europe,* INRP, Paris

Bynner, J, Chisholm, L and Furlong, A (1998) *Youth, Citizenship and Social Change*, LAC 'Occlusions' Paper

European Commission (1995) White Paper: *Teaching and Learning – Towards the Learning Society,* Office for Official Publications of the European Communities, Brussels

European Commission (1997a) *Agenda 2000,* vol 1, Office for Official Publications of the European Communities, Brussels

European Commission (1997b) *European Union: Treaty of Amsterdam,* Office for Official Publications of the European Communities, Brussels

European Commission (1997c) *Presidency Conclusions – Extraordinary European Council Meeting on Employment,* Office for Official Publications of the European Communities, Brussels

European Commission (1998) *Commission Communication – From Guidelines to Action: The national action plans for employment,* Office for Official Publications of the European Communities, Brussels

Eurostat and Eurydice (1997) *Key Data on Education in the European Union,* Office for Official Publications of the European Communities, Brussels

Eurydice (1997) *A Decade of Reforms at Compulsory Education Level in the European Union (1984–1994),* Office for Official Publications of the European Communities, Brussels

Glennerster, H (1998) Tackling poverty at its roots? Education, in *An Inclusive Society: Strategies for tackling poverty,* ed C Oppenheim, Institute for Public Policy Research, London

Green, A, Leney, T and Wolf, A (1997) *Convergences and Divergences in European Education and Training Systems.* The report was prepared for the European Commission's Directorate General 22, who published a shortened Working Paper in 1998

Lasonen, J and Young, M (1998) *Strategies for Achieving Parity of Esteem in European Upper Secondary Education*, Institute for Educational Research, University of Jyväsklä, Finland

Mulgan, G (1998) Social exclusion: joined up solutions to joined up problems, in *An Inclusive Society: Strategies for tackling poverty,* ed C Oppenheim, Institute for Public Policy Research, London

Oppenheim, C (1998) Introduction, in *An Inclusive Society: Strategies for tackling poverty,* ed C Oppenheim, Institute for Public Policy Research, London

Room, G (1995) Poverty and social exclusion: the new European agenda for policy and research, in *Beyond The Threshold: The measurement and analysis of social exclusion,* ed G Room, The Policy Press, Bristol

Rutter, M *et al* (1979) *Fifteen Thousand Hours,* Paul Chapman Publishing, London

Social Exclusion Unit (1997) *Social Exclusion Unit: Purposes, work, priorities and working methods*, Cabinet Office, London

Walker, R (1995) The dynamics of poverty and social exclusion, in *Beyond The Threshold: The measurement and analysis of social exclusion,* The Policy Press, Bristol

Whelan, B and Whelan, J (1995) In what sense is poverty multidimensional? in *Beyond the Threshold: The measurement and analysis of social exclusion,* ed G Room, The Policy Press, Bristol

Willis, P (1977) *Learning to Labour, How Working Class Kids Get Working Class Jobs,* Saxon House, Aldershot

Young, M (1971) *Knowledge and Control: New directions for the sociology of education,* Collier Macmillan, London

3

Developing Social Capital: Dilemmas, Possibilities and Limitations in Education

Eva Gamarnikow and Anthony Green

The policy concern in the latter part of the 1990s with poverty, social exclusion and social change has frequently focused on social capital as an explanatory concept and as a policy strategy.[1] The concept of social capital has been used in a variety of policy contexts: health and health promotion,[2] education,[3] economic policy and economic development,[4] politics and democracy[5] and welfare reform.[6] This significantly abridged list highlights two key issues that make social capital worth investigating. The first concerns the concept itself, its plasticity and transdisciplinary applicability. Secondly, there is the convergence of traditionally self-contained policy discourses onto social capital building as a policy strategy to deliver successful outcomes in a variety of policy domains. The common thread is the rediscovery of civil society and its social foundation, trust.

In this chapter our aim is to explore the concept of social capital in relation to education. We shall begin by locating the multidisciplinary origins and definitions of social capital. Then we shall address the connections between social capital and the social policy of the 'Third Way', illustrated with brief reference to the high profile Education Action Zones (EAZs) policy (for a detailed analysis of the EAZ policy in the context of New Labour politics, see Gamarnikow and Green, forthcoming). We end with an outline of critical issues for social capital as these relate to contemporary educational policy.

Defining social capital

The concept of social capital, as it is currently being deployed (we shall turn to Bourdieu's (1986) version of social capital in the conclusion), has at least three very different disciplinary origins: in sociology, political science and economics. In sociology social capital is associated with Coleman's (1988, 1990) rational action theory; in political science with Putnam, Leonardi and Nanetti's (1993) work on Italian politics; and in economics with Fukuyama's (1995) comparative study of national capitalisms. In spite of their different emphases what all these perspectives have in common is the links they postulate between successful social outcomes (such as education, employment, family relationships, health, etc) and the presence of social capital. It is this link which makes social capital a relevant consideration in issues of social policy and policy analysis.

Coleman developed the concept of social capital to try to resolve the traditional sociological methodological problem of how to link micro and macro levels of social analysis. His specific concern was to bridge the theoretical gap between the individualistic, socially disembodied notion of the rational cost–benefit calculator in neo-liberal economics and the 'over-socialized', socially deterministic notion of social action in macro-sociologies. While neo-liberal economics attributes agency to social action through the notion of individual choice in the market, this fails to recognize the social embeddedness of actors and their choices. Meanwhile many sociological perspectives appear to deny agency to actors by seeing them as determined and constrained by social structure, but locate them within the social. The aim of the concept of social capital was to redefine certain aspects of society and to transform them from constraint to resource, thereby explaining how socially embedded actors make rational choices by drawing on social structures and relations as a resource.

Unlike other forms of capital (for example, financial, physical or human), social capital is not the property of individuals but 'inheres in the structure of relations between actors and among actors' (Coleman, 1988: S98). Coleman identified three aspects of social relations that constitute key forms of social capital: obligations, expectations and trustworthiness of structures; networks and information channels; and norms and effective sanctions. The most important of these are trust, shared norms and effective sanctions.

Coleman's concept of social capital as resources, such as trust, norms and sanctions that individuals can draw on is neutral in terms of the ends for which it is used (Foley and Edwards, 1997). For example, trust is as important in legal as for illicit purposes, organizations and institutions. He also claimed that it is context-specific: what functions as social capital in one situation may not work in another.

According to Coleman, there are two ways in which social capital is developed. The first is through its use as a resource: relying on the trustworthiness of structures increases their trustworthiness. The second is by introducing it to succeeding generations in the family and education. In this instance social capital is developed in the family through involved and supportive parenting which functions as investment in children and contributes to their educational achievement. Social capital is further developed when families are linked with each other in a variety of community networks, including schools, which share and reinforce common values. Educational achievement appears to be strongly correlated with family social capital.[7] For Coleman, if social capital is not generationally renewed in the family and education, social stability and cohesion are undermined.

The second key source of social capital conceptualization is Putnam, Leonardi and Nanetti's longitudinal study of the development of regional government institutions in Italy. The conclusions of *Making Democracy Work* (Putnam with Leonardi and Nanetti, 1993) are striking: the regions where regional government developed most effectively over the 20-year period studied (1970–1989) were not the wealthiest (the north), nor those which had received most development aid (the south), but those which had the highest density of networks of civic engagement, as measured by participation in all types of organizations in civil society, ranging from membership of sports clubs to political associations. These 'civic' regions also exhibited the highest levels of social trust and experienced the greatest increase in a variety of positive outcomes, such as educational achievement and levels of morbi-mortality. This finding led the authors to argue that networks of civic engagement constitute a key element of social capital that operates to enhance institutional performance in the production of collective goods, such as education and health.

Putnam, Leonardi and Nanetti (1993: 167) define social capital as 'features of social organization such as trust, norms and networks that can improve the efficiency of society by facilitating co-ordinated actions'. Social trust in modern complex societies arises not from personal relations but from norms of reciprocity and networks of civic engagement. Reciprocity restrains individualism and opportunism. Social networks institutionalize generalized reciprocity and make collective action a fruitful endeavour.

Unlike Coleman's concept, which is technically value-neutral, Putnam, Leonardi and Nanetti's social capital is a normative concept, linked explicitly to specific formations of democracy and democratization. Thus, all communities have social networks, but not all of these networks are productive in terms of social capital. Social networks can be vertical/hierarchical or horizontal/egalitarian. Vertical networks, for example clientism, do not foster trust or reciprocity, but are sustained through 'buying off' social superiors in exchange for protection and exclusionary nepotism or 'amoral familism' (Leonardi, 1995). Horizontal networks, or networks of civic engagement, do tend to foster trust and reciprocity. Societies or communities with dense horizontal social networks can draw on trust and reciprocity to develop more successful political and economic outcomes.

In this perspective social capital is developed in two ways. The first is similar to Coleman's, namely through use: engagement in civic networks fosters trust and trust increases the likelihood and success of collective action. The second is at the institutional level, where institutions are orientated towards producing collective goods that result in improved outcomes and greater trust.

In economics, social capital is seen as the fourth form of capital (Fukuyama, 1995). Unlike physical, financial and human capital which are private goods, social capital is a public good whose role is to lower transaction costs in the market. According to Fukuyama (1995) and other economists (Szreter, 1998) markets are not operated by the proverbial disembodied invisible hand, but by individual actors for whom market relations are forms of sociability. Sociability is formed by culture and, in particular, by the presence or absence of social capital. Societies with high levels of social capital can draw on trust in social relations to reduce the need for insurance and litigation and the costs associated with corruption, and to develop more co-operative, hence productive, ways of working in markets.

Fukuyama develops this argument further and claims that the neo-classical conception of the rational utility-maximizing actor is only 80 per cent correct because individual actors are socially embedded in families, communities, organizations and countries. These are all cultural institutions, embracing norms, values, symbols, meanings, roles and role expectations that impact very directly on the context and nature of individual choice in markets. Culture is arational, but provides the framework within which rational utility-maximizing decisions are made. In fact, Fukuyama's critique of neo-classical economics extends to the claim that markets are culturally determined and will take different forms in low trust/low social capital and high trust/high social capital societies.

Fukuyama (1995) defines social capital as trust and a thriving civil society. Trust is developed initially in the traditional nuclear family, within communities embodying a strong sense of norms, values and sanctions. However, intra-family social capital is insufficient for economic development, and familistic societies that do not have cultural traditions of trusting non-kin can move into the 'amoral familism' of, for example, southern Italy (Putnam with Leonardi and Nanetti, 1993; Leonardi, 1995) or reliance on criminality as an alternative form of association, as in Colombia (Rubio, 1997). High trust societies are those which have cultural traditions of co-operation and trust among non-kin in the realm of civil society, and, in particular, in economic institutions. These are the societies that will be able to develop large, productive corporations and become key economic players in global markets.

To sum up, trust is the constitutive element of social capital. The key social locations for its development are in the interconnected social institutions of: families, particularly in parent–child relations; communities with strong norms, values and sanctions; generalized cultural norms of reliability, reciprocity and accountability; dense social networks; and civic engagement (Hall, 1997). Their connectedness may take the form of benign spirals of reinforcement of social capital resources or of vicious circles of deteriorating stocks of social capital and accompanying social disintegration.

However, such formal accounts of social capital provide only part of the story and ignore significant tensions between different formulations. It is possible to discern a continuum of social capital manifestations. At one end of the continuum, social capital embraces progressive, liberal and civic notions of co-operation, empowerment, participation and community action in the construction of needs and priorities. As such the culture supports responsive, dynamic and sensitive state policy implementation in relation to an active and confident citizenry. Here civic engagement thrives. At the other extreme social capital may be realized in a normative order of traditional institutional forms, for instance, favouring two-parent nuclear families; locating the 'parenting deficit' in women's increased labour market activity; and arguing for a collective non-relativist moral regime of duties and responsibilities to which all are expected to conform, particularly those least well placed in the system. This may be reinforced by much hardened sanctions, 'tough love', 'tough on crime and tough on the causes of crime', 'three strikes and you're out', 'naming and shaming' and 'workfare not welfare' to put metal into social capital. At this end of the continuum traditional forms of power relations, although invisible in the accounts, appear to form an essential feature of social capital, rendering citizenship ambiguous in relation to subjecthood.

Social capital theory is multi-dimensional, thus slippery and ambiguous. As such it provides fertile ground for conceptualizing the politics of the 'Third Way'. It appears to offer rationales for encouraging both greater participation and democratization, as well as for greater conformity to traditional structures. While these are not necessarily in contradiction, in complex, socially and culturally heterodox societies tensions are inherent in social relations and structures. Not surprisingly perhaps, the concepts associated with social capital appear to have found favour with a variety of writers representing diametrically opposed political and economic perspectives: for example, Fukuyama (1995) on the right, and left-of-centre think tanks and networks, such as Demos (Demos, 1997; Perri 6, 1997a, 1997b), Institute for Public Policy Research (Oppenheim, 1998) and the Nexus Web site (http://www.netnexus.org/3wayecon).

'Third Way' policy and social capital

These formulations and definitions are significant in the context where it is claimed that there is an alternative approach to social policy which can avoid both the fragmentation of neo-liberal marketization and the bureaucracy and dependency culture of the welfare state. The discourses of social capital provide rationales for the 'Third Way,' the so-called 'radical centre' associated with the Blair government (Driver and Martell, 1998; Giddens, 1994, 1998). This accepts the logic of capitalist globalization, with free markets for goods and services and flexible markets for labour, but recognizes that certain individuals and groups who have been excluded from the 'success' of Tory Britain require the state to provide support and opportunities to help themselves. The basic ideas entailed in 'The Third Way' focus on empowering individuals, families and communities to move out of poverty, unemployment and social exclusion by a combination of individual responsibility, social support, education and welfare to work initiatives.

Thus, New Labour provides continuity with the Tory idea that the state should not do things 'for' people through macro-economic management and bureaucratic welfare provision. But in place of the Conservative preference for a non-interfering state and the Old Labour commitment to redistribution and welfare, New Labour ideology constructs the state as partner, enabler and provider of frameworks for opportunities for improved outcomes by regenerating social capital.

Although New Labour's 'Third Way' (Blair, 1997a, 1997b, 1998; Giddens, 1998) may still be no more than a constellation of statements and propositions about a political project concerned with developing an alternative to neo-liberal marketization and social democratic corporatism, there is a key notion binding them together. This is the concern with 'society', that aspect of the social world whose existence was specifically denied by Margaret Thatcher in her by now infamous statement made in an interview in *Woman's Own* in 1987: 'There is no society. There are only individuals and families'. The 'Third Way' project has a very eclectic view of society (terms such as community, stakeholders or partnership have been used), but the disparate elements are linked to populist notions of social cohesion and a commitment to addressing poverty and social exclusion. This brings civil society and building its social capital infrastructure into the policy frame.

If, as social capital theorists argue, abundance of social capital can be used to explain (positive or negative) social, political and economic outcomes in individuals, families and communities, then at the level of social policy social capital can be regarded as a tool to change society. If positive social outcomes are the result of the social capital resources of a community, then one of the ways in which unsuccessful communities can be helped is through the building of social capital. As we have seen, social capital consists of responsible families, thriving communities, strong norms, values and sanctions, dense social networks and civic engagement. Building social capital has come to signify interventions aimed at the constituent elements of social capital: deployment of parental, family and individual responsibilities and obligations (Social Exclusion Unit, 1998a); community participation in defining objectives and setting priorities (Social Exclusion Unit, 1998b); and structures and institutions of social support, such as community-level programmes using multi-agency or one-stop-shop approaches in which collaboration, co-operation and partnerships among agencies are key notions (Gamarnikow, 1998). Taken together, these provide integrated services and draw individuals and families into wider social networks. The underpinning assumption is that problems of poverty and social exclusion can best be dealt with by providing opportunities which individuals, families and communities are expected to take advantage of, in order to empower themselves. The community is then able to become an effective social context for mutually supportive institutional development.

The State and social capital

There are a number of important tensions at the heart of the notion of building social capital through state social policy. In the first instance, social capital is a feature of civil society, and in liberal democratic conceptions civil society and the state are mutually exclusive social arenas. It is this very separation which guarantees democracy and liberty and, more importantly, provides the space for the social relations and networks, the social capital of civil society, to flourish. State intervention in building social capital through social policy involves the state in fashioning and moulding civil society, thus undermining the latter's autonomy and, hence paradoxically, it might be argued, its social capital. If the social norms and values to which we are expected to adhere are prescribed by state policy, little space is left for communities to develop their own, except perhaps, in opposition to the state.

Secondly, because social capital is a feature of an autonomous civil society, it is difficult for sections of societies lacking social capital to build it, since its development is linked to its autonomous, self-sustaining use. In order to address this apparent infinite critical regress whereby social capital can only be developed if it already exists and the contradictions inherent in the idea of state involvement in building social capital, Leonardi (1995) developed a model that links social capital and social policy through the operation of institutions in civil society. He argues that social capital is not an end in itself, but a means for effecting positive collective outcomes. This shifts the analysis from an exclusive focus on individuals and communities and includes institutional performances and their effectiveness. In fact, Leonardi argues that institutional performance can affect, positively or negatively, the norms and values of individuals and communities. Key policy issues arise around addressing the problem of how the state can operate to support and develop social institutions which in themselves constitute positive social capital generators: 'Where local institutions have shown their ability to produce collective goods, it has a positive impact on the patterns of social values, and over time it helps to build up social capital' (Leonardi, 1995: 176).

If the two key elements in building social capital are, firstly, supporting individual attitudes and values and, secondly, strengthening institutional performance, it is possible to conceptualize the state's problem for social policy in relation to social capital building as one of intervening in any one of three different models. Leonardi's own model provides one sequence of social capital building as:

MODEL 1

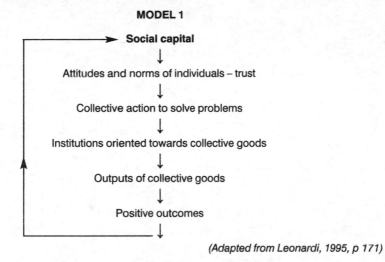

(Adapted from Leonardi, 1995, p 171)

Figure 3.1: *Model 1: Individual integrity for collective goods*

Maintaining the key elements of the model but with the sequence starting with institutions oriented to the production of collective goods, rather than with individuals, the logic of Leonardi's argument suggests another model of the virtuous sequence of building social capital which we depict as:

MODEL 2

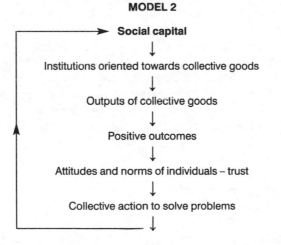

Figure 3.2: *Model 2: Institutional action for collective goods*

This second model is an interesting way to try to conceptualize the link between policy orientation, institutional change and social outcomes in the context of building social capital. It situates the policy focus in partnerships of providers and multi-agency working (Gamarnikow, 1998).

There is a possible third model, however. We might accept that Leonardi has set out the main constituents that are required for social capital forma-

MODEL 3

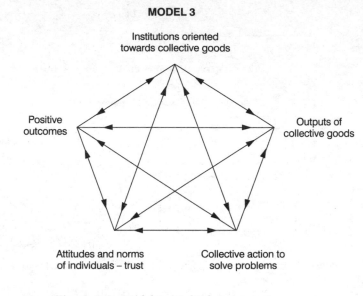

Figure 3.3: *Model 3: Multiple interventions*

tion but it is possible to conceive of non-linear sequencing such that the elements are all interconnected and mutually constitutive. This allows for a possible figure (Figure 3.3: multiple interventions). Here no particular sequencing is assumed but each element is taken to be necessary in a network of mutually reinforcing relations. Taken thus, there is no reduction in the essential complexity of procedures for policy analysis and diagnosis, nor in the contestability of any particular policy form, content or procedures for implementation. Causal dogmatism is potentially displaced by a form of atheoretical pragmatism with the emphasis on mutual co-operation and partnership. This may well be indicative of 'Third Way' policy presentation, as in the SEU's paradigmatic 'joined up solutions to joined up problems'.

'Third Way' politics of policy formation and implementation recognize that the liberal assumption of clear boundaries between state and civil society cannot apply. It offers rethinking and recognizing that top-down and bottom-up policy regimes are not alternatives, but exist at a dynamic interface consisting of often intractable cultural processes of governmentality (Foucault, 1980). While 'Third Way' policy glimpses this in some respects, we should not underestimate the difficulties which may frequently be glossed over with a rhetoric of 'networks' and 'partnerships', nor the theoretical shortcomings of this perspective or its practical effectiveness. We will outline some of the key issues, taking the Education Action Zones policy as illustrative of these general concerns.

Education Action Zones

The overall focus of New Labour's education policy is to raise educational standards by setting ambitious targets for literacy and numeracy achievement, and adopting a principle of 'zero tolerance of underperformance' applying to all schools and local education authorities (Secretary of State for Education, 1997). Instead of relying on the market logic of parental choice imposed by Tory educational reforms, which resulted in predicted winners and failing schools and widened the education gap, measured by GCSE results, between the top 10 per cent and bottom 10 per cent of schools (Ofsted, 1998: 20), the aim of New Labour policy is to raise standards in all schools, and to reduce the education gap:

> Our goal is a society in which everyone is well educated. . . . Britain's economic prosperity and social cohesion both depend upon achieving that goal. . . . Our aim is excellence for everyone. If this is to be more than rhetoric, then persistent failure must be eradicated. Hence our commitment to zero tolerance of underperformance.
>
> (Secretary of State for Education, 1997: 9–10)

Education Action Zones (EAZs)[8] are a key policy initiative within this overall framework, focusing on raising educational standards in 'new and imaginative ways' (Secretary of State for Education, 1997: 39) in areas of severe social and economic deprivation and educational underachievement.

EAZs are local clusters of around 20 schools, one or two secondary schools, with feeder primaries and, optionally, special schools, 'working in a new partnership with the LEA, local parents, businesses, TECs and others . . . encourage[ing] innovative approaches to tackling disadvantage and raising standards' (DfEE, 1997: 4). The partnership, whose composition is flexible enough to encompass local needs, traditions and resources and ideas for creative collaboration, will run an EAZ through an Action Forum. There is extra funding of £1 million per annum over three years for each 'first wave' EAZ.

EAZs will be able to develop specialist schools; improve access to, and teaching of, information and communication technology; establish closer links between education and employment through work-related learning and pilots of GNVQ part one projects; and move into community education through family literacy schemes and early excellence centres.

Particularly controversial are the ideas associated with 'flexibility' in the Education Action Zones.[9] Proposals include: opting out of national agreements on teachers' pay and conditions in order to provide incentives to attract 'super teachers' and 'super heads'; experimenting with extending the school day and academic year, including before and after school, Saturday and holiday provision; opting out of the National Curriculum to make 'additional opportunities for work-related learning and community work or . . . literacy and numeracy' (DfEE, 1997: 8); the ceding of some or a majority of the powers of governing bodies to the Action Forum; encouraging non-educational bodies to take the lead in partnerships, for example 'a business, community or voluntary organization . . . new and exciting groups' (DfEE, 1997: 10).

Education Action Zones and social capital: critical challenges

The main focus of the EAZs is to raise educational achievement in areas of severe deprivation and educational underperformance by building social capital. The policy model is to focus on small geographical spaces bounded by the 'catchment areas' (in theory obsolete since the 1988 Education Reform Act) of several primary schools and their main receiver secondary school(s), co-ordinated by an Action Forum constituting a partnership including non-educational bodies, with clear local interests. In view of this, all EAZ bids contain very explicit and ambitious commitments regarding achievement targets in numeracy, literacy and, in many cases, at GCSE. In line with concerns about truancy, school exclusions and social exclusion (Social Exclusion Unit, 1998a) EAZs also have clear targets for increasing attendance rates, and all are committed to reducing exclusions.

Collaboration and experimentation, for example in respect of opting out of the National Curriculum, and flexibility, for instance in terms of possible opting out of national pay agreements for teachers, are all in the service of discovering 'what works'. These seem central to the initiative, as does the requirement of the social capital resource of trust in building on existing, and developing new, partnerships crossing professional, administrative, commercial and cultural lines. While in principle this appears to reflect a pragmatic multiple intervention strategy in which transferable new knowledge should be generated for application as 'good practice' elsewhere, many critical challenges arise if this initiative is to have any recognizable success in social capital terms.

The focus on levels of poverty, unemployment and social exclusion indicates a concern for the wider social ramifications within which educational underperformance occurs. EAZs have an explicit commitment to address these wider social issues. This is where social capital enters the picture. In earlier parts of this chapter we identified key elements of social capital. We shall now explore these aspects of social capital which embody critical challenges for this kind of policy.

Parenting deficit rediscovered

A source of difficulty will be if EAZ families are regarded as fundamentally non-educogenic. Discussions of problematic families tend to focus on single parents and benefit dependency, lack of parenting skills, and inadequate care and concern among parents for their children's education.

What will be significant from the perspective of social capital is if EAZ families are viewed as repositories of inappropriate attitudes and practices and as lacking social capital. This will devalue working-class family life and operate within the discourses of the parenting deficit outlined in that wing of social capital theorizing somewhat reminiscent of conservative communitarian literature (Etzioni, 1995; Morrow, 1998). Trust and active partnerships between lay and professional educational interests are unlikely to thrive on assumptions of cultural deprivation. This has been evident for at least 30 years of educational research, not least in the Educational Priority Area policies of the 1960s and 1970s (Bernstein, 1973; Centre for Contemporary Cultural Studies, 1981; Halsey, 1972; Silver, 1973).

Community and context

Here what is relevant is the extent to which EAZ operational assumptions fall within a social exclusion discourse which tends to regard the effects of poverty, unemployment, racism and other forms of social inequality as attributes of individuals and neighbourhoods. Thus little progress will be made if relations between de-industrialization, unemployment, poverty and social exclusion are not brought into focus, particularly if the approach prioritizes responsibilities to the exclusion of rights.

A key feature of contemporary policy discourses is the corrosive effects of crime on communities. However, the social capital literature is interestingly ambiguous on this and views criminal activity as a formally viable option in communities that lack the legitimate social capital to make appropriate non-criminal choices. Thus it is an open question as to the contribution of the 'hidden economy' and other networks of trust which emerge as alternatives to the state and dominant social forms to reproducing social capital which 'works'. To the extent that the challenge of involving such structures remains beyond the scope of such policy and, indeed, provides the rationale for 'toughening' in relation to illicit institutions, paradoxically it may reinforce and drive further underground such sources of local social capital which make things 'work' in the absence of wider social and economic considerations.

Norms and values

Little in recent education policy has worked to shift the ground where the central function of education is to control, sort and classify through offering competitive opportunities to demonstrate relative success in which there are always losers. This is so particularly where educational success is linked directly in local cultural assumptions about the prospects of employment. Educational demoralization is endemic in such a system and the social capital developed to cope on the part of the losers has to be taken seriously by all constituent elements of the 'partnerships' being proposed. Problems will occur if EAZ policy initiatives over-focus on anti-education and anti-school cultures among parents and pupils, regarding EAZ resources and innovations simply as a way of changing local cultures towards what is provided locally in education without addressing their sources.

Differentiation of social networks

Dense social networks are a key ingredient of social capital (Perri 6, 1997a; Putnam with Leonardi and Nanetti, 1993). They foster connectedness, social inclusion and norms of trust and reciprocity. However, there is a serious danger if the social networks these policies are aimed to encourage are effectively networks for professional providers. This is very likely, as it is partnerships that tend to be responsible for the bids for funding and central government support.

This is to be expected as EAZ bids were required to provide clear information about who was involved in the bid and which of the partners would be involved in a more direct way in the Action Forum running the EAZ. Furthermore, past evidence of such successful partnerships becomes a way of demonstrating the viability of EAZ partnerships in the current bidding process. If, as Perri 6 (1997a) has argued, social exclusion is an effect of network poverty, then EAZs will fail if they do not address this issue. Paradoxically, the results will be developing greater trust and re-moralization in the social networks of the network-rich.

Civic engagement and citizenship

To succeed in terms of building social capital, EAZs should be the products of community civic engagement, including 'civic entrepreneurship' (Leadbetter and Goss, 1998; Thake and Zadek, 1997), evidenced perhaps in the work of headteacher Norma Redfearn. She turned around West Walker primary school in Newcastle by working with parents and their concerns and priorities: 'There is nothing in this [school] that does not come from the parents. Unemployment had created an area in which people were used to other agencies doing things for them. . . . That is what we have to change: not just how children are educated but how the community sees itself' (Redfearn, quoted in Leadbetter and Goss, 1998: 22–23).

While 'employability' is a major concern and focus for curriculum development in the EAZ policy, this will be a problem if it is at the expense of both pupils' and parents' citizenship. The challenge will be to build democratic and participatory citizenship discourses in the EAZs. Thus if the EAZ policy directs its focus on the two issues of changing the values of EAZ families and the attitudes of pupils and parents towards education, it could simply refashion the Thatcherite notion of the citizen as consumer (Hall and Jacques, 1989), and effectively undermine participatory civic engagement.

Conclusion: capital for redesigning civil society?

We argued that it is possible to identify a social capital continuum: at the progressive end there is concern with citizenship, empowerment, pluralism and democratization. At the more conservative end social capital is located in commitment to traditional family structures and relationships and a collective moral order of 'normative consensus' around traditional values, duties and responsibilities. Where the EAZ partnerships are focused on building the latter form of social capital, not the former, they are likely to contribute more to the problem than the solution.

A fundamental criticism of social capital theory running through our thinking is that it ignores structured social inequalities, particularly those traditionally conceptualized as social class inequalities. So it is interesting to note that there may be a recognition that there are strong correlations between social trust, civic participation and education (Brehm and Rahn, 1997), or between types of networks and education (Perri 6, 1997a), or between education and civic participation (Bynner and Parsons, 1997). Education is frequently seen as a marker for social class (Whitty *et al* in Chapter 4), yet there seems to be a marked reluctance in 'Third Way' Britain to talk about it in terms of access to economic and other resources, as a key mediating variable, let alone as structured by production and with massive effects on distribution. If EAZs are to have no connection with economic redistribution their effects are likely to be negligible, and we will have learned very little from the failures of anti-poverty programmes of the 1960s (Halsey, 1977).

If they focus on the conservative elements of social capital, explaining poverty, social exclusion and educational underachievement in terms of family, community and values deficits, the discourses and practices of the EAZs will obscure the cultural links between social class and educational success. It can be argued that if unsuccessful communities are defined by deficits of social capital, then successful communities maintain their socially privileged access to education and employment by privileged access to virtuous spirals of social capital.

In the previous social democratic era of concern with educational achievement, Bourdieu and Passeron (Bourdieu, 1986; Bourdieu and Passeron, 1977) argued that educational success is mediated by unequal access to economic, social and cultural capital. The outcomes are manifested in the habitus, discipline and dispositions engendered in the social relations to education in middle class families and the symbolic capital accumulation of the just rewards of meritocratic status attainment. The effects of these outcomes are compounded by hierarchical valorizations of particular social capitals manifested in class-specific forms of sociability and networks. These processes are obscured by the institutional cloak of broadly reproductive outcomes, particularly across wide ranges at the upper and lower regions of the social structure. Educational provision by the state does not, and arguably could not alone, provide cultural capital to those without it. Schools nonetheless operate as if all pupils possess it, thus, in effect, discriminating against those children who lack it. Cultural capital is therefore the expression of class privilege within educational institutions. Educational underachievement of working class children is not the result of their deficits of ability, but should be understood in relation to middle-class cultural privilege and class cultural discrimination, the cultural violence of arbitrarily defining thinkable cultural distinctions.

If appreciation of these dimensions of class privilege and discrimination as Bourdieu and others elaborated have now all but disappeared from educational policy discourse, then we must consider whether this serves to obscure perceptions of patterns of social inequality. 'Third Way' discourse, while trumpeting the oxymoronic rhetoric of 'excellence for everyone', may well be shifting us back to a deficit approach to educational underachievement. This contributes to the institutional redesigning of authority for the network-rich to have a role in managing the network-poor and may provide yet another manifestation in the long tradition of the professionalizing of *noblesse oblige* in which teachers are likely to find themselves ambiguously placed.

At best it is an open question as to whether what appears to be a great concern to enable pupils, parents and communities to develop educational 'know-how', or cultural capital, will be realized by providing access to the means for educational achievement to social groups who traditionally have been excluded from cultural capital. In a highly and increasingly competitive and differentiating social order there are many indications that this is doubtful. Current policy discourse and government policies are concerned with social capital, not the critical possibilities of cultural capital. While the latter offers a set of critical themes in relation to inequalities, it has little to offer strategically to those at the wrong end of cultural capital formation, unless articulated with critical themes for economic capital formation. By contrast, current social capital ideas are concerned with endorsing conventional success within a victorious global capitalism: educational achievement, employment, two-parent families, active commitment to the norms and values of the work ethic and labour market competitiveness. Building social capital in the current political context may turn out to be yet another reworking of social inequalities, rewarding those already well placed, according to the Matthew Principle, and failing to interrogate the wider origins of social injustice, thereby offering a strategy for successful adaptation to existing social relations and structures.

Notes

1. Demos, 1997; Kelly, Kelly and Gamble, 1997; Oppenheim, 1998.
2. Freudenberg, 1998; Gillies, 1997; Whitty *et al*, 1998.
3. Coleman, 1994; Glennerster, 1998; Schuller and Field, 1998.
4. Fukuyama, 1995; Szreter, 1998; World Bank, 1997.
5. Putnam with Leonardi and Nanetti, 1993; Putnam, 1995, 1996; Foley and Edwards, 1997; Newton, 1997.
6. Demos, 1997; Perri 6, 1997a; Oppenheim, 1998; Leadbetter and Goss, 1998.

7. We will return to the echoes this has with critical sociological tradition associated, for instance, with the concept of 'cultural capital' in the work of Bourdieu in the conclusion to this chapter (Coleman, 1988; Wadsworth, 1996; Whitty *et al* in this volume).

8. The EAZ policy was briefly outlined in the Government's first education policy document, *Excellence in Schools* (Secretary of State for Education, 1997, p 39–40) and developed in the School Standards and Frameworks Act, 1998. The Department for Education and Employment Standards and Effectiveness Unit published a short explanatory booklet in December 1997 (DfEE, 1997). Invitations to bid for EAZ status went out in January 1998, with a 20 March deadline (DfEE, 1998a). The first 25 successful bids were announced on 23 June, with 12 EAZs beginning in September 1998 and 13 starting in January 1999 (DfEE, 1998b).

9. Our own experience provides an interesting illustration. We contacted all the HAZs and EAZs by telephone to obtain copies of the bids. HAZ bids tend to be located in Health Authority press and publicity departments and were routinely sent out to inquirers; many indicated their delight in our interest and included unsolicited additional material. By contrast, EAZ bids tended to be held in the offices of the Directors of Education or headteachers, and there appeared to be some concern about the precise nature of our interest. At the time of writing we have received only half the EAZ bids. Repeated inquiries in August failed as many key officials were on holiday and unavailable to 'vet' our request. Moreover, at least one EAZ, Lambeth, has an explicit policy of refusing to send out its bid, and instead, compiled a short press release-style résumé.

References

Bernstein, B (1973) Education cannot compensate for society, in *Equality and City Schools: Readings in urban education,* ed J Raynor and J Harden, vol 2, Routledge and Kegan Paul, London

Blair, T (1997a) *The Will to Win*, speech, 2 June, Aylesbury Estate, Southwark, *Social Exclusion Unit: Background and structure* (1997), Social Exclusion Unit, London

Blair, T (1997b) *Bringing Britain Together,* speech launching the SEU, 8 December, Stockwell Park School, Lambeth, in *Social Exclusion Unit: Background and structure* (1997), Social Exclusion Unit, London

Blair, T (1998) *The Third Way: New politics for the new century*, Fabian Pamphlet 588, Fabian Society, London

Bourdieu, P (1977) Cultural reproduction and social reproduction, in *Power and Ideology in Education*, ed J Karabel and A H Halsey, Oxford University Press, Oxford and New York

Bourdieu, P (1986) The forms of capital, in *Handbook of Theory and Research for the Sociology of Education*, ed J G Richardson, Greenwood Press, New York

Bourdieu, P and Passeron, J-C (1977) *Reproduction in Education, Society and Culture*, Sage, London

Brehm, J and Rahn, W (1997) Individual-level evidence for the causes and consequences of social capital, *American Journal of Political Science*, **41** (3), pp 999–1023, July

Bynner, J and Parsons, S (1997) *It Doesn't Get Any Better: The impact of poor basic skills on the lives of 37-year-olds*, The Basic Skills Agency, London

Centre For Contemporary Cultural Studies (1981) *Unpopular Education: Schooling and social democracy in England since 1944*, Hutchinson, London

Coleman, J S (1988) Social capital in the creation of human capital, *American Journal of Sociology*, 94 (Suppl. 95), pp S95–S120

Coleman, J S (1990) *Foundations of Social Theory*, Harvard University Press, Cambridge, MA

Coleman, J S (1994) Social capital, human capital, and investment in youth, in *Youth Unemployment and Society*, ed A C Peterson and J T Mortimer, Cambridge University Press, Cambridge

Demos (1997) *The Wealth and Poverty of Networks: Tackling social exclusion*, Demos Collection issue 12, Demos, London

DfEE (1997) *Education Action Zones: An introduction,* Department for Education and Employment, London

DfEE (1998a) *Education Action Zones: General briefing pack*, Department for Education and Employment, London

DfEE (1998b) £75 million boosts radical Education Action Zones to raise educational standards, *DfEE News*, 23 June, Department for Education and Employment, London

Driver, S and Martell, L (1998) *New Labour: Politics after Thatcherism,* Polity Press, Cambridge

Etzioni, A (1995) *The Spirit of Community*, Fontana Press, London

Foley, M W and Edwards, B (1997) Editors' introduction: escape from politics? Social theory and the social capital debate, *American Behavioral Scientist*, **40** (5), pp 550–61, March/April

Foucault, M (1980) The juridical apparatus, in *Power/Knowledge*, ed C Gordon, Pantheon Books, London

Freudenberg, N (1998) Community-based health education for urban populations: an overview, *Health Education and Behavior*, **25** (1), pp 11–23

Fukuyama, F (1995) *Trust: The social virtues and the creation of prosperity*, Hamish Hamilton, London

Gamarnikow, E (1998) *Social Capital and the Health Action Zones*, paper presented at the meeting of the Social Capital Empirical Research Group, LSE, Gender Institute, 15 July, London

Gamarnikow, E and Green, A (1999) Education Action Zones, the 'Third Way' and Social Capital: a new agenda for education, parents and community?, *International Studies in Sociology of Education*

Giddens, A (1994) *Beyond Left and Right*, Polity Press, Cambridge

Giddens, A (1998) *The Third Way: The renewal of social democracy*, Polity Press, Cambridge

Gillies, P (1997) Review and evaluation of health promotion – the effectiveness of alliances or partnerships for health promotion: a global review of progress and potential consideration of the relationship to building social capital for health, Conference Working Paper presented to the Fourth International Conference on Health Promotion, 21–25 July, Jakarta, Indonesia

Glennerster, H (1998) Tackling poverty at its roots? Education, in *An Inclusive Society: Strategies for tackling poverty*, ed C Oppenheim, Institute for Public Policy Research, London

Hall, P A (1997) Social capital: a fragile asset, in *The Wealth and Poverty of Networks*, Demos Collection issue 12, Demos, London

Hall, S and Jacques, M (eds) (1989) *New Times: The changing face of politics in the 1990s*, Lawrence and Wishart, London

Halsey, A H (1972) *Educational Priority: EPA problems and policies*, HMSO, London

Halsey, A H (1977) Government against poverty in school and community, in *School and Society: A sociological reader*, ed B R Cosin *et al*, Routledge and Kegan Paul, London

Kelly, G, Kelly, D and Gamble, A (eds) (1997) *Stakeholder Capitalism*, Macmillan, Basingstoke

Leadbetter, C and Goss, S (1998) *Civic Entrepreneurship*, Demos, London

Leonardi, R (1995) Regional development in Italy: social capital and the Mezzogiorno, *Oxford Review of Economic Policy*, **11** (2), pp 165–79

Morrow, V (1998) *What is Social Capital and How Does it Relate to Children and Young People?*, unpublished paper, LSE Gender Institute, London

Newton, K (1997) Social capital and democracy, *American Behavioral Scientist*, **40** (5), April/May, pp 575–86

Ofsted (1998) *Secondary Education 1993–97: A review of secondary schools in England*, Office For Standards In Education, Stationery Office, London

Oppenheim, C (ed) (1998) *An Inclusive Society: Strategies for tackling poverty*, Institute for Public Policy Research, London

Perri 6 (1997a) *Escaping Poverty: From safety nets to networks of opportunity*, Demos, London

Perri 6 (1997b) Social exclusion: time to be optimistic, in *The Wealth and Poverty of Networks*, Demos Collection issue 12, Demos, London

Putnam, R D (1995) Bowling alone: America's declining social capital, *Journal of Democracy*, **6**, pp 66–78

Putnam, R D (1996) The strange disappearance of civic America, *American Prospect*, **24**, pp 34–49

Putnam, R D with Leonardi, R and Nanetti, R (1993) *Making Democracy Work: Civic traditions in modern Italy*, Princeton University Press, Princeton, New Jersey

Rubio, M (1997) Perverse social capital: some evidence from Colombia, *Journal of Economic Issues*, **31** (3), pp 805–16, September

Schuller, T and Field, J (1998) Social capital, human capital and the learning society, *International Journal of Lifelong Education*, **17** (4), pp 226–35, July–August

Secretary of State for Education (1997) *Excellence in Schools*, Cm 3681, Stationery Office, London

Silver, H (ed) (1973) *Equal Opportunity in Education*, Methuen, London

Social Exclusion Unit (1997) *Social Exclusion Unit: Background and structure*, Social Exclusion Unit, London

Social Exclusion Unit (1998a) *Truancy and School Exclusion,* Cm 3957, Stationery Office, London

Social Exclusion Unit (1998b) *Bringing Britain Together: A national strategy for neighbourhood renewal*, Cm 4045, Stationery Office, London

Szreter, S (1998) *Social Capital, the Economy and the Third Way*, paper presented to the Nexus Conference 'From Principles to Policies: Mapping out the Third Way', 3 July, King's College, London

Thake, S and Zadek, S (1997) *Practical People, Noble Causes: How to support community-based social entrepreneurs*, New Economics Foundation, London

Wadsworth, M E J (1996) Family and Education as determinants of health, in *Health and Social Organization: Towards a health policy for the 21st century*, ed D Blane, E Brunner and R Wilkinson, Routledge, London

Whitty, G *et al* (1998) Education and health inequalities: Input Paper 10 to the Independent Inquiry into Inequalities in Health, January 1998, *Journal of Education Policy*, **13** (5), pp 641–52

World Bank (1997) *World Development Report 1997: The state in a changing world*, Oxford University Press, New York and Oxford

Part 2

Developing Education Policy to Tackle Social Exclusion

4

Health, Housing and Education: Tackling Multiple Disadvantage

Geoff Whitty, Sally Power, Eva Gamarnikow, Peter Aggleton, Paul Tyrer and Deborah Youdell

Introduction

Paradoxically, at the same time as governments have tried to apply similar sets of policy solutions (eg quasi-markets, target-setting, etc) across a whole range of social policy fields, they have also sought to downplay the relationship between those fields. Thus, in recent years, it has been fashionable to treat the solution to educational problems as largely to be found within the educational arena. As Mortimore and Whitty indicate in this volume, this has often produced an over-inflated notion of what school-centred initiatives can achieve. At its most extreme, the argument that poverty should not be used as an excuse for underachievement has been taken to mean that poverty is not an explanation for underachievement. This chapter seeks to demonstrate the intimate connections between education and other fields of social policy in creating social exclusion and argues for the forging of similar links in developing means of combating it.

Education and health inequalities

We begin by offering some examples of connections between educational inequalities and health inequalities. According to recently published data from the 1970 birth cohort study, those without educational qualifications are, at age 26, four times more likely to report poor general health (23 per cent) than those with the highest educational qualifications (6 per cent). There is also an inverse relationship between educational qualifications and depression, measured by the Malaise Inventory, where very high levels of depression are evident, particularly among women without educational qualifications (Montgomery and Schoon, 1997). There are strikingly similar findings in research on those with poor basic skills in the 1958 cohort study: 36 per cent of women and 18 per cent of men with very low literacy skills suffered from depression, compared with around 6 per cent of those with good literacy skills (Bynner and Parsons, 1997). Another conclusion to be drawn from cohort studies is that 'children who do well in education tend strongly to make better choices in adult life in health-related habits of diet, alcohol consumption, smoking and exercise' (Wadsworth, 1997a: 200).

In many studies, level of education acts as a marker for the effects of other influences, such as class, occupational level or lifestyle (Marmot *et al,* 1997). Because so few studies have controlled adequately for relevant variables, the exact nature of the relationship between educational, health and other forms of disadvantage remain obscure. Nevertheless, many studies have drawn attention to the cumulative effects of low social class of origin, poor educational achievement, reduced employment prospects, low levels of psychosocial well-being and poor physical and mental health (Benzeval *et al*, 1995; Wilkinson, 1994, 1996). Life course perspectives on human development hypothesize a chain of causality which links critical periods of biological development, sensitive periods of psychosocial development and high risk factors in adult life (Kuh 1997; Wadsworth, 1996, 1997a and 1997b). At each stage risks can accumulate, adding to disadvantage. The 'pathway' perspective advocated by Power and Hertzman (1997) points to the importance of early experience but also to the possibility of changing trajectories through experiences in later life. In this context, educational interventions might be seen as having a particularly important role.

However, many people live in such disadvantaged circumstances that their opportunities to benefit from education, and from the role it may have in countering other forms of social exclusion, are severely limited. Robinson (1997: 17) rightly argues that 'a serious programme to alleviate child poverty might do far more for boosting attainment . . . than any modest intervention in schooling'. Nevertheless, even though substantial increases in material resources for disadvantaged groups may seem the most obvious way of tackling inequalities, interventions that increase 'social capital' (as discussed by Gamarnikow and Green in Chapter 3) may also be useful in reducing risk and lead to consequent improvements in health, education and, indeed, economic prosperity.

For example, Furstenberg and Hughes (1995: 589) have suggested that social capital is a factor determining school staying-on rates among disadvantaged African-American young people in the USA. They further found that those with a higher level of social capital are less likely to be depressed, more likely to be in work, less likely to be teenage parents and more likely to have 'avoided serious trouble'. Fuchs and Reklis (1994) have concluded that the strength of parental relationships and the influence of other social networks is crucial in affecting children's 'readiness to learn' in pre-school contexts.

Data from British birth cohort studies similarly suggest the importance of social capital in maximizing educational potential, thus bringing likely health benefits. For example, Wadsworth's analyses (1996, 1997a, 1997b) indicate that parental interest in children's education impacts positively on educational outcomes, and on achievements and opportunities in adult-hood, irrespective of social class. Willms (1997) cites studies in Catholic schools, suggesting that the success of these institutions may be in part dependent upon strong levels of social capital within the communities that the schools serve. School effectiveness and improvement research similarly provides evidence that high levels of trust between headteacher and staff, between staff and students and between home and school are associated with beneficial outcomes. Moreover, although participation in community and voluntary organizations is strongly differentiated by social class and education, women with low literacy and numeracy skills appear more likely to be involved in schools' PTA activities (6 per cent and 12 per cent respec-tively) than in any other local networks (Bynner and Parsons, 1997).

Early interventions seem likely to be particularly effective in this respect and Wadsworth argues that the 'chances of reduction of inequalities for any given generation will be greater the earlier attempts at reduction are begun. It is unlikely that inequalities can be easily or rapidly reduced, increasingly so as the individuals carry an accumulation of health potential which is hard to change' (1997b: 867). In view of this, it is interesting to note that early years' educational initiatives tend to take a more holistic approach and recognize the importance of building social capital to a much greater extent than interventions in other phases. Although still controversial, findings from two of the longest established US initiatives, High/Scope and Project Headstart, do seem to demonstrate impressive gains in health and social outcomes – particularly when students are compared with those who stay at home or experience other forms of intervention (Schweinhart, Barnes and Weikart, 1993; Case, 1997). For example, only 6 per cent of those attending High/Scope – a programme based on a constructivist theory of child development – are reported as having received treatment for emotional difficulties during their primary or secondary education, compared with 47 per cent of a group that had undergone an intervention involving direct instruction. Similarly, Headstart students have been reported as staying on at secondary school for an average of two years longer than those who did not attend a pre-school programme. They also seem to have experienced fewer teenage pregnancies, less delinquency, 'higher feelings of empowerment and a more positive attitude towards the education of their children' than the control group (Case, 1997: 10). These direct and indirect social benefits suggest that every dollar invested in High/Scope-style pre-school education nets $7 in long-term savings on crime, health, and other social expenditure (Schweinhart and Weikart, 1997).

As Law (1997) has pointed out, we cannot assume that findings from the United States are necessarily applicable here. However, there is some evidence – from a range of initiatives piloted in the last 20 years – to suggest that good quality pre-school interventions can have positive effects in the UK too (see, for example, Jowett and Sylva, 1986; Athey, 1990; Shorrocks *et al*, 1992; Sylva and Wilshire, 1993). Interventions that focus on developing what has sometimes been called a 'readiness to learn' seem likely to bring particular benefits to disadvantaged children (Ball, 1994; Sylva and Wilshire, 1993). Support for parents can also be of vital importance in this context (Smith and Pugh, 1996). Although, over the years, many UK-based programmes have either been marginalized or abandoned before their outcomes could be properly evaluated, there is now a broad consensus amongst educationalists, developmental psychologists, child and adolescent psychiatrists and researchers that high-quality interventions in the early years are among the more effective ways of improving educational performance, self-esteem and emotional well-being.

It is important to note, however, that interventions in the later years of education may also have an effect on reducing health and education inequalities, as work by Power and Hertzman (1997) has suggested. This is particularly the case when such interventions are linked to broader efforts to build social capital. For example, health education in schools organized within whole school PSHE frameworks provides some interesting examples of these kinds of interventions. A key feature of newer approaches to PSHE lies in the links they propose between learning how to develop relationships characterized by trust and reciprocity, gaining familiarity with structures for effective involvement and participation, and positive health and educational outcomes.

The notion of Health-Promoting Schools operates within a broadly based approach, where health promotion is a whole-school undertaking, encompassing not only health education but, more importantly from the point of view of social capital, its ethos and environment and links between the school, parents and community. A recent evaluation of the English schools in the European Network of Health-Promoting Schools (Hamilton and Saunders, 1997) suggests that such approaches to health promotion may lead to student gains in knowledge, attitudes, self-esteem and health behaviours.

Whether such changes in attitudes and health behaviours will be sufficient to ameliorate health and education inequalities between groups and on any long-term basis remains to be seen. The new initiative, *Healthy Schools* (DfEE, 1998), attempts to make links between health-related activities, school improvement and academic achievement. Advocates of the approach imply that partnerships between schools, businesses and community-based agencies can be an important conduit for building social capital. Evidence from one local project (McInnes and Toft, 1998) suggests that health-related activities can impact positively on levels of achievement, school attendance and bullying. Further research will be needed to see whether these improvements can be sustained or extended in the absence of parallel work that more directly addresses the disadvantaged conditions in which many students live.

Programmes and interventions that shift opportunities towards disadvantaged individuals, families and communities are more likely to reduce educational and other inequalities, than are more broadly based initiatives catering for all. As Mortimore and Whitty argue in this volume, if we seek to reduce inequalities, rather than merely raise standards overall, policies will need to be more effectively targeted towards disadvantaged groups than has previously been the case. In what follows, we take the example of homelessness and education to illustrate the need for co-ordinated policies and interventions to tackle disadvantage and social exclusion.

Homelessness and education

As might be expected, housing is also intimately connected with both health and education. A range of studies has shown that poor housing in general, and temporary accommodation in particular, has adverse consequences for the physical and psycho-social development of children. In terms of physical well-being, the Black Report, published in 1980, established a causal relationship between type of housing tenure and health. Seven years later, the National Children's Bureau (1987) provided further evidence that poor housing and homelessness were detrimental to child health. Other research and surveys reveal that living in temporary accommodation, particularly bed and breakfast hotels, has negative health aspects (eg Howarth, 1987), which are likely to be anything but temporary (Morton, 1988).

In addition to ill health (eg Furley, 1989; Woodroffe *et al*, 1993), poor housing adversely affects other aspects of a child's development. Overcrowding has also been shown to result in a range of socio-emotional problems for children. Edwards (1992) reports on the problems caused by poor living conditions and lack of play space. The limitations of living in bed and breakfast accommodation can be particularly restrictive. Isolation is a recurrent theme. Crane (1990) argues that living in temporary accommodation separates children from friend and family networks.

Research from the United States has clearly linked homelessness to lower student achievement. For example, Bassuk and Rosenburg (1988) found that 40 per cent of students from a sample of homeless families were failing or producing 'below average' work, and one quarter were in 'special' classes. Kozol (1988) found that children living in welfare hotels were, on average, two or three grades behind their peers. Stronge (1992) found that homeless students scored one year below their grade level in standardized achievement tests in reading, spelling and mathematics, a deficit that increased to between one to three years as students grew older. He also estimated that 43 per cent of homeless children in the United States were not attending school on a regular basis.

British work has shown similar connections between poor housing and lack of educational progress. An early report from the National Child Development Study (1972) found that overcrowded housing and lack of basic amenities were clearly correlated with lower reading ages and arithmetical achievement at primary school. More recently, Stepien *et al* (1996) found that the vocabulary development of homeless children was behind that of others. Some of our own research, funded by the homelessness charity Shelter (Power, Whitty and Youdell, 1995), has tried to explore some of the processes that lie behind such patterns of disadvantage. It showed that the nature and organization of current services, and professional responses to disadvantaged groups, were often as much part of the problem as part of the solution.

At central government level, policy and provision relating to housing is the responsibility of the Department for the Environment, Transport and the Regions (DETR), while the Department for Education and Employment (DfEE) oversees the education system. In both areas of welfare, national policies are interpreted and implemented at local government level, where the division between housing and education remains as sharply demarcated. The picture is further complicated by a lack of congruence between boundaries. Although housing and education departments in unitary authorities share administrative boundaries, those in shire counties do not. The effects of these divisions became evident when we conducted a postal questionnaire asking LEAs about their administrative arrangements relating to the education of homeless children. It was soon apparent that many LEAs experienced difficulties in responding to the survey. Although the overall return rate was 64 per cent (70/109), this was only achieved after intensive follow-up through fax and telephone. Late and reluctant responses were found to reflect perceptions that LEAs had only limited responsibility for issues relating specifically to the education of homeless children. Some asserted that homeless children were the responsibility of the housing and social services departments. Others said that their scarce resources had to be concentrated entirely on meeting their own statutory obligations. Some reported that they had no one in a position to pull together the relevant information. On three occasions, we were given conflicting information from different people within the same local authority. Not only do these 'duplicate' returns indicate the problem of co-ordination within the authority, they also reveal interesting discrepancies. For instance, in one authority, the level of homelessness was reported by one respondent as 'low', while another from the same department claimed it was 'significant and on the increase'.

These instances of non-response, confusion and lack of consistency indicate the kind of demarcated and fragmented bureaucracy which homeless families themselves have to confront when trying to obtain appropriate services. This not only presents them with practical difficulties, it also prevents policy-makers and service providers from seeing the multiple effects of their policies on 'whole' persons and households. There is little doubt that this makes it easier to 'pass off' responsibility to other sectors and influences the kind of provision homeless families receive. It also means that professional responses take the form of crisis management rather than developing ongoing liaison and support.

Schools, as well as families, experience a range of problems when they have high numbers of students living in temporary accommodation. Although geographic mobility is not necessarily related to homelessness, the nature of temporary accommodation means that homeless students often face frequent changes of school. Nearly two-thirds of head teachers whose schools had homeless children attending reported that the high turnover of homeless students had a noticeable impact on student population. Whilst the level of student turnover varies from school to school, many schools reported having registered far more individual children each year than indicated by the total school roll. Within schools with significant numbers of homeless children, notably those in close proximity to bed and breakfast hotels, hostels and homeless units, there were very high rates of student turnover with students arriving and leaving on an almost constant basis.

There is little doubt that this turbulence creates difficulties for schools. Almost 60 per cent of schools with homeless students reported having to deal with additional administration. The extra work associated with the transience of homeless students appeared to have a significant impact on the central task of the school – facilitating teaching and learning. The high student turnover rate associated with having high numbers of homeless children in a class also had an impact on continuity and progression. Nearly half the schools in the survey reported that homelessness had a detrimental effect on the educational experiences of other students as well. Again, it is the high degree of transience associated with living in temporary accommodation that appears to be the significant factor. The group dynamics of a class might certainly be affected by newly admitted students. When there was a sudden influx, the class could be quite severely disrupted. In addition, the extra amount of time a teacher needed to spend with newly admitted homeless students also affected other students on occasions, as did the need to amend lesson plans and to account for the previous schooling of new students. In addition to militating against a stable working environment, having significant numbers of homeless children appeared to put a strain on teachers' time and morale and can have significant knock-on effects throughout the school organization.

Such difficulties are not new, but recent reforms have exacerbated the situation and the extent to which schools can overcome turbulence. For instance, although at one level the introduction of the National Curriculum would initially appear to provide a common framework that students can slot into when they join a new school, the reality is somewhat different. The general impression given was that the problems associated with missed assessments and partial or lost records of transient students outweighed the potential advantages. Some teachers also felt that the fairly rigorous teaching and assessment demands of the National Curriculum diverted attention away from other areas.

But it is the devolution of budgets to schools that creates some of the most serious problems for schools with high numbers of homeless children. A number of head teachers felt that their schools were losing resources as a result of the financial climate and changes in the funding mechanisms. They reported that, prior to formula funding, they had been 'generously funded' in order to maintain staffing levels which were able to cushion the effects of unexpected intakes. This was no longer possible under a formula that had to be applicable across all schools.

Because so much of the education budget is devolved to individual schools, LEAs have only limited scope to provide extra funding to deal with special factors affecting particular schools. Only 1 in 10 LEAs said they provided additional formula-based funding to schools to take account of the effects of homelessness. In five cases this was distributed according to an element relating to 'transience' or 'turbulence'. In only two LEAs was there an element specifically relating to students living in temporary accommodation.

Educational welfare and psychology services that are frequently required in relation to homeless students have traditionally been supplied by LEAs on the basis of need. However, the financial delegation and site-based management of LMS means that much of the cost is now incurred by individual schools. In one of the areas researched, the LEA had delegated its education welfare services to individual schools. Although the LEA had retained a centralized service, this provided only the barest minimum of support that is required by law. Schools were then able to buy back into the service at various levels if they so wished. Thus, although schools were obliged to spend £300 on EWO support, they could chose to buy in extra time at a rate of about £100 per day. Whilst this allowed schools to respond to the specific needs of their school population, it might mean that some schools would choose to buy less welfare support than they really needed.

The formula itself can handicap schools with turbulent populations. Per capita based funding, such as LMS, relies on an accurate head count. This is normally conducted in January, with adjustments made in relation to a further school roll count in September. However, the high turnover associated with homelessness makes such 'snapshot' assessments problematic. Some head teachers indicated that they had lost out significantly. They claimed that they not only incurred the additional financial burden of accommodating an ever-changing population, but the school roll was under assessed. Where student numbers had peaked at the point of the head count, this was generally felt to be little more than good fortune. But temporary 'dips' in student numbers could lead to significant shortfalls in budgets.

Apart from the immediate shortfall created by unstable registers, the recent reforms may severely damage some schools' ability to attract students and thereby funds in the longer term. Schools are increasingly obliged to compete with each other for students in order to ensure their income, making the public image of a school increasingly important. Several schools expressed concerns about the impact that the presence of homeless children would have on their position within local school 'league tables', although this varied with the incidence of homelessness. Schools with many homeless children felt they had a potentially disproportionate number of students in lower attainment levels. One headteacher in particular was concerned that their reputation for success with students with difficulties would no longer be valued according to the current criteria of success. These include not only achievement statistics, but also attendance rates that are often lower among homeless families for a variety of understandable reasons connected with the nature of their accommodation and the other pressures facing them.

Some families and housing workers felt that certain schools claimed to be full as an excuse not to admit homeless children. Although there was no evidence of this in the schools we visited, it has recently been reported in relation to refugee children – many of whom will also be living in temporary accommodation (Ghouri, 1998). But, in other instances, lack of co-ordination between housing and welfare services meant parents felt obliged to keep their children at home. Parents often felt that successive school moves were not in the child's best interest. They claimed that multiple school moves could be more unsettling and distressing to a child than keeping them out of school for a short time. In particular, families may not seek school placements when they expect to be moved quickly into permanent accommodation in another area.

However, temporary accommodation placements are frequently not as temporary as homeless households hope and the families involved are often unaware of the potential wait before a permanent placement. One mother reported that she had not sought school places near to her temporary accommodation because she had been told her stay there would be around two weeks. Ten weeks later she deeply regretted her decision and said that with hindsight she would have sought school places immediately.

Even when places had been allocated, there were insufficient funds to help with the direct and incidental expenses of going to school. In particular, not having the proper school uniform can make students reluctant to attend school. With successive school moves, the costs of uniforms can build up. And although there are clothing grants to help, these take time to administer. Furthermore, in some authorities, like the inner London boroughs, no such grants are available for children of primary school age. Even more disturbingly, a family of children in a refuge reported that they had been unable to attend school since they arrived because they did not have any shoes with them and were waiting for a DSS payment. No other sources of financial support in meeting clothing needs seemed to be available.

Some parents claimed that schools were unsympathetic to their plight. They reported that teachers often saw their children as 'problems' rather than actively helping them. Several homeless students mentioned bullying as something that had to be endured. Homeless students felt they were seen as 'outsiders'. The response to their transience and such stigmatization was often a form of withdrawal, for instance a refusal to make friends, which then further endorsed their isolation.

In summary, governmental, institutional and interpersonal level processes and practices, underpinned by implicit and explicit assumptions and expectations of homeless families, act to compound significantly barriers to educational inclusion which homeless children face. Only when the issues are seen as interrelated and co-ordinated strategies developed is there any real likelihood of changing that situation.

Recent initiatives

The example of homelessness and education is, of course, merely illustrative of broader issues that have now, to some extent, been recognized by the creation of the Social Exclusion Unit (SEU) and the government's talk of 'joined-up' rather than departmental policies. Interestingly, both homelessness and education have been among the first priorities of the SEU, though the issue-based approach runs its own risks of fragmentation in the absence of a clear recognition of their connectedness.

That danger has also been apparent in New Labour's 'zones' policy. Initially, the government announced a series of zones for Employment, Health and Education. They seemed responsive to some of the arguments we have been advocating here, particularly about concentrating resources in areas of greatest disadvantage and working through networks, partnerships and inter-agency collaboration. Yet, initially, Education Action Zones seemed to be conceived separately from Health Action Zones and Employment Zones, though there have since been promising moves to link at least some of them, while the proposed Estates Renewal Initiative does clearly recognize the relationship between different aspects of social policy. In Scotland, plans have recently been announced to develop a new breed of 'community schools', based on the US experience of 'full-service' schools.

What remains depressing about these various plans, though, is how little interest New Labour seems to have taken in research on past initiatives. There is little evidence that it has looked systematically at the positive and negative lessons that might be learned from Educational Priority Areas, Urban Development Corporations or City Technology Colleges. These all have some echoes in the proposals for zones and could yield important lessons for current initiatives. Plewis (1998) implies that lessons from the experience of France and The Netherlands have similarly been ignored in the planning of Education Action Zones.

Although we now tend to use the currently fashionable language of social capital and social inclusion, some of the arguments we have made in this chapter must seem all too familiar to those who were involved in the community development and EPA interventions of the 1960s and 1970s. As A H Halsey pointed out over 20 years ago: '. . . the teacher cannot reconstruct the community unaided. . . the needs of the neighbourhood for health, housing, employment and other services will be found to impinge directly on. . . teaching tasks. The implication is clear: educational priorities must be integrated into community development' (Halsey, 1977: 241).

It is to be hoped that it will not take another 20 years for this implication to be acted upon, especially as similar conclusions are to be drawn from a recent OECD survey of integrated services for children and families at risk in 14 countries (OECD, 1996).

Acknowledgement

Parts of this paper draw upon work carried out for the homclessness charity, Shelter, and for the Independent Inquiry on Inequalities in Health, chaired by Sir Donald Acheson. See Power *et al* (1995) and Whitty *et al* (1998) respectively.

References

Athey, C (1990) *Extending Thought in Young Children: A parent–teacher partnership*, Paul Chapman, London

Ball, C (1994) *Start Right: The importance of early learning*, RSA, London

Bassuk, E and Rosenberg, L (1988) Why does family homelessness occur? A case-control study, *American Journal of Public Health*, **78**, pp 783–88

Benzeval, M, Judge, K and Whitehead, M (1995) *Tackling Inequalities in Health,* King's Fund, London

Bynner, J and Parsons, S (1997) *It Doesn't Get Any Better: The impact of poor basic skills on the lives of 37-year-olds*, Basic Skills Agency, London

Case, R (1997) Socio-economic gradients in mathematical ability and their responsiveness to compensatory education, in *Tomorrow's Children*, ed D Keating and C Herzman, Guildford and New York

Crane, H (1990) *Speaking from Experience – Working with Homeless Families*, Bayswater Hotel Homcless Project, London

DfEE (1998) Press release on *Healthy Schools Initiative,* May, Department for Education and Employment, London

Edwards, R (1992) Co-ordination, fragmentation and definitions of need: the new Under Fives Initiative and homeless families, *Children & Society*, **6** (4), pp 336–52

Fuchs, V R and Reklis, D M (1994) Mathematical achievement in eighth grade: interstate and racial differences, NBER Working Paper 4784, NBER, Stanford

Furley, A (1989) *A Bad Start in Life – Children, Health and Housing*, Shelter, London

Furstenberg Jr, F F and Hughes, M E (1995) Social capital and successful development among at-risk youth, *Journal of Marriage and the Family*, **57**, pp 580–92

Ghouri, N (1998) Refugees spurned 'to improvc tables', *Times Educational Supplement*, 10 April, p 3

Halsey, A H (1977) Government against poverty in school and community, in *School and Society: A sociological reader,* ed B R Cosin *et al,* Routledge and Kegan Paul, London

Hamilton, K and Saunders, L (1997) The Health-promoting school: A summary of the ENHPS Evaluation Project in England, Health Education Authority/National Foundation for Educational Research, London/Windsor

Howarth, V (1987) *Survey of Families in Bed and Breakfast Hotels*, Thomas Coram Foundation for Children, London

Jowett, S and Sylva, K (1986) Does the kind of pre-school matter? *Educational Research,* **25** (1), pp 21–31

Kozol, J (1988) *Rachel and Her Children: Homeless families in America,* Crown, New York

Kuh, D (1997) The life course and social inequalities in health, Evidence to the Independent Inquiry into Health Inequalities

Law, C (1997) Mother/fetus, infant, child and family: socio-economic inequalities, Input Paper No. 1, Evidence to the Independent Inquiry into Inequalities in Health

McInnes, C and Toft, M (1998) *Healthier School Partnership Project: Monitoring Report,* Lewisham Education and Community Services, London

Marmot, M *et al* (1997) Social inequalities in health: next questions and converging evidence, *Social Science and Medicine,* **44** (6), pp 901–10

Montgomery, S M and Schoon, I (1997) Health and health behaviour, in *Twentysomething in the 1990s: Getting on, getting by, getting nowhere,* ed E Bynner, E Ferri and P Shepherd, Ashgate, Aldershot

Morton, S (1988) *Homeless Families in Manchester,* Faculty of Community Medicine, University of Manchester, Manchester

National Child Development Study (1972) *From Birth to Seven: The Second Report of the National Child Development Study (1958 Cohort),* Longman/National Children's Bureau, London

National Children's Bureau (1987) *Investing in the Future – Child Health Ten Years After the Court Report,* National Children's Bureau, London

OECD (1996) *Successful Services for Our Children and Families at Risk,* Organization for Economic Co-operation and Development, Paris

Plewis, I (1998) Inequalities, targets and zones, *New Economy,* **5** (2), 104–08

Power, C and Hertzman, C (1997) Social and biological pathways linking early life and adult disease, *British Medical Bulletin,* **53** (1), pp 210–21

Power, S, Whitty, G and Youdell, D (1995) *No Place to Learn: Homelessness and education,* Shelter, London

Robinson, P (1997) *Literacy, Numeracy and Economic Performance,* CEP, School of Economics and Political Science, London

Schweinhart, L J and Weikart, D P (1997) Lasting differences: the High/Scope preschool curriculum comparison study through age 23, *Early Childhood Research Quarterly,* **12**, pp 117–43

Schweinhart, L J, Barnes, H V and Weikart, D P (1993) Significant benefits: the High/Scope Perry preschool study through age 27, *Monographs of the High/Scope Educational Research Foundation,* 10

Shorrocks, D *et al* (1992) Enca 1 project: The Evaluation of National Curriculum Assessment at Key Stage 1, School of Education, University of Leeds

Smith, C and Pugh, G (1996) *Learning to be a Parent: A survey of group-based parenting programmes,* Family Policies Studies Centre, London

Stepien, D *et al* (1996) *Homelessness, Schooling and Attainment: An interim report,* University of Portsmouth, Portsmouth

Stronge, J H (1992) The background: history and problems of schooling for the homeless, in *Educating Homeless Children and Adolescents: Evaluating policy and practice,* ed J H Strong, Sage Publications, Newbury Park, USA

Sylva, K and Wilshire, J (1993) The impact of early learning on children's later development: a review prepared for the RSA Inquiry 'Start Right', *European Early Childhood Education Research Journal,* **1** (1), pp 17–40

Wadsworth, M E J (1996) Family and education as determinants of health, in *Health and Social Organization: Towards a health policy for the 21st century,* ed D Blane, E Brunner and R Wilkinson, Routledge, London

Wadsworth, M E J (1997a) Changing social factors and their long-term implications for health, *British Medical Bulletin,* **53** (1), pp 198–209

Wadsworth, M E J (1997b) Health inequalities in the life course perspective, *Social Science and Medicine,* **44** (6), pp 859–69

Whitty, G *et al* (1998) Education and health inequalities, *Journal of Education Policy,* **13** (5), pp 641–52

Wilkinson, R G (1994) Health, redistribution and growth, in *Paying for Inequality: The economic cost of social justice,* ed A Glyn and D Miliband, IPPR/Rivers Oram, London

Wilkinson, R G (1996) *Unhealthy Societies: The afflictions of inequality,* Routledge, London

Willms, J D (1997) *Quality and Inequality in Children's Literacy: The effects of families, schools and communities,* Mimeo, Faculty of Education, University of New Brunswick

Woodroffe, C, Glickman, M, Barker, M and Power, C (1993) *Children, Teenagers and Health: The key data,* Open University Press, Milton Keynes

5

School Improvement: A Remedy for Social Exclusion?

Peter Mortimore and Geoff Whitty

Introduction

There is longstanding – and continuing – evidence that students from disadvantaged social backgrounds fare relatively badly within formal educational systems (Douglas, 1964; Davie *et al*, 1972; Essen and Wedge, 1982; Mortimore and Mortimore, 1986; Osborne and Milbank, 1987; Gorman and Fernandes, 1992; OECD, 1995). Whilst some outstanding individuals have achieved the highest levels despite (or, in some cases, motivated by) their inauspicious backgrounds, the overall social distribution of educational success and failure has remained depressingly consistent. There is a strong negative correlation between most measures of social disadvantage and school achievement, as even a cursory glance at the league tables of school by school results demonstrates.

According to some commentators, this topic has been 'almost a taboo subject in public policy debate in recent years' (Smith and Noble, 1995: 133). Teachers who have dared to mention the subject have been branded defeatist or patronizing for even considering that social background can make a difference. Yet, despite the Thatcher and Major governments' refusal to acknowledge the importance of the relationship between social disadvantage and educational achievement, stark differences in the lives of students with different family backgrounds have not gone away. Although some members of the Blair government have shown an alarming tendency to perpetuate the Conservative position, the change of government could provide an opportunity to reopen this important public policy debate. In this chapter, we seek to contribute to this debate by examining both the possibilities and the limitations of attempts to overcome the impact of social disadvantage on educational achievement, with particular reference to the sorts of school improvement strategies that are currently fashionable. In particular, we argue that it cannot just be assumed that such strategies will contribute to greater social inclusiveness. We therefore point to some of the conditions that will need to be met if school improvement policies are not to perpetuate or even exacerbate the problem of disadvantage and social exclusion.

Social disadvantage

More than fifteen years ago Mortimore and Blackstone (1982) commented that 'The concept of social disadvantage is not easy to define partly because it is a relative concept, tied to the social context of time and place' (1982: 3). Townsend (1996) sees poverty in the same relative way, as 'the absence or inadequacy of those diets, amenities, standards, services and activities which are common or customary in society'. In an attempt to provide objective measures, studies carried out by the National Children's Bureau on the effects of disadvantage adopted three 'hard' criteria: membership of a large or a single parent family; being in receipt of a low family income; and living in poor quality housing (Essen and Wedge, 1982). The Organization for Economic Co-operation and Development draws attention to the multiplicative effects of such factors, with one form of disadvantage often leading to the experience of other forms (OECD, 1995).

Despite the general improvement over recent years in most people's living standards, conditions have worsened for a significant minority. The number of people living in poverty (50 per cent of average national earnings or less) has shown a threefold increase since 1979 and now stands at one quarter of the population (Walker and Walker, 1997). In Britain, the increasing difference between the 'haves' and the 'have-nots' during the 1980s seems to have resulted from official policies designed to lift the constraints affecting the rich. These policies also seemed designed to penalize the poor in the interests of freeing them from a so-called 'dependency culture'. 'Britain stands out internationally in having experienced the largest percentage increase in income inequality between 1967 and 1992' (Dennehy, *et al*, 1997: 280). The proportion of children living in poor households is now 32 per cent compared to the European Union average of 20 per cent (Eurostat, 1997).

As noted by Holtermann (1997) social disadvantage is frequently associated with poorer health. Children tend to be physically weaker and have less energy for learning than their peers. They are also more likely to be emotionally upset by the tensions in their lives. Finally, they are less likely to have the opportunity for study and for educational help at home. These are just the conditions in which children will be vulnerable to low levels of self-efficacy: 'an inability to exert influence over things that adversely affect one's life, which breeds apprehension, apathy, or despair' (Bandura, 1995: 1). They, in turn, will work against children's development as effective school learners and, ultimately, according to Wilkinson (1997), their chance of a long healthy life. Thus, the effects of disadvantage are cumulative. Each new factor adds to the problem, as discussed in the chapter on health, housing and education by Whitty *et al* (Chapter 4).

Remedies already tried

There have been a number of distinct educational approaches to the amelioration of the effects of poverty on educational opportunities. One approach rests on the concept of meritocracy, which was the basis of the scholarship ladder introduced at the turn of the century, subsequent 11-plus selection procedures and, most recently, the assisted places scheme. It has also informed the thinking behind public examinations generally. The evidence from studies of social mobility shows that such a meritocratic approach does help overcome the effects of disadvantage by promoting some individuals with outstanding talents. What such studies also show, however, is that although this works for some, it fails to do so for many more (Brown *et al*, 1997) and does nothing to improve the standard of education for those left behind.

The second approach has involved the use of compensatory mechanisms. These include individual benefits, such as free school meals, uniform grants and other special measures for low-income families. The problems with individual benefits are that the levels of funding have always been relatively modest and have thus been unable to compensate for the major differences in the conditions of children's lives (Smith and Noble, 1995). Compensatory mechanisms have also included the allocation of additional resources to schools, such as in the Educational Priority Area programmes of the 1960s and 1970s, when extra payments were made to schools with high proportions of disadvantaged students (Halsey, 1972; Smith, 1987). One drawback of such schemes is that some advantaged students gain access to extra resources within the chosen schools, whilst many disadvantaged students, in other schools, do not (Plewis, 1997). Later versions of this idea, adopted by the (former) Inner London Education Authority, provided extra resources on a sliding scale rather than on an all or nothing basis (Sammons *et al*, 1983). The local management formulae for schools approved by governments over the last few years, however, allow little scope for radical positive discrimination.

The third approach involves the creation of specific intervention projects, which can be used with the disadvantaged with a view to accelerating their educational development. Examples of such projects in the USA include the High/Scope programme (Weikart, 1972; Schweinhart and Weikart, 1997) the Comer Approach (Comer, 1980) and Success for All (Slavin *et al*, 1993; Herman and Stringfield, 1995). In New Zealand, Clay has developed the Reading Recovery Programme, a structured approach to overcoming early reading failure that has been shown to be effective for disadvantaged students (Clay, 1982; Rowe, 1995). In the United Kingdom, the Early Years Nursery Study, which focused on ways of increasing children's capacity to learn (Athey, 1990), has claimed some success. A series of British parent involvement schemes designed to encourage children and parents to read together (see, for example, Tizard *et al*, 1982) has been shown to have positive effects, while a Scottish project on the use of homework has demonstrated gains in disadvantaged areas (MacBeath and Turner, 1990). Despite the enthusiastic support of teachers and local authorities in the UK for each of these projects, official support and hence widespread implementation was, under the last government, extremely limited.

The present government's policies seem to embrace elements of all three approaches, but its White Paper, *Excellence in Schools* (DfEE, 1997b), and the subsequent School Standards and Framework Act 1998 have placed a particular emphasis on school improvement strategies, backed by a strengthened accountability framework.

Change through school improvement

The roots of school improvement lie in 20 years of research into school effectiveness carried out mainly in England, The Netherlands and the United States (Hopkins *et al*, 1994). The central tenet of school improvement is that the responsibility for change must lie in the hands of the school itself (Stoll and Fink, 1996). In contrast to centrally driven projects, and the thinking behind some recent policies, those working in school improvement believe that the head teacher, staff and school governing body – having listened to the views and advice of school inspectors, consultants or researchers – are usually the best placed to decide how to improve their own institutions (Mortimore, 1996).

Established school improvement projects usually have a common pattern (Stoll and Fink, 1996). Initially, the school improvement team carries out an audit of the current state of the school: the student outcomes, the curriculum, the pedagogy, the management of learning, behaviour and resources, and the state of the premises. In the light of this, the team draws up an action plan. This is often based on a series of hypotheses about what has probably caused which outcome, and what might, if changed, produce a different result. It is far from being an exact science and in the third stage – the evaluation – the team may discover that many outcomes are the result of a complex web of influences and that some changes have produced unintended negative results.

The National Commission on Education (NCE, 1996) undertook a project designed to uncover how some schools with disadvantaged students had improved and succeeded against the odds. The authors of one school case study (Mortimore *et al*, 1996) were particularly impressed with the quality of the leadership team and the way it had trusted the majority of the staff to create a set of school aims around the idea of achievement. Students were committed to learning and staff held high expectations about examination performance and social behaviour. The confidence of the teachers in the good sense of the students – even to the radical point of encouraging them to draw up a code of what they expected of the staff – was impressive.

Maden's and Hillman's (1996) discussion of the findings from all the case studies in the project emphasizes the importance of: a leadership stance which builds on and develops a team approach; a vision of success which includes a view of how the school can improve; the careful use of targets; the improvement of the physical environment; common expectations about students' behaviour and success; and an investment in good relations with parents and the community. The project demonstrates that committed and talented heads and teachers can improve schools even if such schools contain a proportion of disadvantaged students. In order to achieve improvement, however, such schools have to exceed what could be termed 'normal' efforts. Members of staff have to be more committed and work harder than their peers elsewhere. What is more, they have to maintain the effort so as to sustain the improvement. There can be no switching on the 'automatic pilot' if schools are aiming to buck the trend. We must, however, be aware of the dangers of basing a national strategy for change on the efforts of outstanding individuals working in exceptional circumstances.

Further evidence about the circumstances in which schools with disadvantaged students have been able to improve comes from the first tranche of case studies published by the DfEE (1997a). These studies describe some of the ways in which improvement was brought about in schools that had failed their Ofsted inspections. In contrast to much of the rhetoric about resources not mattering, what stands out is the impact of the extra resources invested by the LEAs in their efforts to turn the schools round. MacGilchrist (1997) has argued forcefully that some of the special interventions noted earlier that have been mounted to support the learning of students with special difficulties – and, in many cases, disadvantaged backgrounds – demonstrate that more schools, given adequate support, could help such students.

In theory, researchers should be able to estimate fairly precisely how many individual students have been helped by their schools to overcome the effects of personal disadvantage. By addressing the GCSE results of secondary schools and noting their intake information from five years before (for example, what student attainment was at the end of primary schooling and how many students were eligible for free school meals) it should be possible to estimate some 'value added' scores for their schools in relation to other institutions. Those that had raised the achievement of their 'disadvantaged students' significantly beyond what had been achieved by similar students in other schools could be assumed to have helped, especially, this group of students. Retrospective investigations could then attempt to explore how the schools had helped these students and, in particular, whether improvement had been the result of a planned programme or whether it had occurred seemingly spontaneously. Other information, such as whether the 'disadvantaged' group had been a particularly high or low proportion of the total, could also be collected to inform us about the importance of the educational context in which a student learns.

Unfortunately, such an investigation remains a theoretical possibility because not only would it be difficult to ensure that one really was 'comparing like with like' but also there is not a suitable national database which brings together accurate intake and examination outcome data. It is worth noting, anyway, that attributing causal effects to particular initiatives in complex organizations such as schools is always likely to be difficult. Without appropriate data and suitably robust analytical techniques, therefore, the evidence for the ability of schools to help individual disadvantaged students has to rest on theory and on the historical evidence of those institutions which, in the absence of alternative explanations, do appear to have bucked the trend. The current government's plans to create a national database of school pupils offers the possibility of exploring the progress made by disadvantaged pupils at some time in the future. This could illuminate what is meant by 'value added' and enable the identification of how some schools promote, to a much greater extent than others, the progress of the disadvantaged.

Cultural and structural change

Many sociologists of education have hitherto been rather critical of work on school effectiveness and school improvement for failing 'to explore the relationship of specific practices to wider social and cultural constructions and political and economic interests' (Angus, 1993: 335). Angus argues that it 'shifts attention away from the nature of knowledge, the culture of schooling and, most importantly, the question of for whom and in whose interests schools are to be effective' (p 342). Hatcher (1996) sees school improvement as downplaying the significance of social class, with similar consequences.

Angus's questions suggest that the curriculum itself may be implicated in perpetuating disadvantage by marginalizing the culture of the least powerful groups in society. There is certainly a case for broadening the scope of what counts as legitimate knowledge in schools (Whitty, 1985). Some of the National Curriculum Orders have been criticized for adopting an unduly narrow view of worthwhile knowledge and ignoring the pluralism and multi-culturalism of late twentieth century Britain (Ball, 1993). The recent relaxation of National Curriculum requirements in order to focus on the 'basics' may even exacerbate this problem.

Although these issues will need to be addressed by the Qualifications and Curriculum Authority (QCA) in its review of the National Curriculum, individual schools can also play some part in the way they choose to interpret the current requirements. Trying to counter the cultural bias of curricular arrangements and making schools more 'inclusive' of diverse communities is sometimes seen as a watering down of standards. Yet schools that are successful with students from a variety of backgrounds recognize that high standards can be achieved in a number of ways. While some learning goals need to be tackled by all students in the same way, others can be achieved through a variety of routes that take account of different backgrounds. This is not the same as adjusting standards to the lowest common denominator, which is an unacceptable option, especially in the light of the increasing globalization of labour and the need to ensure that young people from the United Kingdom can compete with their peers from elsewhere in the world.

Such considerations also demand that we find ways to ensure that a greater proportion of our students can succeed. This may require a restructuring of the assessment system so that a much higher proportion of candidates reaches the currently accepted level of success. Unfortunately, the experience of assessing the progress of students through the National Curriculum is not very promising and efforts to combine a student's need for diagnostic assessment with a system need for certification and monitoring have generally proved unsatisfactory for each of these needs. There are, however, a number of ways in which our national approach to assessment could be improved: the standards set for performance could be better defined; feedback could be more positive; a range of performance tasks and modes could be provided (Gipps, 1994). Nevertheless, this would not necessarily solve the problem with which we are concerned in this chapter, as such improvements would be more likely to lift overall standards than specifically help the disadvantaged.

Whatever changes occur in the curriculum and means of assessment, it seems inevitable that schools will be affected by their role within a wider society that still maintains social divisions and a powerful sense of hierarchy. A particular criticism of school improvement work is that it has tended to exaggerate the extent to which individual schools can challenge such structural inequalities. Whilst some schools can succeed against the odds, the possibility of them all doing so, year in and year out, still appears remote given that the long-term patterning of educational inequality has been strikingly consistent throughout the history of public education in most countries. Doubts have recently even been cast on whether Sweden, usually seen as a shining exception, has actually been bucking this particular trend in recent years (Erikson and Jonsson, 1996). Although there are different theories about how the social and cultural patterning of educational outcomes occurs (Goldthorpe, 1996), these patterns reflect quite closely the relative chances of different groups entering different segments of the labour market. Accordingly, whilst it might be possible, for example, for the ethos of a particular school to help transform the aspirations of a particular group of students within it, it seems highly unlikely that all schools could do this in the absence of more substantial social changes.

As noted earlier, one of the depressing findings is that the relative performance of the disadvantaged has remained similar even when the absolute performance of such groups has improved. Just as poverty is a relative concept, we are faced with a situation in which educational success also appears to be partly relative. A large-scale longitudinal study of primary schools (Mortimore *et al*, 1988) found that no school reversed the usual 'within school' pattern of advantaged students performing better than the disadvantaged. However, some of the disadvantaged students in the most effective schools made more progress than their advantaged peers in the least effective schools and even did better in absolute terms. Yet, encouraging as this is, it would appear that, if all primary schools were to improve so that they performed at the level of the most effective, the difference between the overall achievement of the most advantaged social groups and that of the disadvantaged might actually increase.

At secondary level, schools only rarely overcome the relative differences between the performance of different social groups, as the latest evidence on differential school effects demonstrates (Thomas *et al*, 1997). Moreover, despite the optimism of some school improvement literature, it is still difficult to counter the conclusion to be drawn from the pioneering *Fifteen Thousand Hours* research (Rutter *et al*, 1979) that if all schools performed as well as the best schools, the stratification of achievement by social class would be even more stark than it is now. This would happen because socially advantaged children in highly effective schools would achieve even more than they might do in a less conducive environment and the gap between them and their less advantaged peers would increase. In those circumstances, theories of 'relative deprivation' would suggest that the social exclusion of disadvantaged groups, as well as a disproportionate incidence of disaffection among individuals from those groups, would continue despite the overall improvement.

This issue is particularly important in the light of considerable evidence from a number of countries that the recent marketization of education has enabled advantaged parents and advantaged schools to further enhance their advantages and thus increase educational inequalities and social polarization (Whitty *et al*, 1998). These findings have very recently been challenged by Gorard and Fitz (1998; in press) who have claimed that the tendency towards increased polarization in both England and Wales and New Zealand may have been merely an initial effect of marketization policies and that social polarization may actually be reduced in subsequent years. Educational polarization between successful and unsuccessful schools, however, has been confirmed in the case of England by Her Majesty's Chief Inspector of Schools (HMCI, 1998) and the 1998 GCSE results brought an increase in the failure rate alongside an increase in the numbers gaining five grades A–C.

Despite some outstanding exceptions, it remains the case that schools located in contexts of multiple disadvantage have overall levels of performance well below the national average and tend to be relatively ineffective at boosting students' progress (Gray, 1998; Gibson and Asthana, 1998). The problems and dilemmas facing schools with large numbers of disadvantaged students, compared with those with advantaged intakes, are much greater than current policies recognize (Proudford and Baker, 1995; Thrupp, 1995). This suggests a continuing need for positive discrimination and the effective targeting of human and material resources. Smith *et al* (1997) recommend three sets of actions to support schools in disadvantaged areas.

They argue that, because of the competitive market that has been created, education in poor areas must not be considered in isolation. Given the existence of this competitive market between schools, they recommend a stronger interventionist role for the LEA. They suggest that 'choice' is too blunt an instrument for improvement and recommend the targeting of resources to schools in disadvantaged areas and possibly a transfer of resources from inspection to school improvement.

Robinson claims that educational measures are unlikely to alleviate the impact of disadvantage. He rightly sees the tackling of social and economic disadvantage as more likely to succeed, arguing that 'a serious programme to alleviate child poverty might do far more for boosting attainment and literacy than any modest intervention in schooling' (Robinson, 1997: 17). However, schools with disadvantaged students can lift achievement levels, provided those who work in them invest the energy and the dedication to maintain momentum even while working against the grain. Within any school, however, the powerful factors associated with a more advantaged home background appear, in general, to be paramount and this is even more evident when we look across the education system as a whole. It is, therefore, important for government, LEAs and school governors to set challenging goals, but it is also important to be clear about the limits of school-based actions. Setting unrealistic goals and adopting a strategy of 'shame and blame' will lead only to cynicism and a lowering of morale amongst those teachers at the heart of the struggle to raise the achievement of disadvantaged students.

Grace has argued that too many urban education reformers have been guilty of 'producing naive school-centred solutions with no sense of the structural, the political and the historical as constraints' (Grace, 1984: xii). If disadvantage has multiple causes, tackling it requires strategies that bring together multiple agencies rather than expecting schools to seek their own salvation. A major priority for the government must be to provide incentives for effective multi-agency work to counter disadvantage, as argued by Whitty *et al* in Chapter 4. This is not just a matter of ensuring greater efficiency in the delivery of public services, important as that is. It can also be done in such a way as to rebuild 'social capital' in disadvantaged communities, as discussed by Gamarnikow and Green in Chapter 3.

The enhancement of social and cultural capital in disadvantaged areas also requires that more be done to provide opportunities for learning beyond the years of compulsory schooling. Traditionally this has been one of the tasks of further education colleges and adult institutes committed to continuing life-long learning, but these institutions and their clientele have too often been marginalized within the system as a whole. If more people are to continue their education and, in particular, if the disadvantaged are to play any part in the formation of a learning society, much more needs to be done. It is only likely to succeed, however, in the context of a culture – as well as a structure – of inclusiveness. Too much of our previous history of education has been built on a culture of exclusiveness, and it is how to change this culture that probably represents the new government's greatest challenge in this field.

Recently, the Kennedy Report (1997a) made a number of detailed recommendations for government, the Training and Enterprise Councils and individual further education colleges. These included: the launching of a lottery-funded government campaign for the creation of a learning nation; the redistribution of public resources towards those with less success in earlier learning; the encouragement of company-funded learning centres for adult workers; and the creation of a unitized system for recognizing achievement. In a comment on the Report, Kennedy argued (Kennedy, 1997b: 3) that drawing more people into the community of learning is not only central to economic prosperity but also 'one of the most effective ways of tackling social exclusion'. She claimed that 'we have been seeing the most terrible separation between rich and poor over the past decades and education has a vital role in redressing the consequences of that division'. This requires 'a redistribution of public resources towards those with less success in earlier learning'. It is not yet clear how far the new government is prepared to move in this direction and its Green Paper on Lifelong Learning (DfEE, 1998) contains some contradictory messages.

Nevertheless, the establishment of a Social Exclusion Unit based at the heart of government has signalled a recognition that tackling social exclusion will involve inter-agency collaboration. Meanwhile, a recognition of the necessity of positive discrimination is evident in one of the few New Labour education initiatives that signals a clear break with the policies of the Conservatives. Its pilot programme of 25 Education Action Zones in areas with a mix of underperforming schools and the highest levels of disadvantage is intended to lever up standards and cut truancy rates. Zones will have at their centre a forum of local parents and representatives from local business and community interests in which an action plan and targets will be formulated, implemented and monitored.

It is anticipated that the zones will be 'test-beds for innovation', with some run by LEAs, others by a group of self-selecting schools, and still others led by private sector organizations. It has been suggested that they thus epitomize New Labour's 'third way' approach to public service reform (Hackett, 1998). It remains to be seen how they actually develop and whether their existence does indeed channel more help and energy into disadvantaged areas. Whether they will, in practice, help schools and children in disadvantaged areas or further isolate them from the mainstream depends not only on what happens in the zones themselves but also on what happens in more advantaged areas.

In the light of what we have said earlier, we believe that some aspects of the idea are certainly worth pursuing, provided each zone's forum gives a voice to all relevant constituencies and if there is a significant redistribution of resources into these areas. At the same time, it will be important not to neglect the needs of disadvantaged groups beyond these zones. There will also need to be a clearer policy for forging links with other interventions both within and beyond education. Initially, Education Action Zones seemed to be conceived as concerned with schools, with little reference to pre-school provision or lifelong learning. As Whitty *et al* argue (in Chapter 4), they seemed similarly isolated from Health Action Zones and Employment Zones, though useful links are now being forged in some areas.

Conclusions

The re-engineering of the educational system, so that disadvantaged groups can succeed, will certainly not be easy, nor will it be achieved by the education service alone. As Bernstein (1970) noted nearly 30 years ago, 'Education cannot compensate for society'. Probably the single most significant factor that currently distinguishes the most academically successful schools (even if not the most 'effective' ones in value-added terms) is that only a small proportion of their students come from disadvantaged homes. To that extent, policies that tackle poverty and related aspects of disadvantage at their roots are likely to be more successful than purely educational interventions in influencing overall patterns of educational inequality. Yet if dynamic school improvement strategies can be developed as one aspect of a broader social policy, then they will have an important role to play.

What we have been concerned to stress in this chapter is that society needs to be clearer about what schools can and cannot be expected to do. The relationship between individuals, institutions and society is complex and blaming schools for the problems of society is unfair and unproductive. Teachers who choose to work in these schools because they want to help the disadvantaged need their commitment recognized and supported rather than being 'blamed', as has happened so shamefully in the recent past. But they will also need to work closely with other agencies if their work is to make a significant and sustained impact on relative levels of achievement among disadvantaged communities.

In short, we do not consider that there is any single factor that could reverse longstanding patterns of disadvantage but neither do we regard them as an unchangeable fact of life. With such a perspective, we consider four clusters of immediate action to be vital:

- better co-ordination of the work of the support agencies by the government and by local authorities;
- early interventions that provide additional educational opportunities for the disadvantaged, funded from an increased education budget;
- reconsideration of the approaches to learning and teaching used with disadvantaged students;
- extra support for students with disadvantaged backgrounds in school improvement programmes.

Even with these actions we accept that there is unlikely to be a sudden reversal of long-established patterns of disadvantage or any significant long-term change in the absence of concurrent strategies to tackle poverty and disadvantage at their roots. We do consider, however, that the current waste of human resources caused by the educational failure and social exclusion of those from disadvantaged backgrounds is unacceptable in a modern society and that now is an opportune time to make a concerted effort to confront the problem in a coherent manner.

Acknowledgement

This paper has been developed from P Mortimore and G Whitty: *Can School Improvement Help Overcome the Effects of Disadvantage?* (1997) Institute of Education, London.

References

Angus, L (1993) The sociology of school effectiveness, *British Journal of Sociology of Education,* **14** (3), 333–45

Athey, C (1990) *Extending Thought in Young Children,* Paul Chapman Publishing, London.

Ball, S J (1993) Education, Majorism and 'the Curriculum of the Dead', *Curriculum Studies,* **1** (2), 195–214

Bandura, A (1995) Exercise of personal and collective efficacy in changing societies, in *Self Efficacy in Changing Societies*, ed A Bandura, Cambridge University Press, Cambridge

Bernstein, B (1970) Education cannot compensate for society, *New Society,* **387**, pp 344–47

Brown, P *et al* (1997) The Transformation of Education and Society: An introduction, in *Education: Culture, economy and society,* ed A H Halsey, H Lauder, P Brown and A Wells, Oxford University Press, Oxford

Clay, M M (1982) *Observing Young Readers,* Heinemann, New Hampshire

Comer, J P (1980) *School Power: Implication of an intervention project,* Free Press, New York

Davie, R, Butler, N and Goldstein, H (1972) *From Birth to Seven,* Longman, Harlow

Dennehy, A, Smith, L and Harker, P (1997) Not to be ignored: young people, poverty and health, in *Britain Divided: The growth of social exclusion in the 1980s and 1990s,* ed A Walker and C Walker, CPAG, London

DfEE (1997a) *The Road to Success,* Institute of Education/DfEE, London

DfEE (1997b) *Excellence in Schools,* Cm 3681, The Stationery Office, London

DfEE (1998) *The Learning Age: A renaissance for a new Britain,* The Stationery Office, London

Douglas, J W B (1964) *The Home and the School,* MacGibbon and Kee, London

Erikson, R and Jonsson, J O (eds) (1996) Can education be equalized? The Swedish case, in *Comparative Perspective*, Westview Press, Boulder, CO

Essen, J and Wedge, P (1982) *Continuities in Childhood Disadvantage,* Heinemann, London

Eurostat (1997) Reported in *The Guardian*, 28 April

Gibson, A and Asthana, S (1998) School performance, school effectiveness and the 1997 White Paper, *Oxford Review of Education,* **24** (2), 195–210

Gipps, C (1994) *Beyond Testing: Towards a theory of educational assessment*, Falmer Press, London

Goldthorpe, J H (1996) Class analysis and the reorientation of class theory: the case of persisting differentials in educational attainment, *British Journal of Sociology,* **47** (3), pp 482–505

Gorard, S and Fitz, J (1998) The more things change. . . the missing impact of marketization, *British Journal of Sociology of Education,* **19** (3), pp 365–76

Gorard, S and Fitz, J (in press) Under starters' orders: the established market, the Cardiff study and the Smithfield project, *International Studies in Sociology of Education*

Gorman, T and Fernandes, C (1992) *Reading in Recession,* NFER, Slough

Grace, G (1984) *Education in the City,* Routledge and Kegan Paul, London

Gray, J (1998) The Contribution of Educational Research to School Improvement, *Professorial Lecture*, Institute of Education, University of London

Hackett, J (1998) Historical ideology seeks a third way, *Times Educational Supplement*, **24**, 4 April

Halsey, A H (ed) (1972) *Educational Priority, EPA Problems and Policies,* vol 1, HMSO, London

Hatcher, R (1996) The limitations of the new social democratic agendas, in *Education after the Conservatives*, ed R Hatcher and K Jones, Trentham Books, Stoke-on-Trent

Herman, R and Stringfield, S (1995) *Ten Promising Programmes for Educating Disadvantaged Students,* Johns Hopkins University Press, Baltimore

HMCI (1998) *Secondary Education 1993–97: A review of secondary schools in England,* Ofsted, London

Holtermann, S (1997) All our futures: the impact of public expenditure and fiscal policies on children and young people, in *Britain Divided: The growth of social exclusion in 1980s and 1990s*, ed A Walker and C Walker, CPAG, London

Hopkins, D, Ainscow, M and West, M (1994) *School Improvement in an Era of Change*, Cassell, London

Kennedy, H (1997a) *Learning Works: Widening participation in further education,* FEFC, London

Kennedy, H (1997b) The Report, *Guardian Education*, pp 2–3, 1 July

MacBeath, J and Turner, M (1990) Learning out of school: homework, policy and practice, A research study commissioned by the Scottish Education Department, Jordanhill College, Glasgow

MacGilchrist, B (1997) Reading and Achievement, *Research Papers in Education*, **12** (2), pp 157–76

Maden, M and Hillman, J (1996) Lessons in Success, in *National Commission on Education, Success Against the Odds*, Routledge, London

Mortimore, J and Blackstone, T (1982) *Education and Disadvantage*, Heinemann, London

Mortimore, P (1996) Partnership and co-operation in school improvement, Paper presented at the Association for Teacher Education in Europe Conference, Glasgow, September

Mortimore, P and Mortimore, J (1986) Education and social class, in *Education and Social Class*, ed R Rogers, Falmer, Lewes

Mortimore, P *et al* (1988) The effects of school membership on students' educational outcomes, *Research Papers in Education*, **3** (1), pp 3–26

Mortimore, P, Davies, H and Portway, S (1996) Burntwood School: a case study, in *National Commission on Education, Success Against the Odds*, Routledge, London

NCE (National Commission on Education) (1996) *Success Against the Odds: Effective schools in disadvantaged areas*, Routledge, London

OECD (1995) *Our Children at Risk*, OECD, Paris

Osborne, A F and Milbank, J E (1987) *The Effects of Early Education*, Clarendon Press, Oxford

Plewis, I (1997) Letter to the *Times Educational Supplement*, 9 May

Proudford, C and Baker, R (1995) Schools that make a difference: a sociological perspective on effective schooling, *British Journal of Sociology of Education*, **16** (3), pp 277–92

Robinson, P (1997) *Literacy, Numeracy and Economic Performance*, CEP/London School of Economics, London

Rowe, K J (1995) Factors affecting students' progress in reading: key findings from a longitudinal study in literacy, *Teaching and Learning, An International Journal of Early Literacy*, **1** (2), pp 57–110

Rutter, M *et al* (1979) *Fifteen Thousand Hours*, Paul Chapman Publishing, London

Sammons, P, Kysel, F and Mortimore, P (1983) Educational priority indices: a new perspective, *British Educational Research Journal*, **9** (1), pp 27–40

Schweinhart, L J and Weikart, D P (1997) The High/Scope pre-school curriculum comparison study through age 23, *Early Childhood Research Quarterly*, **12**, pp 117–143

Slavin, R E *et al* (1993) Success for all: longitudinal effects of a restructuring program for inner city elementary schools, *American Educational Research Journal*, **30**, pp 123–48

Smith, G (1987) Whatever happened to EPAS?, *Oxford Review of Education*, **13** (1), pp 23–38

Smith, G, Smith, T and Wright, G (1997) Poverty and schooling: choice, diversity or division? in *Britain Divided: The growth of social exclusion in the 1980s and 1990s,* ed A Walker and C Walker, CPAG, London

Smith, T and Noble, M (1995) *Education Divides: Poverty and schooling in the 1990s,* CPAG, London

Stoll, L and Fink, D (1996) *Changing our Schools,* Open University Press, Buckingham

Thomas, S *et al* (1997) Differential secondary school effectiveness: comparing the performance of different pupil groups, *British Educational Research Journal,* **23** (4), pp 451–69

Thrupp, M (1995) The school mix effect: the history of an enduring problem in educational research, policy and practice, *British Journal of Sociology of Education,* **16**, pp 183–203

Tizard, J, Schofield, W and Hewison, J (1982) Symposium: reading-collaboration between teachers and parents in assisting children's reading, *British Journal of Educational Psychology,* **52** (1), pp 1–15

Townsend, P (1996) Comment quoted in Richards, H, Perspectives, *Times Higher Educational Supplement,* p 13, 30 August

Walker, A and Walker, C (ed) (1997) *Britain Divided: The growth of social exclusion in the 1980s and 1990s,* CPAG, London

Weikart, D P (1972) Relationship of curriculum, teaching and learning in pre-school education, in *Preschool Programs for the Disadvantaged*, ed J C Stanley, Johns Hopkins University Press, Baltimore

Whitty, G (1985) *Sociology and School Knowledge*, Methuen, London

Whitty, G, Power, S and Halpin, D (1998) *Devolution and Choice in Education: The school, the state and the market,* Open University Press, Buckingham

Wilkinson, R (1997) *Unfair Shares: The effects of widening income differences on the welfare of the young,* Barnardos, London

6

Widening Participation in Pursuit of the Learning Society: Kennedy, Dearing and *The Learning Age*

Gareth Parry and Heather Fry

Following a decade or more of major reform and rapid expansion in the education of young people and adults, policies for 'education and training' addressed to national and individual competitiveness have since given way to policies for 'learning' directed, more broadly, to personal well-being, social cohesion and economic success. Over the same period, growing importance has been attached to education and learning beyond the compulsory phase, whether viewed as a means of remedying deficiencies in the initial system or aimed at renewing the skills base in search of improved productivity, employability and prosperity. While concepts of education throughout life and lifetime learning had entered into the policy discourse of previous administrations, it was a new Labour government which sought to place investment and participation in lifelong learning at the centre of a strategy to build human and social capital in a knowledge economy.

Lifelong learning: a policy for inclusion?

The key statement of this new strategy was the publication of a Green Paper on lifelong learning – *The Learning Age* (DfEE, 1998a) – which declared that success in the information and knowledge economy of the 21st century would need to be built on a very different foundation than in the past: one that necessitated an investment in the intellect, creativity and enterprise of 'all our people', not just the few; and one that nurtured and sustained a regard for learning 'at whatever age', not just for the opportunities and advantages it brought to individuals, employers and the wider society, but also 'for its own sake'. In short, investment in skills and ideas, together with the development of a culture of lifelong learning for all, were 'essential' to continue to compete, to generate new wealth, and to equip individuals and organizations to cope with enormous economic and social change:

We have no choice but to prepare for this new age in which the key to success will be the continuous education and development of the human mind and imagination.

(DfEE, 1998a: 9)

We will succeed by transforming inventions into new wealth, just as we did a hundred years ago. But unlike then, *everyone* [emphasis in original] must have the opportunity to innovate and to gain reward – not just in the research laboratories, but on the production line, in design studios, in retailing outlets and in providing services.

(DfEE, 1998a: 10)

In the new age of information and global competition, the most productive investment would be linked to best educated and best trained workforces, and 'the most effective way of getting and keeping a job will be to have the skills needed by employers'. Yet, we were assured, the 'vision' of *The Learning Age* was about more than employment and employability:

The development of a culture of learning will help to build a united society, assist in the creation of personal independence, and encourage our creativity and innovation.

(DfEE, 1998a: 10)

It will mean changing the culture in many homes and workplaces where learning is not seen as having any relevance. It is a social as well as an economic challenge.

(DfEE, 1998a: 13)

In these and other respects, the Green Paper was, unlike its Conservative predecessor, a consultation document on 'lifetime learning' (DfEE, Scottish Office and Welsh Office, 1995) that chose to focus on the continuing education and training of the workforce and the need to increase commitment to, and individual responsibility for, vocational lifetime learning. In contrast to the narrow emphasis on personal competitiveness and economic returns in this earlier document, the Green Paper was expansive, inventive and assertive, conferring learning with a powerful potential and almost limitless reach.

For individuals, learning offered 'excitement and the opportunity for discovery'; it stimulated 'enquiring minds and nourished our souls'. For businesses, it added value and kept them up-to-date, developing the intellectual capital of the organization and providing the tools to manage industrial and technological change. Within communities, learning contributed to social cohesion and fostered 'a sense of belonging, responsibility and identity'. And for the nation as a whole, learning was 'essential to a strong economy and an inclusive society', offering 'a way out of dependency and low expectation and capable of overcoming a vicious circle of underachievement, self-deprecation, and petty crime'.

Because it benefited everyone, investing in learning was to be seen as a shared responsibility between individuals, employers and the state. In this new partnership, each would contribute, directly or through earnings foregone, to the cost of learning over a lifetime. Individuals were expected to invest in their own learning to improve their employability, professional competence and earning potential, as well as for the purpose of leisure. Employers would continue to have responsibility for investing in the job and career-related training of their employees. Both would increasingly 'take charge of their own learning and of meeting their need for skills', so giving more importance to their decisions and choices, and requiring education and training providers to 'transform themselves' in order to meet their needs.

What was different about this partnership, compared to the balance of responsibilities described in the 1995 document on lifetime learning, was the larger role for the state and for public funding in supporting social, economic and strategic purposes. While there was little that was remarkable about a pledge to 'help create a framework of opportunities for people to learn and to lift barriers that prevent them from taking up those opportunities' (DfEE 1998a: 13) the priorities for public funding were now to widen participation, increase achievement and promote inclusion. The challenge for government and its partners was to bridge the deep 'learning divide' between those who had benefited most from education and training and those who had gained least. Such funds were to be directed at areas of most benefit to society and targeted on learners in greatest need:

> The aim of public funding should be to widen participation and increase attainment at all levels where this will benefit society most.
>
> (DfEE, 1998a: 25)

> Public financial support for learners should be designed to: bring back into learning those who stopped after leaving school; address particular shortages; widen access for those who are disadvantaged; and enable individuals to choose the method of learning that suits them best.
>
> (DfEE, 1998a: 26)

To carry forward its strategy for lifelong learning and its commitment to widening participation, a range of initiatives were outlined, some announced earlier, some already under development and others signalled for the first time in the Green Paper. The two most significant of these, the creation of the University for Industry and the introduction of individual learning accounts, were concerned with building investment and stimulating demand as much as increasing accessibility, flexibility and capacity in the supply and delivery of education and training. In the example of the University for Industry, modern communication technologies were to support 'a brand new learning network' designed to link businesses and individuals to relevant and cost-effective forms of education and training. In the case of individual learning accounts, individuals would be able to save and borrow for investment in their own learning, with the Government proposing to make an initial, if modest, contribution to each account. Neither initiative was focused exclusively on widening participation or improving attainment. However, the idea of individual learning accounts was intended to act 'as a catalyst for the learning revolution', with 'universal' and 'targeted' approaches being tested. The latter were to be used to support particular learning or skill needs, such as among people without qualifications or in low-skill jobs and among those seeking to return to work.

Other initiatives, including proposals to strengthen learning in the family and in communities, to improve provision specifically for people with disabilities or learning difficulties, and to implement a national childcare strategy, were more clearly referenced to social inclusion and active citizenship. Elsewhere, however, an employment-related agenda was able to assert itself, as registered in proposals for new national targets that would 'help employers and employees in changing the culture of the workplace'. A National Skills Task Force would assess the future skill needs of the economy and the development of 'employability skills' for unemployed people. Together with a whole series of other steps, they would ensure that people 'have the right skills in the right place at the right time' in order to operate in a modern competitive world.

The combination and intersection of rival agendas in *The Learning Age* was to be expected of a document which spanned the territories of adult, community, further and higher education on the one side and learning at work on the other. Cutting across these interests, and informing the careful balances achieved in the consultation paper, were other oppositions and familiar tensions: between access and standards, competition and collaboration, autonomy and accountability, freedom and compulsion, and – ever present – the liberal and the vocational. Leaving aside civil service machineries and Cabinet politics, these were probably reasons enough to explain the delay in the appearance of *The Learning Age* and its downgrading from a White to a Green Paper.

Yet another source of complexity was introduced by the need for the new administration to draw on, and respond to, the work and reports of a number of expert committees and advisory groups, each charged to make recommendations about the future of their part of the education and learning scene. In the Green Paper, the work of five groups in particular was mentioned, all but two of which had been established under the previous Conservative Government. One of these exercises – a review of qualifications for 16–19-year-olds conducted by Sir Ron (now Lord) Dearing – was undertaken as a personal commission and had reported its interim findings and final conclusions as early as 1996 (Dearing, 1995, 1996).

Of the other two early inquiries, about which we have more to say in subsequent sections, one chose to report after the general election and the second was required to do so by its terms of reference. The first was a committee on widening participation set up by the Further Education Council and chaired by Helena Kennedy QC (now Baroness Kennedy). The second was a national committee of inquiry into the future development of higher education chaired by (the same) Sir Ron Dearing. The remaining two groups, both quickly put in place following the change of government in May 1997, were convened with a policy or strategy for lifelong learning in mind: one an advisory body on the design and implementation of the University for Industry (chaired by David Brown); and the other a national advisory group for continuing education and lifelong learning (chaired by

Professor Bob Fryer). The Fryer advisory group was set up by the Secretary of State to advise him on matters concerning adult learning and, more directly, on the preparation of the anticipated White Paper on lifelong learning (NAGCELL, 1997).

In the rest of this chapter we examine how the Kennedy committee on further education and the Dearing committee on higher education addressed questions of widening participation and lifelong learning in their separate reports; how they viewed the roles of further education and higher education in the creation of 'a learning society'; and how their arguments were received and represented in *The Learning Age*. At the end of the chapter, and with reference to three interlocking themes, we comment briefly but critically on some of the assumptions, judgements and silences operating in the Kennedy, Dearing and *The Learning Age* texts.

Kennedy and widening participation: a radical project?

Established in December 1994, the Widening Participation Committee chaired by Helena Kennedy QC was one of three such bodies set up by the funding council for further education in England to advise on its strategy for allocating funds to colleges and other providers in the further education sector. However, unlike the Committee on Learning Difficulties and/or Disabilities (FEFC, 1996a) and the Committee on Learning and Technology (FEFC, 1996b), the Widening Participation Committee chose to broaden its remit to include 'post-16 learning' as well as provision for further education. It presented proposals to the government as well as to the funding council. Indeed, its main report – *Learning Works* (FEFC, 1997a) – was published one month after the coming to office of the Labour Government and ahead of the report of the Dearing committee on higher education. As a measure of the regard and status accorded to the work of the Widening Participation Committee, the new Labour administration published its formal response to the Kennedy and Dearing reports in parallel volumes (DfEE, 1998b, 1998c), even though only one of these committees had been set up by central government (rather than by one of its regional funding agencies) and had terms of reference asking it to make recommendations on the United Kingdom as a whole.

Asked to advise on the identification of under-represented groups in further education and how funding arrangements should be developed to increase and improve the quality of participation, the Kennedy committee placed further education at the centre of a national strategy to widen participation and to build a learning society which was inclusive and cohesive:

> Widening participation means increasing access to learning and providing opportunities for success and progression to a much wider cross-section of the population than now. All those who are not fulfilling their potential or who have underachieved in the past must be drawn into successful learning. Widening participation in post-16 learning will create a self-perpetuating learning society.

(FEFC, 1997a: 15)

99

This, it was emphasized, would require a dramatic shift in public policy for post-compulsory learning, involving a powerful vision of a 'learning nation' and communicating 'a new philosophy' about the purposes of education. More controversially it would necessitate a redistribution of resources in favour of further education in recognition of the costs of drawing disaffected and excluded groups 'back to the social embrace'. While autonomy for the colleges, together with the introduction of a new funding methodology linked to individual success in the attainment of qualifications, had encouraged institutions to be more active in their recruitment and retention of students, there was a tendency for too many colleges to go in pursuit of those most likely to succeed. These more competitive conditions had stimulated expansion but, it was argued, the application of market principles had often operated to the detriment of potential learners and had displaced or undermined the social and public purposes of learning:

> Education must be at the heart of any inspired project for regeneration in Britain. It should be a springboard for the revitalisation that our communities so urgently need. However, in all the political debates, it is the economic rationale for increasing participation in education that has been paramount. Prosperity depends upon there being a vibrant economy, but an economy which regards its own success as the highest good is a dangerous one. Justice and equity must also have their claim upon the arguments for educational growth. In a social landscape where there is a growing gulf between those who have and those who have not, the importance of social cohesion cannot be ignored.
>
> (FEFC, 1997a: 5–6)

Because the achievement of economic goals and social cohesion were 'intertwined' it was important therefore to find the right balance or articulation between public service values 'which have been the pulse of further education' and business imperatives. Learning was central to the achievement of economic success and social cohesion: a healthy society was a necessary condition for a thriving economy and, equally, economic prosperity was a major factor enabling people to play a full part in social and cultural life. Given this 'new synthesis', all types of learning were to be seen as 'valuable': not only were distinctions between vocational and non-vocational learning becoming less and less valid but notions of learning for work and learning for life were 'inseparable'.

By emphasizing the centrality of human and social capital in economic success, the Widening Participation Committee sought to recover a notion of education as a public good, as a common endeavour and, more boldly, as 'a weapon against poverty':

> Education has always been a source of social vitality and the more people we can include in the community of learning, the greater the benefits to us all. The very process involves interaction between people; it is the means by which the values and wisdom of a society are shared and transmitted across the generations. Education strengthens the ties that bind people, takes the fear out of difference

and encourages tolerance. It helps people to see what makes the world tick and the ways in which they, individually and together, can make a difference. It is the likeliest means of creating a modern, well-skilled workforce, reducing levels of crime, and creating participating citizens.

(FEFC, 1997a: 6–7)

Realizing these collective goals meant remedying past deficiencies and reaching out both to the majority of adults who received no further learning opportunities after completing their initial education and training, and to the large number of young people who started adult life 'in need of compensatory education'. Positioned between schools and higher education, and overlapping both, further education was in a 'unique' position to tackle this 'backlog of thwarted potential', providing first and second chance opportunities to engage with general, academic and vocational learning, whether in formal, informal or workplace settings. Its comprehensiveness, richness and diversity made further education the most 'economical' way of encouraging and broadening participation. It was also the 'only' means of enabling all to have the opportunity to achieve and qualify at level 3 – the platform needed to widen participation and to provide for lifelong learning and for employment in a learning society.

In the first of some 49 recommendations to the government, the Kennedy committee called for national leadership in the creation of a learning society and a national strategy for post-16 learning to widen and not simply increase participation. It was for the government to state its aspiration for all to achieve a level 3 qualification 'including key skills' and to set new and comprehensive national learning targets to support this aim. At the same time, it was necessary to establish a strategic focus at local level through a national network of permanent partnerships, 'covering all post-16 learners and learning' and involving all the key stakeholders in producing participation plans for their localities and setting out agreed local targets for widening participation. Such partnerships would be closely linked to the regional committees of the funding council and would support that body in its duty to secure the provision of sufficient and adequate further education.

Furthermore, if progress in widening participation was to be monitored in a consistent fashion, at national and local levels, then systems for measuring participation and achievement in post-16 learning would need to be harmonized and arrangements for sharing information improved. Both the government and the funding council would be expected to make an annual report on progress in extending participation and strengthening achievement, with the funding council invited to make use of a new framework for measurement developed by the Widening Participation Committee.

Consideration was also to be given to the development of a nationally agreed system to measure the value-added or 'learning gain' achieved in post-16 learning, although the setting of national performance indicators for widening participation in the college sector was seen as 'inappropriate at this stage'. Learners would be able to chart their learning gain through the creation of a national framework for credit, receiving recognition for interim achievement and accumulating credit across the lifespan. Those with low levels of attainment in education and training would be able to take advantage of a 'New Learning Pathway' to make learning gains at a level and pace suited to their needs. It was for the government to create a national partnership to develop a credit framework 'for implementation within the next five years' and for the funding council to play a leading role in this enterprise, to support the introduction of the new pathway and to promote the good practice guide on widening participation produced by the Kennedy committee.

Colleges and other providers intending to offer the new pathway would be expected to devise an individual learning programme, to provide a planned programme of learning support, and to ensure that good quality information, advice and guidance was made readily available. The importance of the latter to widening participation was not to be underestimated, with the government being asked to establish a national entitlement to guidance as part of its strategy for post-16 learning. To be included in this entitlement was a new 'Charter for Learning' which would set out the rights of all individual learners aged over 16. The launch of the Charter was to be part of a national publicity campaign to stimulate demand for learning, with the government calling upon the expertise of media professionals to help design the best approaches.

Notwithstanding the range and potential of these and other recommendations, it was funding which offered the most important lever for change in widening participation and it was the inequity of the current arrangements which provided the most compelling reason for radical overhaul of funding principles and priorities:

> Those who have already succeeded are now most likely to take part in further learning. The successful take priority for public funding with funding skewed towards the minority who are already high achievers.

> (FEFC, 1997a: 50)

The task for government was to create a national framework for the funding of post-16 learning founded on the principle of equity and based on a recognition of the relative costs required to widen participation:

> The principle of equity should apply across post-16 funding. Levels of funding as well as funding systems should be harmonised. All students and providers should be entitled to a fair share of funding based on common principles. Equity does not mean uniformity. Funding principles would need to take account of students' needs and the circumstances of the providers. Differences should be soundly based and transparent. Funding differences for providers would need to be carefully justified, for example, on grounds of higher costs. The system should aim to deliver common outcomes for all.

> (FEFC, 1997a: 51)

Moreover:

> Resources are required both for new students and for the additional support, guidance and enrichment that under-represented groups need if more are to

participate successfully in education and training. Investment is required in curriculum, institutional and technological change. Staff development is a particular concern. Redistribution of resources both to further education and within it is required if widening participation is to become a reality.

(FEFC, 1997a: 52)

To contribute the necessary investment, the committee recommended that funds from the national lottery should be released after the millennium to create a 'Learning Nation Fund' to tackle the national backlog of under-achievement in the population. While learning would continue to be free for all young people and for those without basic skills, those who had done well from previous public investment in learning, and who could afford to pay more than at present, would be expected to do so. In short, public subsidy was to be aimed at those who had not yet reached level 3, with tax relief available for any learning programme up to level 3 which was funded by individuals and with tax incentives being used to stimulate the spread of employee development schemes. Given that the present system of financial support for post-16 learning was judged neither fair nor transparent, it was necessary for the government to embark on a root and branch review of these arrangements, although some changes were to be made immediately. The principles laid down for the national funding framework were also to apply to the funding council. A whole set of revisions and adjustments to the funding methodology were proposed to give much higher priority to widening participation in the distribution of funds to colleges and other organizations in the further education sector.

Dearing and widening participation: a core concern?

Both the Kennedy committee and the Dearing inquiry on higher education owed their origins to contemporary issues and problems of funding. The context for Kennedy was the development of a new funding system for the further education sector to be operated for the first time in 1994–95, being specifically designed to promote learning and reward achievement. However, the setting up of the Dearing inquiry was essentially a product of a deepening crisis in the funding of universities, with an on-going internal review unable to deflect calls from vice-chancellors for urgent and immediate action. After year-on-year reductions in the unit of funding, which accompanied the shift to a mass system and which continued during the period of consolidation imposed since 1994, a number of universities in January 1996 threatened to introduce top-up fees for students if no additional public funds were able to be found for higher education. In the following month, the Government, with bipartisan support, announced the establishment of a National Committee of Inquiry into Higher Education under the chairmanship of Sir Ron Dearing which was asked to report to a new administration in the summer of 1997. Since neither the Government nor the main opposition party was minded to debate funding matters ahead of a general election, the promise a national inquiry – the first since the Robbins committee of 1961–63 – offered an opportunity to buy time and win consent for a thorough examination of funding and related questions.

Unlike the Kennedy committee which trailed its emerging conclusions (FEFC, 1997b), consulted on them immediately before the general election (FEFC, 1997c), and published its pocket-sized main report in June 1997, the Dearing inquiry announced its findings and recommendations at the close of the inquiry in July 1997. Its main report extended to 466 pages and was published alongside a summary report and a further eight volumes of evidence and analysis. On the same day as its publication, the Government chose to reject one its key recommendations on funding: that support for the living costs of students be kept in its existing form. Rather than retain the maintenance grant and require a contribution to the cost of tuition, the preferred option of the new Labour Government was to abolish the maintenance grant altogether and introduce a means-tested contribution to tuition fees backed by an income-contingent loan. It was this policy, and its implications for future demand and wider participation, which were to be a subject of major criticism and continuing concern following publication of the inquiry report.

The need for Dearing and his committee to come up with short-term and longer-term solutions to the funding problem was always going to be a major preoccupation, yet the terms of reference for the inquiry were extensive. The committee was asked to report on 'how the purposes, shape, structure, size and funding of higher education, including support for students, should develop to meet the needs of the United Kingdom over the next twenty years'. Of the additional seven general principles offered to the committee, each to be considered 'within the constraints of the Government's other spending priorities and affordability', one bore directly on participation and underlined the importance of both initial and lifelong participation in higher education:

> there should be maximum participation in initial higher education by young and mature students and in lifetime learning by adults, having regard to the needs of individuals, the nation and the future labour market.
>
> (NCIHE, 1997a: 3)

A second principle emphasized 'choice and diversity' in the provision of higher education and another reminded members that arrangements for student support should be 'fair and transparent'. Learning was expected to be increasingly responsive to employment needs (and to include the development of 'general skills') and the effectiveness of teaching and learning was to be enhanced. However these principles might be interpreted or applied, the maintenance and assurance of standards was not to be compromised, 'standards of degrees and other higher education qualifications should be at least maintained, and assured' (NCIHE, 1997a: 13).

Accelerating demand, growing diversity and increasing competitiveness in international markets were among the many contextual features that the committee was asked to take into account. There was expanding demand from applicants of all ages as 'more people achieve qualifications at level 3' and as those who already held higher level qualifications looked to upgrade or update them. In addition, the rise of information societies and knowledge economies, together with the investment of competitor nations in higher level education and skills formation, meant a 'key role' for British higher education in regenerating the workforce and providing 'a basis for responding to social and economic change through innovation and lifelong learning'. Again, new technology was opening up the possibility of new forms of teaching and learning (in the workplace and in the home through distance learning), and links between higher education and other parts of the education and training system (particularly further education) were increasing in importance.

With economic and employment imperatives emphasized in the terms of reference, the invitation to consider the wider roles and responsibilities of higher education was less than likely to inspire questions about the political and social economy of the higher education enterprise, 'higher education continues to have a role in the nation's social, moral and spiritual life; in transmitting citizenship and culture in all its variety; and in enabling personal development for the benefit of individuals and society as a whole' (NCIHE, 1997a: 4).

As it was, the committee chose to introduce and frame its report in terms of a 'vision' of education as 'life-enhancing', with the most economically successful nations being those where 'all are committed, through effective education and training, to lifelong learning'. Central to this vision of the future was the judgement that the United Kingdom will need to develop as 'a learning society', investing in education to compete with the best in the world and contributing to the maintenance of 'a cohesive society and a rich culture'. For Dearing, a learning society was one 'in which people in all walks of life recognize the need to continue in education and training throughout their working lives and who see learning as enhancing the quality of life throughout its stages' (NCIHE, 1997a: 9). It was one focused largely, but not exclusively, on individuals and their working lives; and one which, looking twenty years ahead, demanded 'further and faster progress' in this direction to 'sustain a competitive economy'.

In a similar fashion, higher education was seen as primarily serving individual and economic ends, rather than advancing social goals or promoting cultural changes. Its success in expanding opportunities for students and maintaining its international standing in research were qualities which, for Dearing, marked the 'distinctive' contribution of higher education to a learning society. This contribution was defined in two main ways: the first, in terms of continuity and excellence in its core functions of teaching, scholarship and research; and the second, in terms of its capacity to expand numbers, safeguard standards and maintain a diverse range of autonomous institutions with different characters and missions. Given that this contribution would increasingly be made through lifelong learning, higher education was expected to find innovative and effective ways to extend the opportunity for learning to a larger and broader section of the community. On the other hand, the pattern and balance of excellence was different across the sector, and for institutions which already had an established world reputation 'there should be no pressure to change their character':

> Higher education needs continuity in the framework within which it operates to support its achievement of quality and distinctiveness. Government should avoid sudden changes in the funding or scope and direction of higher education. In return, the community, as represented by the government, has a right to expect higher education to be responsive to the developing needs of society and to be as zealous in the use of resources as it is in the pursuit of excellence in teaching and research.
>
> (NCIHE, 1997a: 8)

The attempt to reconcile the traditional claims of institutional autonomy and the national policy demands of lifelong learning was well illustrated by the recommendations put forward on widening participation. Although not highlighted in the terms of reference, nor the subject of a separate working group within the inquiry, the recommendations in support of widening participation, and those in respect of resumed expansion, occupied a prominent place in the Dearing report. They headed the list of 93 recommendations and were referenced to three of the fourteen research and analytical projects commissioned by the committee (NCIHE, 1997b, 1997c, 1997d).

With an assortment of evidence to hand, together with the results of commissioned research into the private and social rates of return of undergraduate education, the committee concluded that demand from the economy and from individuals, for initial qualifications and lifelong learning, was likely to grow, with much of that demand expressed at 'sub-degree' level. Both the changing nature of the economy and the changing requirements of the labour market demanded a more highly skilled workforce, and there were economic benefits to be gained for individuals and society. Accordingly, it was proposed that the cap on full-time sub-degree places should be lifted immediately; and that the limit on full-time first degree places should be relaxed over the next two to three years.

In recommending a resumption of expansion, the committee looked to employer and student demand, rather than social justice or the collective good, as the main determinants of future participation. Hence, intervention was only likely to be necessary in the case of strategic and shortage subjects, or to ensure that participation did not fall behind that of major competitor countries. Nor did the committee see any value in setting targets for participation, even though these were a feature of policy outside of higher education.

Nevertheless, it was recognized that expansion on its own was unlikely to achieve a significant broadening of the social base of higher education. While the recent and rapid movement to mass higher education had produced some considerable achievements, especially the increased participation by women, by mature students, by students from minority ethnic groups and by those with new kinds of entry qualifications, there remained 'substantial problems' which needed to be tackled as 'a matter of urgency':

> Apart from the economic imperative, there are other influences pointing to resumed growth. Unless we address the under-representation of those from lower socio-economic groups we may face increasingly socially divisive consequences. As a matter of equity, we need to reduce the under-representation of certain ethnic groups and of those with disabilities.
>
> (NCIHE, 1997a: 10)

To reduce these 'disparities' and 'discrepancies', the committee recommended that the government, when allocating funds for the expansion of higher education, should:

> give priority to those institutions which can demonstrate a commitment to widening participation, and have in place a participation strategy, a mechanism for monitoring progress, and provision for review by the governing body of achievement.
>
> (NCIHE, 1997a: 107)

It would be for governing bodies to devise a clear policy about its strategic aims for participation by under-represented groups, to monitor admissions and participation against these aims and, as a condition of public funding, to publish the results of a systematic review of these and related matters. However, it was less clear whether some rather than all institutions would be expected to embrace an access mission or identity. On the one side, the committee indicated that priority in funding should go to those establishments which had demonstrated a commitment to widening participation 'in the recent past' and which had 'a robust strategy' for doing so in the future. On the other hand, it was important – particularly in the context of 'a new compact' between higher education and society – that institutions individually and collectively 'command public confidence in the way they address participation matters'. For Dearing, it was legitimate for the government to prompt and encourage, but not to plan or intervene; and certainly not to query the right of institutions – always jealously guarded – to select individuals for their courses. Nor, it would seem, did the committee envisage any weakening of the competitive and selective basis for entry to undergraduate education. It was for individuals to demonstrate their 'ability to benefit'; there was to be no entitlement to a higher education, no guarantee of a place in the system for those who met the requirements for entry. 'In a system where the providers of higher education are autonomous institutions, there can be no absolute statutory or government-backed guarantee of a place for all who want one' (NCIHE, 1997a: 82).

In short, while higher education was 'not powerless to affect participation', the committee saw only limited ways in which the sector and its institutions might be in a position to extend access for previously excluded groups. This was particularly so in relation to young people, where the primary causes of their uneven participation were seen 'to lie outside higher education'. Even so, it was recommended that the funding bodies in further education and higher education collaborate to sponsor development projects designed to address low expectations and achievement, and that they consider financing pilot projects which allocated additional funds to institutions which enrolled students from 'particularly disadvantaged localities'. In the case of students with disabilities, these measures were seen as unlikely on their own to give sufficient support to these individuals and specific recommendations were made to encourage higher education to adapt its teaching and learning strategies.

Again, while institutions were charged with 'a moral obligation' to concern themselves with these matters, there was a role for the state and its agencies to ensure that higher education was 'an active partner' in the 'developing strategy' to raise achievement and extend participation.

Kennedy, Dearing and The Learning Age: some critical comments

In *The Learning Age*, the 'radical vision' of the Kennedy report and its placing of further education at the centre of widening participation were endorsed by the new Labour Government. The sector was praised for an excellent track record in reaching disadvantaged people, helping to reduce social exclusion and promoting employability. In realizing the learning age, further education was seen as 'the key to breaking the vicious circle of poor economic performance and an inadequate standard of living'. These were themes echoed and amplified in other parts of the Green Paper where the influence of the Kennedy agenda was evident in the support for new national targets, for more coherent planning and funding arrangements in post-16 education, and for the idea of a national credit framework.

The influence of the Dearing report, on the other hand, was less marked. Higher education, offering high quality and high standards, had a 'central role' to play in the learning age, in producing and disseminating new knowledge, in sharing and transferring its expertise, and in the meeting the expected demand from young people and adults. Given the priority in the Green Paper to 'reach out and include', the Government signalled its wish to see the Dearing recommendations on widening participation implemented in full.

One obvious reason for this lower profile was the focus in much of the Green Paper on basic and intermediate skills. Whereas the world class standards of the universities were 'a great strength', the 'serious weaknesses' in national educational performance were to be found in the failure of many young people to reach level 2 by the age of nineteen and in the large number of adults who held no formal qualifications and had poor literacy and numeracy skills. It was further education rather than higher education which was positioned to correct these deficiencies and the 'grand project' set out in the Kennedy report was one which aligned with the spirit, if not necessarily the substance, of *The Learning Age*. Rather than pursue an assessment of their relative contributions, we conclude this chapter with some critical comments about various omissions and silences in these texts as well as their significant meanings and messages.

Encouraging or discouraging participation?

In a document otherwise celebrating the rich variety and diversity of learning, and its potential to include and unite, there remain assumptions about 'learning' and judgements about 'learners' in the Green Paper which invite a constricted, distorted and negative understanding of these new keywords in the policy lexicon. In *The Learning Age*, and in Kennedy in particular, the word 'learning' was commonly used when 'education' was more clearly and more properly the subject of the narrative. In the consultation paper, people were expected to 'return to learning throughout their lives' and to 'enter and re-enter learning at every point' as if learning somehow stopped after leaving school or had been interrupted or extinguished by subsequent life events. Similarly (though more routinely) in Kennedy, people were to be 'brought into learning', to 'make a fresh start in learning' or, alternatively, to be 'helped to stay in learning'. In these constructions, learning was something divorced or detached from the normal, everyday continuous process of living, rather than intrinsic to that process.

To associate 'learning' with formal, planned and directed (even self-directed) learning episodes, and to leave out of account the way that adults engage in incidental and informal learning activities throughout their lives, was to assume that those who did not participate in planned programmes were without any learning. As Rogers (1997) has contended, it was to make a value judgement about people and their everyday experience: 'It demeans the natural learning processes, it says they are not important'. What was a submerged set of messages in the Green Paper was a firm set of categories in the Kennedy report where the challenge was to reach the 'non-learners', to convert 'potential learners' into 'new learners', and to close the gap between those people and their families 'who know and can do, and those who do not know and cannot do'. Not only did the description 'non-learner' do scant justice to the multiple forms of disadvantage which served to deter the participation of many people; it also betrayed a tendency, most evident perhaps in the Green Paper, to blame non-participants for the 'learning divide' while placing responsibility on them for doing something about it. For Tight (1998a), such 'victim blaming' was both off-putting and unrealistic: 'Stigmatizing non-participants from the start hardly seems the most sensible approach.'

At the same time, lifelong learning was portrayed as unavoidable, even semi-compulsory. 'We cannot force anyone to learn', declared the Green Paper, but to make ourselves ready for the digital age 'we must all develop and sustain a regard for learning': 'We have no choice but to prepare for this new age'. For Kennedy, as for *The Learning Age*, success and achievement were necessary requirements for 'learning gain'. It was not sufficient to draw under-represented groups into education and learning: 'making sure that they succeed and progress' was equally important as was enabling them to 'recognize their learning gains and have them celebrated'. To a significant extent, in both documents, achievement was equated with success in qualifications – especially those which appeared on the national 'scoreboard' of learning achievement or which featured in the national targets for education and training. In these and other policy statements, it was formalized and institutionally based learning leading to certification (and progression) that was seemingly privileged, over-informal, unaccredited and most often non-vocational learning. This was to ignore the fact that, for so many people, it was their experience of the formal system had turned them off the idea of learning (Tight, 1998b).

Qualifications, however much they deterred or excluded, were what colleges and universities provided, what funding councils funded, what employers wanted, and what governments measured and reported. While qualifications were 'not an end in themselves' and 'not everyone who learns needs or wants a qualification':

> today qualifications give signals about our employability and allow us to progress. They tell individuals and employers what is needed to achieve a given standard or skill. They help motivate people to stick with learning. They provide step-by-step progress through education and training, thus helping people to move forward or change direction in their careers.
>
> (DfEE, 1998a: 63)

Stimulating or steering demand?

Given its exclusive focus on higher education, where learning and learners were categories applied specifically to that context, the Dearing report avoided some of the elisions that featured in the Kennedy and Green Paper texts. Nevertheless, there were assumptions in Dearing about resuming expansion and widening participation that suggested a limited and circumscribed role for higher education in the creation of a more inclusive learning society.

Whereas in Kennedy the aim was to stimulate a broad and large demand for post-16 learning, thus enabling everyone to have the opportunity to achieve and qualify at level 3, in Dearing the need was to respond to demand from those already qualified at this level or who had otherwise demonstrated their capability to benefit from higher education. Responding to this 'qualified' demand was not, however, to be interpreted as a passive or neutral process.

Although the Dearing committee expected that, at least initially, a large part of future growth 'would' take place in the area of sub-degree education, most of the arguments mobilized in support of this view were about why provision and participation 'should' be increased at these levels. In the inquiry report, the expansion of sub-degree education was seen to be justified variously in terms of: the marked shift in the balance of higher education towards the higher levels brought about by periods of rapid growth; the relative international disadvantage of the United Kingdom in education and training at these levels; the wide scope for access and progression through sub-degree provision, as in the example in Scotland; the importance of short-cycle forms of higher education for lifelong learning; the role of intermediate qualifications in helping to reduce drop-out in mass higher education systems; and a concern coming through in the evidence that 'too high a proportion of students is aiming for a degree rather than a sub-degree qualification'. More bluntly:

> As access to higher education widens, and students with modest prior academic attainments or abilities are admitted to higher education, adaptations to programmes and qualifications will be needed to meet their needs. If such changes are not made, too many people will be set up to fail in higher education, or there will be a natural pressure to compromise on standards of achievement to allow them to succeed.
>
> (NCIHE, 1997a: 83)

Underneath some of these arguments was the assumption that expansion at these intermediate levels might relieve pressure on the standards of the first degree and provide 'alternative progression routes' for students with modest academic qualifications or 'non-standard qualifications'. This was a means of reconciling a growth in numbers with the maintenance of standards, and an echo of the thinking which informed the reform proposals put forward by Sir Ron Dearing in his review of qualifications for 16–19-year-olds (Dearing, 1996a, 1996b). As one of us has commented elsewhere (Parry, 1998), although the committee was aware of evidence indicating that those from the lower socio-economic groups were more likely to be studying for a sub-degree qualification, there was little or no discussion in the main inquiry report about the possibility that social divisions might be reproduced or reinforced within the different levels of undergraduate education. Nor was there much appreciation of the nature and scope of that described – and nowhere defined – in the report as 'sub-degree' higher education.

What was a missing or displaced argument in the decision to focus early growth on levels below the first degree was the reluctance to make any link between sub-degree provision and widening participation. This curious disconnection was no doubt explained, in part, by the late attention given to issues of access and equity in the work of the inquiry (Parry, 1999). What was most surprising about this silence was that the Dearing committee also recommended that, in the medium term, priority in growth in sub-degree provision should be accorded to further education colleges – as a 'special mission' for these establishments. As the location for the majority of students studying for academic, vocational and general vocational qualifications at the level normally required for entry to initial higher education, it might have been expected that the critical role of further education in broadening participation would have been acknowledged or emphasized.

Respecting or removing boundaries?

For all their concern with widening participation and lifelong learning, both the Kennedy and the Dearing inquiries were remarkably respectful of sector boundaries and processes. The Kennedy committee was, of course, set up and serviced by a sector agency, although this did not stop its members 'from the outset' defining further education more broadly than that which took place in colleges. The Dearing inquiry, on the other hand, had the freedom to define higher education in any way it wished. In the event, the inquiry team resisted any broadening of the scope of its activities 'we already faced an enormous task'. They adopted a conventional administrative definition based on education above level 3 and they chose to concentrate on teaching, learning, scholarship and research in the context of establishments of higher education (we had to set some boundaries).

Given that Kennedy sought to champion the cause of further education as well as reform its funding arrangements, it was understandable perhaps that sector demarcations were observed – especially if they seemed to point up inequities in the funding of programmes and students across further education and higher education. Nevertheless, the Kennedy committee would appear to have been relatively untroubled by the need for students at level 3 to compete for places in higher education, rather than achieve progression to a next stage or level of their education. Nowhere in the Kennedy and Dearing reports was serious consideration given to the merits of meritocratic principles or affirmative policies in the 'admission' of young people and adults to undergraduate courses.

Even though a 'redistributive' model of access and funding was to be applied to post-16 learning, the radical vision of the Kennedy report did not extend to a basic questioning of the need for a division between the further education and higher education sectors – each with its separate funding and quality regimes, and each identified with different levels of learning and distinctive sets of qualifications. It was enough for the two domains to continue to build ladders linking their programmes and for colleges of further education themselves to deliver more higher education courses, whether provided in their own right or franchised to them by universities. For Kennedy, the significance of more higher education being offered in the context of further education, and more partnerships being developed to provide the progression opportunities needed by a self-perpetuating learning society, were twofold, 'This will be an economical way of expanding and encouraging participation in ongoing cumulative learning' (FEFC, 1997a: 10). 'Not only will further education provide a means of bringing all to the level 3 platform, it will provide the most cost effective way of broadening the entry base for higher education' (FEFC, 1997a: 28).

A very different attitude to collaborative relationships was displayed by the Dearing committee. In their report, they attempted to specify a new division of labour between institutions of higher education and colleges of further education. In so doing they tried to check the franchising ambitions of some further education establishments: especially those which were considered to be extending themselves too broadly and entering into too many relationships to be able to ensure quality and standards. The committee wanted to limit the special mission of further education colleges to the provision of directly funded sub-degree higher education and it saw no case for expanding degree or postgraduate work in this sector, 'In our view, this extra discipline to the level of higher education qualifications offered by further and higher education institutions will offer each sector distinctive opportunities and best meet growing individual, local and national needs' (NCIHE, 1997a: 260). Furthermore:

> We believe that in the interests of extending opportunity and encouraging lifelong learning, franchising should continue, but only on the strict understanding that it must not prejudice the assurance of quality and maintenance of standards. To that end, there needs to be a proper contractual relationship between the franchiser and the franchisees which describes clearly the responsibilities of the partners. We would expect further education colleges to enter into partnership with only one higher education institution, unless there were exceptional circumstances relating to geographical proximity or subject provision.
>
> (NCIHE, 1997a: 159)

These were among the most prescriptive parts of the inquiry report and, like much of the Kennedy document, they invited no radical transformation of constitutional and structural arrangements. As Wagner (1998) has argued: 'Instead of lifelong learning having to make itself compatible with these existing structures, the relationship needs to be reversed'. The Kennedy, Dearing and *The Learning Age* texts were not designed to achieve such a fundamental overhaul of the language and structures of the post-compulsory system. Without such an undertaking, conceptual as well as political, policies for widening participation and lifelong learning will be denied their ready purchase and radical potential.

References

Dearing, R (1995) *Review of 16–19 Qualifications, Interim Report*, School Curriculum and Assessment Authority, London

Dearing, R (1996) *Review of Qualifications for 16–19-year-olds, Full Report*, School Curriculum and Assessment Authority, London

DfEE (1998a) *The Learning Age: A renaissance for a new Britain*, Department for Education and Employment, Cm 3790, The Stationery Office, London

DfEE (1998b) *Further Education for the New Millennium. Response to the Kennedy Report*, Department for Education and Employment, The Stationery Office, London

DfEE (1998c) *Higher Education for the 21st Century: Response to the Dearing Report*, Department for Education and Employment, The Stationery Office, London

DfEE, Scottish Office and Welsh Office (1995) *Lifetime Learning: A consultation document*, Department for Education and Employment, The Stationery Office, London

FEFC (1996a) *Inclusive Learning: Report of the Learning Difficulties and/or Disabilities Committee*, Further Education Funding Council, Coventry

FEFC (1996b) *Report of the Learning and Technology Committee*, Further Education Funding Council, Coventry

FEFC (1997a) *Learning Works. Widening Participation in Further Education*, Further Education Funding Council, Coventry

FEFC (1997b) *Pathways to Success. The Widening Participation Committee: Emerging conclusions*, Further Education Funding Council, Coventry

FEFC (1997c) *The Widening Participation Committee: Consultation Document*, Further Education Funding Council, Coventry

NAGCELL (1997) *Learning for the 21st Century, First Report*, NAGCELL, London

NCIHE (1997a) *Higher Education in the Learning Society: Main Report*, NCIHE, London

NCIHE (1997b) Widening participation in higher education by ethnic minorities, women and alternative students, *Higher Education in the Learning Society, Report 5,* National Committee of Inquiry into Higher Education, London

NCIHE (1997c) Widening participation for students from lower social classes and students with disabilities, *Higher Education in the Learning Society, Report 6*, National Committee of Inquiry into Higher Education, London

NCIHE (1997d) The contribution of graduates to the economy: rates of return, *Higher Education in the Learning Society, Report 7,* National Committee of Inquiry into Higher Education, London

Parry, G (1998) Size, shape and structure: dimensions of access and equity in proposals for the future development of British higher education, *Journal of Institutional Research in Australasia*, **7** (1), pp 74–89

Parry, G (1999) Education research and policy making in higher education: the case of Dearing, *Journal of Education Policy*, **14** (3), May–June

Rogers, A (1997) Learning: can we change the discourse?, *Adults Learning*, pp 116–17, January

Tight, M (1998a) Education, Education, Education! The vision of lifelong learning in the Kennedy, Dearing and Fryer reports, *Oxford Review of Education*, **24** (4), pp 473–85

Tight, M (1998b) Lifelong learning: opportunity or compulsion?, *British Journal of Educational Studies*, **46** (3), pp 251–63

Wagner, L (1998) *The Radical Implications of Lifelong Learning*, Philip Jones Memorial Lecture, 12 March, National Institute of Adult Continuing Education, Leicester

7

Funding Issues and Social Inclusion: Reflections on the 'Marketization' of Further Education Colleges

Norman Lucas and John Mace

Introduction

Social exclusion is a term widely used by policy makers in both the UK and the European Union. As other chapters in this book illustrate it is a complex and multi-dimensional term embracing many socio-economic and cultural factors. Social inclusion for many policy makers has replaced the debate about economic equality and is seen as a means of bringing hitherto excluded groups into the mainstream. Its application to education has attracted a lot of attention, with the Government seeing education and teachers as central to forging an inclusive society and a key to the 'redistribution of possibilities' (Giddens, 1998: 109). This chapter will look at the implications of this approach and explore the relationship between social exclusion/inclusion and the issue of funding. We will focus on the further education (FE) sector, which is particularly relevant as it is considered of pivotal importance to the New Deal, Widening Participation (Kennedy, 1997) and the recent Government initiative on Lifelong Learning. As the Secretary of State noted 'by reaching out to the community further education can help reduce social exclusion, increase employability and raise the nation's economic strength and morale' (Education and Employment Committee, 1998: 5).

Our argument is that much of the debate about policy initiatives to deal with social exclusion has not been cognisant of economic aspects. Yet the way such policies are funded, both in terms of the quantum and the method of allocation, is a crucial element in its success or failure. At present, although the Government is stressing social inclusion and lifelong learning, it is retaining a funding regime that was constructed in order to foster markets and competition. We will show that whilst markets may be a satisfactory mode for business they are not appropriate for education, particularly if the aim is to develop policies for social inclusion. All too often simply setting targets with attached funding fails to bring about the qualitative shifts needed for a more inclusive system. In other words whilst recent increases in student participation are to be welcomed, broadening participation to embrace those who are currently excluded requires a careful rethink of how such students are to be attracted to colleges, and how they can achieve and progress. It could be argued that the experiment with the marketization of FE has led to an increase in participation. However we shall argue that the qualitative changes necessary to develop a strategy for a socially inclusive FE system have been neglected. Our strategy for social inclusion is not based on competition between providers but on the development of a co-operative, inter-agency approach, on a regional basis across a range of different providers with a structure that provides access and opportunities to reinforce social inclusion.

This chapter is divided into four sections. Section one discusses the nature of markets and how they may affect efficiency and equity. Some empirical evidence is briefly presented and we discuss the practical and conceptual nature of markets. In the second section we describe the further education funding method. We will describe and analyse the 'marketization of education' following incorporation in 1993 and compare it with the experience of other marketization policies. In the following section we evaluate the effects of education markets on social exclusion in general and the FE sector in particular. The fourth section considers ways in which socially inclusive strategies could be developed in the sector. Finally we conclude with some reflections on the policies of the present government concerning social exclusion, suggesting a series of steps that could be taken to build a more socially inclusive system.

The market model: a critique

The market model and its application to education is an important dimension in the context of this book as its use in the past, particularly in the Thatcher and Reagan era, was an assertion of the primacy of economics over politics and planning. The 'marketization' of education has become fashionable around the world, and nowhere has the rhetoric and practice of the 'market' been stronger than in the UK. Most education legislation in the UK, from the Education Reform Act of 1988 onwards, has been concerned with releasing market forces at the school, college and tertiary level. In order to make the 'market' work better a plethora of performance indicators (PIs) has been developed so that consumers (students or their parents) and the Government can make judgements about the effectiveness of colleges (and schools). These PIs are to assist in making informed choices in deciding where students should receive their educational services.

The idea of the market and its supposed benefits have been most fully developed in economics, where it is argued that the unfettered operation of the market would secure the greatest benefit for the greatest number. This is because the individual pursuit of self-interest would result in an efficient ordering of production and distribution of society's goods and services. In order to achieve the benefits of the market, budgets are now delegated to schools and 'open' enrolment has been introduced. The recent Government White Paper *Excellence in School*s shows that 'New Labour' will, with some modifications, be continuing the policies introduced by the Tory Government. Furthermore, although the 'Learning Age' has an important change of emphasis, it does not challenge the existing funding regime. The present British Government and its predecessor are not alone in using markets in education: its proponents straddle international and disciplinary boundaries. For example, Friedman and Friedman (1960), Chubb and Moe (1990) and Tooley (1996) come from different sides of the Atlantic and may be claimed to represent economics, sociology and philosophy respectively. International agencies and in particular the World Bank constantly advocate the increased involvement of markets/privatization within education (World Bank, 1995).

What do economists make of the introduction of markets in education? The first issue is the nature of the education market itself. There is no such thing as a free market in education. In the United Kingdom, after more than a decade of marketization the education system is closely controlled and regulated by the state. Indeed the irony is that without a huge degree of regulation and legislation from the government to underpin the present arrangements the quasi-market arrangements that do exist could not actually work. This point is very forcibly made by the staunch advocate of education markets James Tooley, who argues that the reason for the failure of reforms to bring the promised benefits of markets is that there are actually no real markets in education. The state shackles the system through its interventions in carrying out inspections and controlling the curriculum. There is little basis for confidence in a market model that needs government intervention to survive. The market is in practice a 'quasi-market' organized on market principles, but underpinned by government finance and government regulation. The state controls the supply of, and to a considerable degree the demand for, education and it is important to note that it does so. This undermines the concept of free economic agents exchanging resources in a market system.

Economists have other concerns about applying the term market to education. These concerns focus on the nature of the 'product', who the 'buyers' are and who the producers are. To begin with the product: What do schools and colleges produce? Can the product be clearly identified? Can it be measured meaningfully? Is it places for students to study and learn, examination results, future job opportunities, better attitudes, a fairer society, something else or some combination of these? It is difficult to know and this raises doubts about how to organize a state-regulated market for something which cannot be clearly identified and quantified. It seems that at this level education and schooling are used to mean one and the same thing, but it is doubtful if they really are. If we do not know the product and how to measure it we are left with no means of putting a price on it. The core feature of markets is the operation of a pricing mechanism to which consumers and producers respond. But no such mechanism exists in state-provided education.

The second set of questions is about who the 'buyers' are in this market? Are they the students who actually experience the process of education and emerge as its products? Is it parents, or is it local business or the economy as a whole? Could it be that the true buyer is society as a whole? But what can this mean in practice? Once again the answer is ambivalent, rendering unclear the concept of the customer, a key concept in the ideology of the market.

Who are the producers of education? Initially it seems easy to identify colleges, schools and universities as the producers of education. However, often they produce a product, a curriculum perhaps, which is actually designed by government agencies. The 'producers' are encouraged by Government to train and qualify people with the laudable aim of getting people back into employment. We support this, but, for those in further education this is a rather narrow use of education because it ignores those who can't work, who still need education and training and are also socially excluded. In some respects colleges, even those to which considerable authority has been devolved are no more than individual franchisees selling the same branded product in a particular geographical area. Are they then the real producers? Once again the answer is unclear and it is this lack of clarity in all of these areas that calls into question the relevance of the market metaphor, quasi- or otherwise, to education.

Clearly there are questions as to the extent to which the education system has the characteristics of a market. More fundamental is the question of whether markets are an appropriate mechanism for achieving social efficiency (and equity) in education provision. We will consider four reasons why there may be doubts: three concerned with efficiency, externalities, information flows and the principal-agent problem, and one with equity.

Education externalities occur when some of the benefits of education accrue not only to the individual receiving education, but also to third parties and to society at large. Examples of such benefits might include crime reduction, social cohesion, technological innovation and the inter-generational transfer of knowledge from parents to their offspring. The extent of these benefits is very difficult to quantify precisely, but they would not be considered by education as 'consumers' when deciding how much education to 'buy' in a market system. In the world of the market the driving motive is individual self-interest and not the wider benefits (or costs) that may occur from one's actions. Since individuals will not be concerned with third party effects the result of educational markets will be sub-optimal provision of education i.e. social inefficiency.

For markets to operate efficiently consumers and producers need information about the quality of the product and its price. As already pointed out, there is no price and there is also a problem as to what the educational 'product' is, let alone its quality. One way around this problem is for the state to develop indicators of performance (PI) to which consumers can respond. There are problems with PIs as currently constructed. One is that without agreement as to what the outputs of education are and how to measure them, PIs will merely indicate performance with respect to the narrowly defined outputs selected. These are usually based on the ready availability of data rather than being the most appropriate indicator of educational effectiveness. But perhaps an even more serious criticism is that they do not adequately relate the output indicator to inputs. College A may be much more successful than College B in terms of student academic achievement, but this 'success' may be because the college has better lecturers, resources and, perhaps most important, 'abler' students. College effectiveness and efficiency must be related to the 'value added' by the college and this requires measures of both inputs and outputs of the college. (Precisely the same considerations apply with respect to the PIs developed for schools and universities.)

A further problem with information about colleges is how it is used by the consumers of education. Sophisticated PIs may be developed, but unless consumers respond rationally to them they will not have the effect desired by the proponents of markets. That is, consumers should go to those colleges performing well and leave those not performing well. But students may be more concerned with attending the nearest college and one, moreover, where they will be mixing with students from the same locale. Evidence also suggests that the groups least likely to respond to PIs are the most disadvantaged in society and so their disadvantage by remaining in the least effective colleges may be exacerbated.

A different sort of problem in market oriented education provision is the principal-agent problem: how does the principal, the government, get the agents, the schools and the colleges to carry out its wishes. Put another way how does he who pays the piper ensure that the tune that he wants is played when he wants it played?

In an important paper, Massy states the issue thus:

> Principal-agent problems reject value incongruities between the resource allocator's values and those of the resource recipient. Then the values differ, the agent's solution to the problem will not be the same as the principal's yet it is the principal who pays the piper and should be able to call the tune.

(1994: 18)

Massy appears to be claiming that the issue is a technical issue and higher education is no different from any other activity. However, it appears to us that simple payer–piper relationships are even less valid for education than they are for skilled mechanics that service our modern motor vehicles. We can legitimately expect them to ensure that it works as it is supposed to work at a reasonable price. Beyond that we must trust their judgement and perhaps sue them if their servicing proves to have been incompetent. The technical competence of the college lecturer or the university professor is of an even higher order and should be subject to correspondingly greater respect. It is perhaps relevant to note that the old adage refers to the simple craftsmen piper, not the symphony orchestra, even less Mozart or Beethoven.

This leads to the question of choice and equity. The whole question of choice is central to the critique of markets by Ball. Choice is possible only if there is a surplus of places available. However, to have a substantial surplus of places represents inefficient resource use. As certain schools become more popular they are able to use some other form of selection and become in Ball's words 'in a position, in one way or another, of choosing students, not the other way round' (Ball, 1993: 11). Ball also makes the point even more forcibly when he claims that 'The education market reasserts, reinforces and celebrates in a major way the opportunity advantages of middle class parents' (Ball, 1993: 11). A somewhat more measured conclusion of the effects of the 'marketization' of education is provided in Whitty, Power and Halpin (1998). This book draws on research findings from England and Wales, Australia, New Zealand, Sweden and the United States. The book's conclusion with respect to marketization and its effects on equal opportunity and equity in education provide a note of caution for countries embarking on the market route to the provision of education. Although it is early days, recent research suggests that the fragmentation of bureaucratic systems of education is leading to a polarization of provision, with 'good' schools being rewarded and able to choose their students – usually those that are academically and socially advantaged. However, 'failing' schools are thrown into a cycle of decline from which they and their students – usually the least socially advantaged – find it difficult to recover' (Whitty, Power and Halpin, 1998: 14). This result may be acceptable to policy makers promoting markets in which there will necessarily be losers and winners but if this is their intention they should be prepared to make it public, rather than argue that the introduction of markets, or quasi-markets, into education will benefit all. If these conclusions are accepted then economists' mistrust of the marketization of education seems valid: markets lead to inequity, are no guarantee of efficiency and are not the right mechanism for a policy of social inclusion. This we shall show below by reflecting upon the recent experience of marketization in the FE sector.

The funding of FE since incorporation in 1993

The incorporation of colleges came about in the context of a Conservative Government, in its third term of office, ideologically determined to introduce competition between education and training providers and to further erode the influence of LEAs. As a result both the system of funding and the funding mechanism were designed to meet these needs and there was little or no consideration of equity issues. The central aim of the approach was to get 'value for money' by raising levels of participation particularly for 16–19-year-olds, improve retention rates and create a national sector funded upon national not local formulae which would ensure greater efficiency and effectiveness (Spours and Lucas, 1996). The new system was outlined in the FEFC document 'Funding Learning' (1993), the major features of which are described below. The ground had already been laid for the new system with the steady growth of centrally controlled targeted funding throughout the 1980s and early 1990s and the introduction of Local Management of Colleges in the 1988 Education Act. Units of funding replaced the traditional full-time equivalent (FTE) and were linked directly to funding levels. There was a wide variety of funding levels between different colleges and courses, ranging from just over £1,000 to £7,000 for a student on a three-year A level course outlined in 'Unfinished Business' (Audit Commission/Ofsted, 1993). Parity was to be achieved by a process of convergence towards an Average Level of Funding (ALF). Convergence of ALFs was to be achieved through setting growth targets for high ALF colleges with 90 per cent funded at historic levels but 10 per cent funded at rates below that of other units of funding. Thus, year on year, high ALF colleges were forced to grow at a lower level of funding thus coming down to the to plus/minus 10 per cent of the median level set by the FEFC.

The concept of unit funding was based upon three stages. 'Entry', 'On Programme' and 'Achievement'. The overwhelming majority of units were earned on the 'On Programme' stage with relatively small amounts for entry and achievement. Other units could be gained from fee remission, child care or additional learning support and different types of courses such as Engineering or Construction were cost weighted to reflect the different resource needs of different learning programmes (Atkinson, 1995). Unlike the funding of Training and Enterprise Councils (TECs) the FEFC funding mechanism is not really output related with 8 per cent (an important margin) of the units relating to achievement compared with the TEC level of between 25 and 40 per cent. Growth in student numbers, the retention of students 'On programme' and convergence are the real drivers. This was to be achieved by funding FE colleges with a core 90 per cent based on historic funding levels with 10 per cent marginal funding, based upon lower rates and dependent on achieving certain growth targets. Thus, with the value of the total units falling, colleges had to increase their total number of units in order to maintain their budgets, so achieving an expansion of student numbers and a lower ALF. The priority for colleges was to improve their market share (Kennedy, 1997) which led to colleges spending scarce resources in competition with each other rather then collaborating to reach excluded groups of potential learners. It has been argued (Lucas, 1999) that incorporation can be seen as the creation of a national framework of FE funding, with schools, TECs and colleges competing in an education and training market within a framework of national regulation. As Kennedy pointed out (1997) because colleges acted as businesses they were mistaking this for being business-like. Also if they were acting as businesses in a market there remain the problems concerned with efficiency and equity discussed earlier.

As mentioned above, although incorporation was an attempt at the marketization of FE, it is difficult to conceive of colleges operating in a market because the relationship between colleges and the vast majority of students is not determined by price. Perhaps it is better described as the creation of a 'quasi-market' where on the supply side there is competition between providers, but on the demand side purchasing power is not expressed in money terms but by a centralized purchasing agency influencing policy decisions. However, the belief in the efficiency of the marketization of education and training was a fundamental ideological belief behind the Conservative Government's project of incorporation. This structure, set up for marketization, has been left largely untouched by the Government in its pursuit of greater social inclusion – this we discuss in more detail below.

An evaluation of FEFC funding: implications for social inclusion

In section one we presented an analysis within which the 'education market' concept could be evaluated. In this section we evaluate the funding system in operation, concentrating on the aspects relevant to social inclusion. A more comprehensive discussion of FEFC funding can be found elsewhere (Leney *et al*, 1998; Education and Employment Committee, 1998; Kennedy, 1997; Lucas, 1999). In any analysis of the effects of funding on colleges difficulties are encountered because the experience of funding varies from college to college depending on their ALF. In any analysis of incorporation it is important to distinguish between the overall quantum expenditure given to the sector and the funding methodology. For example, cuts in public expenditure that were being forced on LEAs by the Conservative government throughout the 1980s were already biting colleges prior to incorporation. Perhaps the 'efficiency gains' due to cuts in public expenditure and the policy of convergence were more important than the funding methodology itself. The financial quantum and the growth targets were not set by the FEFC but by the Government. These distinctions are important because the size of the quantum allocated to the FE sector is a political decision whereas the funding allocation is a methodological issue (Spours and Lucas, 1996).

From the experience of the last six years it would seem that the choice and implementation of funding methodologies has had a profound impact on the values and culture of colleges, far more powerful than mere policy shifts from national or local government. The impressive expansion of further and higher education in the last 20 years or so has to a large extent been achieved by funding drivers. However, alongside considerable gains the methodology is proving to be more problematic than foreseen at the time of incorporation (Leney *et al*, 1998). The Kennedy Report (1997) noted there was evidence of potential learners being denied full access to information and a wasteful duplication of effort. Furthermore, Kennedy noted that the priority for some colleges was to improve their market share rather than expand the market for learning, with the funding regime acting as a barrier to the collaboration which was needed to engage groups of excluded learners. These problems are not always apparent when judged by quantitative standards such as increases in the participation rate, however, when judged upon qualitative and curricula criteria, worries emerge such as the cuts in course hours and the difficulty in funding part-time partial achievement – all important for social inclusion. The present FEFC model is based on the dogma that everything can be controlled and influenced by funding; there is no evidence that this dubious assumption is being questioned. Recent evidence suggests (Leney et al, 1998) that funding encourages basic services to be put in place and quantitative targets to be met but it does not sufficiently influence quality of provision.

The gains from the FEFC model of incorporation in relation to social inclusion seem to fall into three categories. Firstly, there has been an increase in the number of people studying in the sector and an evaluation of exam results has concluded that on balance the service to students has improved, an important advance for attracting and retaining hitherto excluded groups (Ainley and Bailey, 1997; Leney et al, 1998). Secondly, the funding mechanism has focused college attention on the processes of induction, tracking and information systems, special needs and student retention – all important elements for an inclusive college. In the short time that it has been in operation, the funding methodology has proved to be surprisingly responsive to some important educational and social issues. These include the emphasis on additional learning support to assist, in particular, those students with special educational needs and the additional units offered for childcare (Cantor et al, 1995). The benefits of identifying and costing students with learning support needs has improved initial guidance and screening at enrolment, particularly for literacy and numeracy. The funding mechanism for additional support has, despite some criticism, brought special needs provision into the mainstream of college work and provision. Thirdly, although there has been a serious decline in the provision of non-vocational adult education, FEFC funding has provided colleges with incentives to take the education and training of adults more seriously. With the levelling off of the spectacular rise in participation of 16 year olds and slight decline in the participation of 16–19-year-olds, colleges are not only turning their attention to questions of retention and progression but are also looking to expand their adult provision to meet future growth targets (Spours, 1995). The implications for a more flexible curriculum, teaching staff and college to cater for this growth in adult participation is beginning to be addressed by some colleges.

However, the current funding regime also has a number of serious limitations in relation to dealing with social exclusion. Firstly, quantity has been emphasized not quality. Colleges give high priority to achieving the performance targets set by the FEFC and qualitative factors, which do not readily lend themselves to measurement through performance indicators, are often ignored (Reeves, 1995). These 'unmeasurables' are often the very factors which appear to encourage participation and retention of excluded groups. As Corbett points out in this volume, the requirement for the precise measurement of special needs relies on a 'medical' definition of disability which both stigmatizes those it can apply to, whilst excluding those with other needs. In the process of efficiency savings and convergence in order to drive down unit costs, the sort of educational values associated with inclusive learning and concerns with the quality of learning have been replaced by funding and financial considerations. A related factor, which may lead to discrimination against the disadvantaged, is that colleges will discriminate against those students unlikely to figure well in the quantity indicators used by the funding council. This phenomenon is called 'cream skimming' and results in the exclusion of the 'less able' either by not accepting them on courses or putting them into lower level courses where they are more likely to succeed, irrespective of their real potential.

Secondly, according to the FEFC Chief Inspector (FEFC, 1996), the 20 per cent efficiency gains achieved since incorporation have been brought about by reducing the number of taught hours rather than increasing class size which remains at an average of 11. (This may well be related to the above point about quality if the number of contact hours is positively related to quality.) Colleges report cuts in teaching hours of as much as seven hours across a range of courses including GNVQs and A levels. Some of the cuts in teaching hours are made to accommodate the 'sixteen hour rule' for those on benefit but for most it is a cost-cutting measure. Although colleges are moving towards more resource-based learning, all too often this is not to encourage wider participation but to compensate for the cuts in teaching hours. Excluded categories of students, particularly those targeted for inclusion by the Kennedy Report, are being disadvantaged by these developments because they require more teacher contact time, not less (Leney et al, 1998).

Thirdly, the funding methodology has introduced rigidities into course design. So far the funding mechanism has been unable to relate to modularization/unitization and credit accumulation because its view of achievement is based on whole-course completion. Leaving a course in order to go on to employment is not funded as a satisfactory achievement. Even where the funding methodology has proved to be responsive, as is the case of additional learning support, it has brought with it rigidities because of the high threshold in the number of hours to be offered before the unit funding can be triggered. This seems to reinforce the view that there are 'normal students' and those with special needs; most FE learners are somewhere in between and receive no extra funding. This relates to 'cream skimming' mentioned above and may have other consequences. For example, the formula has resulted in a reduction in careers advice and enrichment activities such as sports and leisure, for 16–19-year-olds in particular, which may be of general value to the economic and social environment and of particular value to the disadvantaged. This is another example of how the introduction of elements of the market disadvantages certain groups and at the same time ignores the wider benefits, ie externalities, from which society would benefit. Courses that may be popular are closed because they do not accrue the same funding units as less popular courses. The recent expansion of first aid and food hygiene courses in FE has not come about because there are jobs in these areas or because there is massive student demand, but because of the FEFC price tag (Perry, 1998), a result, incidentally, that runs counter to the market philosophy since it is not consumer choice that is driving institutional behaviour but the vagaries of the funding formula. Increasingly, the ones who may have been left out of the equation may become the norm – that is, those who are relatively slow learners, but who, with a little extra support and attention, could achieve progression thresholds. The FEFC methodology, in its present state, fails to recognize partial, unit-based achievement. In this sense, FEFC funding is in need of fundamental reform if it is to meet the more flexible curriculum required by the recommendations of Kennedy (1997), Dearing (1996) and the DfEE's document *Qualifying for Success* (1997). Social inclusion and lifelong learning require the whole structure and purpose of qualifications as we know them to be rethought (Young, 1999). Achieving inclusion must recognize partial achievement and provide progression routes within a more flexible qualification framework and a complete rethink about approaches to teaching and learning (Young and Lucas, 1999). Such radical reform of qualifications is lost in the present set up which has made everything funding driven – not driven by student/learner need.

Fourthly, if carried to the extreme, the funding mechanism is open to abuse. It appears that a proportion of the much applauded expansion of FE has been a result of franchising existing provision to the private sector, reclassifying work and 'unit farming' (sometimes called tariff farming, nesting or additionality). The colleges have thereby been able to gain full funding advantage and increased their units of funding and thus lowered the ALF of their college (Gravatt, 1997). Unit farming is where funding units are increased without increasing student numbers. It is achieved by entering students on extra qualifications around the same course (nesting). According to Perry (1997) one college increased their unit total by 100 per cent whilst actually reducing student numbers. Recent research (Leney *et al*, 1998) suggested that the methodology could be open to abuse with the 'boundaries of accurate recording' of registers being extended particularly at census points. Taking a broader view of unit maximization or 'manipulation' it can be regarded as a form of unit inflation because as the units increase, the value of the unit must lower, unless new resources are found. Some colleges have registered dramatic growth and lowered their ALF through franchising courses and training that already existed in the private sector thus diverted funds from mainstream FE work (Perry, 1997) with FEFC funds subsidising the costs of other providers (Gravatt, 1997).

Fifth, the funding methodology continues to favour full-time students (despite the disappearance of enrichment studies or other extra-curricula activities for 16–19-year-olds that leave them disadvantaged, when compared to those at school). Part-time students, many of whom are adult returners, are precisely those identified by Kennedy as most excluded from education, and are disadvantaged by the funding methodology. It is often a bureaucratic struggle, for relatively small amounts of funding for part-time adult education. For example, in the case of A levels, a college receives only a quarter of the funding units allocated to a full-time student (Derrick, 1997).

In addition to the above points, there may be other tensions developing within the sector that, though difficult to quantify, may militate against efficiency and equity. The funding mechanism has developed internal markets in which there are conflicts between different players in the system. Tensions between staff and management and between departments are likely to undermine efficiency and the provision of the best service for the students. The funding mechanism, because of the uncertainty that it breeds, may inhibit strategic, long-term planning, in the process undermining professionalism and efficiency. Further problems of equity arise when it becomes apparent that schools receive between 5 and 20 per cent higher funding for equivalent courses. Related to this inequity may be the differences in salary and working conditions of those doing similar work in colleges and schools.

Finally, since incorporation in 1993 colleges have become finance driven with curriculum innovation and risk taking inhibited. It was found in recent research that a preoccupation with funding and finance overshadowed every aspect of college activity (Leney et al, 1998). This included rising redundancies of full-time staff and the increased use of part-time agency staff in order to save money (Guile and Lucas, 1996). Bringing about an ethos of social inclusion requires good dedicated staff, which is difficult to achieve when part-timers now number 100,000 in comparison to 48,000 full-time staff (Williams, 1998). More and more resources are being spent on meeting the audit requirements of the FEFC, which are considered 'out of control'. As one college principal noted, 'it is not that responding to the agency gets in the way of the job – it becomes the job' (Perry, 1998: 6).

Our above assessment of the present FEFC funding regime with its foundation in marketization raises real doubts about the FE sectors' ability to respond to the agenda of social inclusion. This is partly because of the relentless pressure to make 'efficiency savings' and partly because the 'units logic' of the FEFC encourages unit maximization and quantity to be put before quality. The crisis facing FE is not just about the need for an increase in funding, although this appears to be essential if widening participation is to become a reality. It is about a lack of strategic thinking with simplistic financial considerations rather then educational/training considerations being foremost. The educational implications of an agenda for social inclusion require colleges to rethink their role within their local and regional context, targeting adult learners (Green and Lucas, 1999) and being far more flexible and inventive in their teaching and learning. We would argue that the present FEFC funding methodology, based on a market-type philosophy, is not conducive to the changes required to meet the agenda raised by social inclusion. In addition it results in inefficiencies in provision through not taking into account externalities, information asymmetries and the principal-agent problem.

Towards social inclusion

FE is now entering a new phase in its development and if the lessons of the recent past inform the new policies there may be grounds for cautious optimism, though on the basis of recent evidence they must be tinged with uncertainty. The FE sector has been given a high and important profile by the new Government with over 80 per cent of the 500,000 additional students expected by 2002 having been allocated to the FE sector. Considerable extra funding has been found albeit with targets for student numbers. The Education Secretary recently announced £725 million for a two year expansion package for the sector, rising to a possible £1 billion if HE provision is expanded in the FE sector (Nash, 1999). The relentless 'efficiency savings' and worst aspects of the 'marketization' of FE identified with the most recent period of incorporation seem to have become less intense. The recent quantum increase and growth targets are evidence of this, as is the FEFC proposal to consider giving more weighting to certain types of students as proposed in the Kennedy Report (1997).

This coming period for FE will be one of organizational change, with colleges having to respond to new initiatives by the Government such as the 'New Deal' and the recommendations of Kennedy to widen participation – in other words to become more inclusive. The Kennedy recommendations include a free lifetime entitlement to education and training up to Level 3 (A level equivalent) for young people and those socially deprived. The report also recommends the creation of pathways for learning with a flexible unitized system for recognizing achievement in a credit accumulation system which the funding arrangement can accommodate. In addition, a revision of the articles of government is proposed to ensure that colleges meet local needs, requiring them to specify how wider community involvement can be achieved. This is to be achieved by financial incentives to widen participation, by awarding extra entry and additional support units, and by recognizing the relative extra costs required to help socially excluded groups. Another idea being piloted is the application of funding levels applied in inverse proportion to the students' previous level of achievement. Another is to calculate social and economic deprivation by taking postcodes into account in the criteria for allocating any funding above the core.

Other recommendations were extending tax incentives to employers and individuals to encourage people to engage in learning programmes, creating a learning regeneration fund to provide incentives and reward local strategic partnership, and allocating extra funding for an 'access and child-care fund'. Finally it was proposed to give financial support to FE students as recommended by the 'Lane Report' (DfEE, 1998a) particularly targeted at those moving beyond intermediate to advanced levels.

The steps outlined by Kennedy involve adjustment of the funding mechanism away from competition to encourage internal planning and inter-institutional co-operation. The main aim would be to stabilize FE colleges and create a level playing field with schools and other providers. There would also have to be moves to bridge the 'democratic deficit' (Scott, 1995) at a local level by giving more LEA and local community representation; this is already proposed in the Green Paper the 'Learning Age' (DfEE, 1998). It will mean the formation of local frameworks to exchange institutional plans and to decide priorities for development. Participation in these could be financed by establishing an Institutional Development Fund at local level. These forums would involve colleges, schools, TECs and other training providers. A further stage could be the formation of a regional planning framework to integrate the providers by devolving the FEFC responsibilities to a regional level and merging these with regional government offices and the TEC structures.

At present the funding of FE is being reviewed but radical changes in the short term are not being contemplated. However, there is a shift away from competition to a more collaborative model. It would seem that, true to the 'third way', there is some effort to balance market forces with more regulation to achieve fairer outcomes (Held, 1998). Our contention is that an accommodation such as this will not end social exclusion in education or, for that matter, other services such as the health service.

Conclusion

We welcome the recent emphasis given to further education as part of the Government's agenda for lifelong learning and social inclusion. We are not critical of the need for greater social inclusion in education and training; indeed, FE has always been concerned with those who need a 'second chance'. Our concern is that 'New Labour' is still working within the structures and confines of a fragmented system based upon a philosophy of competition when their stated aim is co-operation.

We are of the view that the quantum allocated to FE is insufficient. The fact that 28 per cent of colleges are in 'weak financial health' (Williams, 1998) and many more in financial deficit is not a good context for FE colleges to develop socially inclusive policies. As Mortimore and Whitty argue in Chapter 5, whilst quality provision by outstanding teachers and institutions can make a difference to the educational achievement of the most disadvantaged, extra resources are also needed if schools or colleges are to succeed against the odds. The FEFC does not recognize the social and economic context in which colleges exist and the process of convergence in college funding levels is still being pursued regardless of the poverty or wealth of the area. We are not arguing for a bottomless pit of resources. We are concerned to see that available resources are used more efficiently and are targeted more effectively to those who need them most. However, based upon our analysis, this cannot be achieved by a national quango with a rigid funding formula that was designed for competition between providers, for convergence of funding and for quantitative rather than qualitative ends. Moreover, we maintain that a market-based system of funding will result in inefficient provision because it fails to take account of such factors as the existence of externalities, the principal agent problem and inadequate information flows.

The Government seems to be clear about its objectives to reduce social exclusion but does not seem ready to embrace a radical agenda that is the complete reform of the present funding regime. For example, it is important to target funds to encourage participation of those socially excluded. This would require funding student support systems in colleges in addition to extra-curricular activities that are so important to 'weaker' students – but this strategy would require a departure from unit funding. A strategy for promoting social inclusion in post-16 education and training requires moving beyond the FEFC model of funding and incorporation. FE has to deal with many bodies including the world of employment. It is involved in many partnerships and agencies, such as those concerned with the New Deal which include the employment service and the TEC, all of whom compete and collaborate, despite all being funded by the DfEE. Perry (1988) has argued about why they exist as separate bodies and why there cannot be a more strategic approach to Kennedy, Tomlinson (1996), New Deal, Education Action Zones, Lifelong Learning, the UfI and others still to come. We would suggest that a more unified approach to funding and curriculum planning should be at a regional level, including tertiary education and training as a whole. This should include the careers and youth service (Pearce, 1998) if social inclusion is going to be taken seriously. Such an approach would not be easy to bring about but would mean far more for those who are socially excluded than the current strategy of tinkering with the FEFC funding methodology.

We have argued throughout this chapter that markets may be right for business but are not a means of bringing about equity or inclusion (unless you can afford it). On the contrary, we should say that on *prima facie* grounds a funding method premised on market principles will result in inefficient provision, from a societal perspective, and inequities – particularly for those currently excluded. We have shown that the present methodology works against the sort of strategic planning, curriculum reform and new forms of teaching and learning that are required to meet the needs of the socially excluded. Indeed we have shown that the structures set up for the marketization of education led to waste and a funding-driven, rather than people-driven FE system. This is not the way to bring about lasting social inclusion.

References

Ainley, P and Bailey, B (1997) *The Business of Learning: Staff and student experiences of further education in the 1990s*, Cassell, London

Atkinson, D (1995) *The Dan Quayle Guide to FEFC Recurrent Funding*, Coombe Lodge Report, Bristol

Audit Commission/Ofsted (1993) *Unfinished Business: Full–time educational courses for 16–19-year-olds*, Audit Commission/Ofsted, London

Ball, S (1993) Market forces in education, *Education Review*, **7** (1), pp 8–11

Cantor, L, Roberts, I and Prately, B (1995) *A Guide to Further Education in England and Wales*, Cassell, London

Chubb, J and Moe, T (1990) *Politics, Markets and American Schools*, Brookings Institution, Washington, DC

Dearing, R (1996) *Review of Qualifications for 16–19-year-olds*, SCAA, London

Derrick, J (1997) Adult part–time learners in colleges and the FEFC, Working Paper 21, Post-16 Education Centre, University of London Institute of Education

DfEE (1997) *Qualifying for Success*, The Stationery Office, London

DfEE (1998a) *The Learning Age: A renaissance for a new Britain*, The Stationery Office, London

DfEE (1998b) *The Lane Report: New arrangements for effective student support in further education*, The Stationery Office, London

Education and Employment Committee (1998) Hodge Report, Sixth Report of the House of Commons Education and Employment Committee, **1** and **2**, 19 May, The Stationery Office, London

FEFC (1993) *Funding Learning*, Further Education Funding Council, Coventry

FEFC (1996) *Quality and Standards in Further Education in England*, Further Education Funding Council, Coventry

Friedman, M and Friedman, R (1960) *Free to Choose*, Harcourt, New York

Giddens, A (1998) *The Third Way: The renewal of social democracy*, Polity Press, Cambridge

Gravatt, J (1997) *Deepening the Divide: Further Education and the Diversion of Public Funds*, Praxis Paper 6, Lewisham College, London

Green, A and Lucas, N (1999) Repositioning FE: a sector for the 21st century, in *FE and Lifelong Learning: Repositioning the sector for the 21st century*, ed A Green and N Lucas, Bedford Way Publications, London

Guile, D and Lucas, N (1996) Preparing for the future: the training and professional development of staff in the FE sector, *Journal of Teacher Development*, **5** (3), pp 47–54

Held, D (1998) The timid tendency, *Marxism Today*, pp 24–28, Nov/Dec

Kennedy, H (1997) *Learning Works: Widening participation in further education colleges*, FEFC, Coventry

Leney, T, Lucas, N and Taubman, D (1998) *Learning Funding: The impact of FEFC funding, evidence from twelve FE colleges*, NATFHE/University of London Institute of Education

Lucas, N (1999) Incorporated colleges: beyond the FEFC model, in *FE and Lifelong Learning: Repositioning the sector for the 21st century*, ed A Green and N Lucas, Bedford Way Publications, London

Massy, W F (1994) *Resource Allocation Reform in Higher Education*, National Association of Colleges and University Business Officers, Washington, DC

Nash, I (1999) Mackney says it is time to do a deal, FE Focus, *Times Educational Supplement*, 15 January, p 33

Pearce, N (1998) Status zero – life on the outside, FE Focus, *Times Educational Supplement*, 11 December, p 27

Perry, A (1997) *A Pencil Instead: Why we need a new funding system for further education*, Lambeth College, London

Perry, A (1998) *Benchmarks or Trade Marks: How we are managing FE wrong*, Lambeth College, London

Reeves, F (1995) *The Modernity of Further Education*, Bilston College Publications, Bilston

Scott, P (1995) *A Tertiary System*, Report for The Society of Education Officers, Leeds University

Spours, K (1995) Post-16 participation, attainment and progression, Working Paper 17, Post-16 Education Centre, University of London Institute of Education.

Spours, K and Lucas, N (1996) The formation of a national sector of incorporated colleges: developments and contradictions, Working Paper 19, Post-16 Education Centre, University of London Institute of Education

Thomlinson, J (1996) *Inclusive Learning: Report of the Learning Difficulties and/or Disabilities Committee*, HMSO, London

Tooley, J (1996) *Education Without the State*, Institute of Economic Affairs, London

Whitty, G, Power, S and Halpin, D (1998) *Devolution and Choice in Education: The school, the state and the market*, OUP, Buckingham

Williams, E (1998) Leaner and fitter, *FE Now*, (50), pp 8–9, December

World Bank (1995) The Lessons of Experience, World Bank

Young, M (1999) Reconstructing qualifications for further education – towards a system for the 21st century, in *FE and Lifelong Learning: Repositioning the sector for the 21st century*, ed A Green and N Lucas, Bedford Way Publications, London

Young, M and Lucas, N (1999) Pedagogy and learning in further education: new contexts, new theories and new possibilities, in *Pedagogy and its Impact on Learning*, ed P Mortimore, Sage, London

Part 3

Perspectives on Social Exclusion

8

Fifty Years of Failure: 'Race' and Education Policy in Britain

David Gillborn

It would be hard to overstate the constitutive role played by overt and covert racial dynamics historically and currently in the construction of 'official knowledge,' teaching, evaluation, public policies, popular culture, identities, economic divisions, and the state itself in the United States and many other nations. An understanding of education that does not recognize this lives in a world divorced from reality, for race is not an 'add-on'. The realities and predicaments of people of color are neither additions to nor defections from American life. Rather, they are among the *defining* elements of that life. . .

(Apple, 1997: xvi, original emphasis)

In comparison with the United States, public policy discourse in Britain trades less often in the language of 'race' and racism, yet the major fault lines of racist inequity are replicated with frightening regularity. In this chapter the word 'race' is presented in inverted commas to denote its socially constructed nature (cf Gillborn, 1990). Rates of imprisonment, life expectancy, unemployment, educational exclusion and achievement, all these and more are characterized by racialized patterns of inequity (cf Gillborn and Gipps, 1996; Modood *et al*, 1997). In this paper I review some of the major trends concerning the position of 'race' and racism in British education policy over the last half-century. My aim is to identify the changing landscapes of education policy in order to locate critically the actions of the 'New Labour' administration, first elected to power in 1997. I will argue that despite superficial changes that acknowledge ethnic diversity and value 'equal opportunities', contemporary policy is no more able to deliver equitable and anti-racist outcomes than previous policy perspectives. The 'naïve multiculturalism' of Tony Blair's Government remains wedded to uncritical and often deficit notions of failure that continue to blame black students for their situation and fail to identify the deeply racialized and racist nature of contemporary education. (Throughout this paper I use 'racialist' to refer to patters of experience and outcome that are strongly associated with differences in ethnic origin. The term 'racism' is used here to denote social processes and differences in outcome that result in the disproportionate disadvantage of one or more minority ethnic groups.) Worse still, by failing to engage with the multiple and complex ways in which policy works through and upon 'race' inequalities, New Labour's bright new world of 'high standards for all' will continue to be scarred by significant and growing racist inequity of experience and outcome. Labour's policy seems destined to add to a long line of failed policy in this field.

Charting failed policy

Sally Tomlinson produced the first serious attempt to chart the changing position of 'race' issues in British education policy (Tomlinson, 1977). Since then numerous writers have produced their own versions, almost all borrowing terms from Tomlinson's original, and often seeking to add and update as new administrations and changing social movements put their own distinctive mark on the evolving politics of 'race' and racism. The most frequently cited addition to this literature is undoubtedly Mullard's essay *Multicultural Education in Britain: from Assimilation to Cultural Pluralism* (1982). This approach typically categorizes changing perspectives and actions via a series of 'models' or 'phases'. This has its dangers, not least glossing over contradictions and resistance in an attempt to describe (or create) relatively tight categories. One problem can be seen in the fact that authors use a wide variety of terms, sometimes choosing to highlight different trends and periods. My aim here is briefly to map some of the broad shifts in policy during the post-WWII period. My focus on the last 50 years should not be taken as supposing that Britain was in any sense ethnically homogenous before that point, or indeed at any point. Britain has *always* been characterized by ethnic diversity. The timescale for this review, however, necessarily reflects the relatively short period over which ethnic heterogeneity has significantly impacted on education policy. The start/end dates are not precise and, as will become clear, there are points of opposition and counter-developments where national trends contrasted dramatically with local practice in some areas. Nevertheless, it is useful to map these broader periods as a means of contextualizing the specific analysis of New Labour's approach and to identify trends that have persisted across the decades. The particular phases, therefore, are offered as a heuristic device, not a definitive description and categorization.

Ignorance and neglect: 1945 to the late 1950s

The term 'ignorance and neglect' is James Lynch's (1986: 42) description of the early post-war period to the 1960s. The initial education policy response to migration from the Caribbean and Indian subcontinent was to do nothing. Others have variously referred to the same period as one of 'laissez-faire' disregard (Massey, 1991: 9) or 'inaction' (Rose *et al*, 1969 in Massey, 1991).

Assimilation: late 1950s to the late 1960s

In 1958 'riots' in Nottingham and Notting Hill, London, saw white racist attacks on migrant communities misrepresented in the press as demanding action on the 'colour problem', while politicians on both sides of the House of Commons sought to excuse the actions of convicted whites (Ramdin, 1987: 208–10). 'Racial' diversity was, therefore, presented as a threat to order and the migrant communities as a 'problem'. Policy responses at this point were characterized first by action to severely restrict black and Asian migration; and second by the policy goal of *assimilationism*. Tomlinson, for example, points to the view of the Commonwealth Immigrants Advisory Council, who in 1964, stated that 'A national system cannot be expected to perpetuate the different values of immigrant groups' (Commonwealth Immigrants Advisory Council, 1964 quoted in Tomlinson, 1977: 3). This view fuelled attempts to assimilate minorities into the majority culture (or at least the official version of it). It can be seen most clearly in the policy concern with teaching the English language and the physical dispersal of immigrant children to minimize their numbers in any single class or school: a policy that left many children and young people especially vulnerable to racist attacks (cf Dhondy, 1982). The overriding policy objective here was to protect the stability of the system and placate the 'fears' of white racist communities and parents: a circular from the then Department for Education and Science (DES), for example, made explicit the priorities of the period:

> *It will be helpful if the parents of non-immigrant children can see that practical measures have been taken to deal with the problems in their schools, and that the progress of their own children is not being restricted by the undue preoccupation of the teaching staff with the linguistic and other difficulties of immigrant children.*

(DES circular 7/65, quoted in Swann, 1985: 194, original emphasis)

Integration: 1966 to late 1970s

Roy Jenkins (then Labour Home Secretary) famously advocated, in a 1966 speech, 'not a flattening process of assimilation but equal opportunity, accompanied by cultural diversity, in an atmosphere of mutual tolerance' (quoted in Mullard, 1982: 125). This was important symbolically for actually acknowledging the contemporary existence of marked inequalities of opportunity, and for apparently withdrawing support for assumptions of white cultural superiority that had argued the need to 'absorb'/destroy ethnic differences. This period saw some important steps forward, not least the passing of the Race Relations Act (1976) and establishment of the Commission for Racial Equality (CRE). Nevertheless, educational work tended to assume a patronizing and exoticized approach to teaching about 'race' and assumed the need to build 'compensatory' programmes to make good the supposed cultural deficits of minority pupils (Massey, 1991:

11–12). It has been said that during this period 'emphasis was on *lifestyles* rather than life *chances*' (Lynch, 1986: 41, emphasis added). This statement draws attention to the publication of curricular materials frequently reflected and reinforced crude stereotypes of ethnic minorities as at best exotic and strange, at worst backward and primitive, and always as alien. The 'problem', therefore, was still seen as residing in the minority communities themselves: a position that continued to absolve the education system of responsibility. 'Tolerance' and 'diversity' emerged as new watchwords (that are still in vogue today) but essentially protection of the status quo remained the key driving force in policy (just as in assimilationism). 'By allowing limited diversity in respect of religious beliefs, customs, dress and even language, it is assumed within the framework of the [integrationist] model that blacks will be more likely to accept than to reject outright those [values and beliefs] which actually shape our society' (Mullard, 1982: 128).

Cultural pluralism and multiculturalism: late 1970s to late 1980s

This period saw the rhetoric of cultural pluralism assume widespread support (across political parties). Like the other 'phases' there was a borrowing (in more or less altered forms) of some of the key concepts and terms of previous periods. So, for example, 'diversity' and 'tolerance' continued to feature prominently in the discourse, but importantly notions of liberal pluralism were at their height and began to find expression in official policy. An official committee of inquiry was established to examine the education of ethnic minority pupils (cf Rampton, 1981; Swann, 1985) and its analysis traded on a 'radical' perspective which used differences in group outcome as indicative of inequalities of opportunity. The recommendations of the Rampton and Swann reports were highly criticized, from the political right and left. Nevertheless, the reports marked something of a watershed in public policy on 'race' and education in Britain. First, by rejecting IQist notions of innate intellectual differences between 'races', and second, by stating that teachers (in their expectations and actions toward pupils and parents) might actively be implicated in the creation of 'race' inequality. These advances, however, were highly constrained. Not only did the Conservative Government of the day reject the committee's most important recommendations (see below) but its Chairman, Lord Swann, prepared a personal summary that barely used the word 'racism'. This summary, in 13 pages, was meant to promote discussion of the report's 800-plus pages. Not surprisingly it was the Chairman's summary that most readers consulted.

Despite the changed nature of the public policy debate at this time, in education much work continued to trade on superficial 'positive images' stereotypes of the type Barry Troyna devastatingly described as the '3Ss' – saris, samosas and steel bands (see Troyna and Carrington, 1990: 20). As the phrase encapsulated, the concern was with a shallow liberal 'celebration' of difference, in a context where issues of power and racism were conspicuously ignored or silenced. This was the very point pursued by anti-racists who sought to place issues of power centre-stage.

Anti-racist counter-hegemonic developments

I noted earlier that one danger of labelling the past via a series of 'phases' is that counter-trends and points of resistance can be glossed over. One of the most important such 'moments' in British education policy concerns the development of anti-racist analyses and pedagogies. Against the wider thrust of public policy, this period saw important developments on the anti-racist front, symbolized by the establishment of several prominent pressure groups (including the *National Antiracist Movement in Education* and *All London Teachers Against Racism and Fascism*, see Gaine, 1995: 42–44; Massey, 1991: 15–17). Despite its presentation in the media and parts of academia as a Marxist ideology of revolution (cf Flew, 1984; Palmer, 1986), anti-racism was never tightly defined as a single theory or pedagogic approach. Much anti-racist work traded on a critique of previous approaches, only rarely venturing into the realms of suggested classroom practice. Godfrey Brandt's *The Realization of Anti-racist Teaching* (1986) marked a key attempt to synthesize anti-racist critique and pedagogy. Brandt's work, as much as anyone's, captured the spirit of anti-racism at this point. He positioned liberal multiculturalism (with its fascination for positive images and curricular change) as 'the Trojan horse of institutional racism' (p 117) and argued that anti-racism differed fundamentally. In particular, Brandt argued that anti-racism should accord a central role to the 'experience and articulations of the Black community' (p 119) and be characterized by an oppositional form. This involved an analysis that focused on *power* and the need to challenge dominant conceptions of knowledge and pedagogy. Nevertheless, anti-racism took a dynamic and varied form such that, as Sivanandan has stated, 'there was no body of thought called anti-racism, no orthodoxy or dogma, no manual of strategy and tactics, no demonology' (1988: 147).

In many ways anti-racism reached a zenith, so far as education policy was concerned, with the work of the Inner London Education Authority (ILEA). Several local authorities, mostly serving large metropolitan areas, adopted anti-racist policies but the Greater London Council (GLC) and the ILEA (London's education authority) were at the forefront of public campaigns to advance anti-racist issues. In hindsight it is certainly true that the GLC and ILEA made many mistakes. This version of 'municipal anti-racism' (Gilroy, 1987) has subsequently been subject to numerous critiques. These include those of left intellectuals who have criticized both the conceptualization and execution of public anti-racism for trading on essentialized notions of differ-ence and for over-simplifying the complex politics of 'race' and racism (cf Gilroy, 1987, 1990; Modood, 1992; Modood *et al*, 1996). Nevertheless, the GLC and ILEA certainly led the way so far as anti-racist public policy was concerned; ILEA's Research and Statistics branch, for example, made concerted efforts to analyse and understand racialized patterns of achievement in the capital's schools. Ultimately both the GLC and ILEA paid the price for their counter-hegemonic stance in their abolition at the hands of a Thatcher government.

An inquiry into a racist murder at Burnage High School in Manchester (Macdonald, 1989) also became entangled in the wider racialized politics of the time. The report's contributors, all active in combating racism, argued publicly that 'the work of all schools should be informed by a policy that recognizes the pernicious and all-pervasive nature of racism in the lives of students, teachers and parents, black and white, and the need to confront it' (Macdonald, 1989: xxiv). Nevertheless, this message was lost amid a torrent of distorted press coverage that misrepresented the particular criticisms that the panel had made of anti-racism as practised at Burnage. Rather than being recognized as a vital step forward in the attempt to identify workable and critical anti-oppressive strategies, the report was falsely presented as an attack on anti-racism *per se*; as 'signalling the failure of the anti-racist project in education' (Rattansi, 1992: 11). Although anti-racist school practice is far from dead, therefore, the late 1980s and early 1990s witnessed many attacks on anti-racism (from left as well as right) and it has undoubtedly suffered a retreat in many areas (cf Gillborn, 1995).

Although anti-racist initiatives were a vital part of this time period they never reached a widespread position of citation (let alone genuine influence). While multiculturalist and anti-racist advocates fought it out in meetings, on committees and in the pages of books and journals, it was only ever a modest version of multiculturalism that achieved the status necessary for characterizing the policy period as a whole. The peak for liberal pluralist multiculturalism was the publication of the Swann report (1985), which, despite attempts to integrate anti-racist sensitivities, remained largely wedded to (and stands as an exemplar for) the cultural pluralist/multicultural sensibilities of the period. Even as this period reached its peak, however, its destruction was in sight: signalled most obviously in the dismissive response of the Conservative Government of the day. Speaking as the Swann report was presented to Parliament, the then Secretary of State for Education, Keith Joseph, repeated the historic refusal of British governments to take serious targeted action on the inequalities endured by minority communities and their children: 'underachievement is not confined to the ethnic minorities . . . [Our] policies apply to all pupils irrespective of ethnic origin. As they bear fruit, ethnic minority pupils will share in the benefit' (quoted in Gillborn 1990: 166). It was Joseph's rejection of the report's principal recommendations, rather than the Swann report itself, that set the tone for future policy in this field.

Thatcherism: the new racism and colour blind policy: mid-1980s–1997

This period was dominated by what Martin Barker (1981) characterized as 'the new racism', a perspective that asserts a strong cultural homogeneity among the majority population as a basis for privileging the views, needs and assumptions of that group over minority communities. The focus on *'race'* and *superiority* of older times was replaced by a discourse that stressed *culture* and *difference*. This strand in Conservative ideology is strongly associated with Margaret Thatcher but as an over-riding policy force it did not come to dominate until well into her reign as Prime Minister. However, elements of this same perspective certainly outlived her occupancy of No 10 Downing Street and could still be seen in the speeches and policy programmes of both main parties as they fought the 1997 general election (cf Gillborn, 1999). The period was characterized by ferocious individualism; as a prop for the pursuit and acquisition of individual wealth and power, but also as a refusal of wider state responsibilities and diversity around class and ethnic interests. The tone of the period is perhaps best captured by Thatcher's assertion that there is 'no such thing as society' (Thatcher, 1993: 626).

The period witnessed a strong assertion of national homogeneity, where the interests of the majority *have* to come first, not through any supposed superiority (as in the assimilationist phase) but simply because 'we' are 'different' and, after all, it's *'our'* country (cf Ansell, 1997; Barker, 1981; Gillborn, 1995). In education, the phase is neatly signalled by two events: its rise is clear in the rejection of the Swann report (above) and the subsequent publication of the initial consultation on the National Curriculum, in 1987, which made no mention of cultural diversity. The phase ends with the Tories' election defeat in May 1997.

Education policy in this period was characterized by *equiphobia* (Myers, 1990) wedded to market economics and the tyranny of 'standards' discourse. This was seen most graphically in the sweeping education reforms of the decade (eg the introduction of the National Curriculum, testing regimes, and opting out of local authority control). Each one was pursued vigorously, with no reference to cultural diversity and with complete disregard (often contempt) for the likely consequences for minority pupils, parents and communities. 'Colour-blindness' (ie the obstinate refusal to consider ethnic diversity despite a wealth of evidence that minorities are *not* sharing equally) became the officially sanctioned approach. During his final year as Prime Minister, for example, John Major openly fixed colour-blindness as official government policy:

Few things would inflame racial tension more than trying to bias systems in favour of one colour – a reverse discrimination that fuels resentment. An artificial bias would damage the harmony we treasure. Equality under the law – yes;

> equality of opportunity and reward – yes. These promote harmony.
> Policy must be colour blind – it must just tackle disadvantage. Faced by British citizens, whatever their background might be.
>
> (Major, 1997: 7)

And what would this look like in education? More of the same market policies:

> But how do you achieve equality of opportunity?
> It begins with education.
> Over the last few years we've opened up our schools so parents – and taxpayers – can see how well they're performing. That hasn't always made comfortable reading. Too often bad schools are found where we need good schools the most – in areas where education is a life line of hope . . . Testing children on the basic skills, and giving parents the results. Inspecting schools on a regular basis. And, when it's really necessary, closing down failing schools. . . . Specialist schools, grant-maintained schools, city technology colleges and – yes, if parents want them – grammar schools. This is the choice we're opening up.
>
> (Major, 1997: 7–8)

Under successive Conservative administrations, therefore, race inequalities were removed from the agenda; subsumed amid other issues; and denied legitimacy as a topic for concerted action.

During this period, of course, there was also a running contest for influence between different factions within right-wing ideology, most obviously between the neo-liberals and the neo-conservatives (cf Whitty, 1992, 1997). The influence of both factions can be detected in the overall shape of the Tories' reforms, with the neo-liberal pursuit of market-driven reform somewhat tempered by the neo-conservative requirement to retain a core entitlement and National Curriculum. The latter strand of neo-conservative thought was also apparent in the Tories' repeated refusal to grant state funding to Islamic schools. The latter area is one where an incoming Labour administration made an immediate difference (see below); so just how different is New Labour's approach to 'race' and education policy?

New Labour: how new is 'new'

At the time of writing Tony Blair's self-styled *'New'* Labour has not yet enjoyed a full term in office; it is early to be talking about a new phase in the politics of race and education in Britain. Nevertheless, the first Labour Government for 18 years has already established an approach that is very different (in some ways) from that of its Conservative predecessors.

The first White Paper of Blair's Government, *Excellence in Schools* (published just 67 days after the general election) took education as its theme and struck a sharp contrast with the previous decade of Conservative education policy. In his opening paragraph David Blunkett, the new Secretary of State for Education and Employment, stated 'the Government's core commitment to equality of opportunity and high standards for all' (DfEE, 1997: 3). This is very different to the Conservative's open hostility to equal opportunities issues, which they had sought to represent as antithetical to the dominant discursive symbols of Conservative reform: 'standards and choice'. 'The Opposition like to talk about equality in education, but they do not mean equality, they mean uniformity. They mean pushing children together, *en masse*, to be treated exactly the same. . .' (John Patten, then Conservative Secretary of State for Education, opening the second reading of the Education Bill 1992: quoted in CRE/Runnymede Trust, 1993).

The rehabilitation of equal opportunity as a policy objective is an important change. It was followed by a further significant break with Tory education discourse, the readiness openly to acknowledge *ethnic* inequalities in attainment and opportunity. The 1997 White Paper, for example, included several discrete references to inequalities of experience and outcome by ethnicity. The main body of the document carried a section entitled 'Ethnic minority pupils' which referred, among other things, to inequalities in achievement and offered modest commitments to consult on ethnic monitoring and 'best practice' in multi-ethnic schools (DfEE, 1997: 34–35). In the document's appendix a further paragraph, paraphrasing a review of research published by the Office for Standards in Education (Gillborn and Gipps, 1996), offered a little more detail on inequalities of attainment (DfEE, 1997: 81). In a document of more than 80 pages, the provision of three paragraphs is, at best, a small beginning. In fact, *Excellence in Schools* set a pattern that was repeated later by another flagship policy document, the first report of the new Social Exclusion Unit (SEU), which, once again, took education as its first theme.

Like the education White Paper, the SEU's first report, on truancy and school exclusion, included a discrete section acknowledging ethnic inequalities and sketching current research evidence on the issue. The SEU report draws attention to the massive over-representation of black students among those expelled from school and, citing an Ofsted-special inspection (Ofsted, 1996), acknowledges the different profile of excluded black young people (often judged of higher ability and less likely to have suffered deep-seated trauma at home than white excludees: SEU, 1998: 11). One study revealed that children of Black Caribbean origin were almost six times more likely to be expelled than their white counterparts (Gillborn and Gipps, 1996: 53–53). Additionally, a wider review of academic research is cited, including the view that white teachers might actively be involved in producing the inequalities via a range of differential expectations and responses to pupil behaviour.

The first education White Paper, *Excellence in Schools*, and the first report of the Social Exclusion Unit, therefore, share important characteristics:

- *Both break with the aggressively 'colour-blind' stance of Conservative policy*. The documents openly acknowledge 'race' inequalities. Both detail the extent of 'race' inequality and cite research that suggests an active role for schools and teachers in creating and/or amplifying inequality.

However, the two reports share less fortunate characteristics also:

- *Both treat 'race' and ethnicity as an 'add-on'*. The consideration of ethnic inequalities is separate from the rest of the discussion and does not impinge on the arguments feeding into the wider formulation of policy. Consequently, an understanding of racism and 'race' inequality remains completely absent from how the principal policy issues are conceived.

As a result, policy continues to pursue colour-blind targets that:

- *fail to address existing 'race' inequality;*
- *are likely actually to make the situation even more inequitable.*

For example, *Excellence in Schools* argues the need to extend the use of selection within schools so that students are grouped according to 'ability':

> The demands for equality and increased opportunity in the 1950s and 1960s led to the introduction of comprehensive schools. All-in secondary schooling rightly became the normal pattern, but the search for equality of opportunity in some cases became a tendency to uniformity. *The idea that all children had the same rights to develop their abilities led too easily to the doctrine that all had the same ability*. The pursuit of excellence was too often equated with elitism.
>
> (DfEE, 1997: 11, emphasis added)

Labour has been keen to dismiss as dogma any attempt to question the common-sense notion that pupils differ in their ability and therefore should be taught separately. This position was articulated in speeches leading up to the general election and in the Party's election manifesto: 'We must modernize comprehensive schools. *Children are not all of the same ability, nor do they learn at the same speed*. That means 'setting' children in classes to maximize progress, for the benefit of high fliers and slower learners alike' (Labour Party Manifesto 1997: 7, emphasis added).

These proposals, to extend selection within schools by the widespread adoption of 'setting by ability', will probably provide an institutional means by which racialized differential teacher expectations will be given even greater force within the highly competitive and selective school-experience now emerging in the post-Thatcher system (cf Gillborn and Youdell, 1999). The proposals completely fail to recognize the *racialized* nature of the processes in question. That is, a student's chances of being failed by tests of 'ability' vary according to ethnic origin. An individual's position, of course, is not pre-determined, but the overall differences in group position could not be clearer. Selection by 'ability' unfairly disadvantages minority ethnic students (for summaries of the relevant literature see Gillborn and Gipps, 1996; Hallam and Toutounji, 1996; Hatcher, 1997; Slavin, 1996). The colour-blind nature of specific policy proposals belies the racialized reality of life in contemporary Britain and, therefore, threatens racist consequences. That is, people's experiences of success and failure are not independent of ethnic origin, the demographics of educational attainment and economic success display clear and consistent patterns in relation to ethnic origin; *the patterns are racialized*. By failing to take these realities in account policy will at best miss the opportunity to close existing ethnic inequalities, at worse it will strengthen processes that will further entrench ethnic inequality, that is, *its consequences will be racist*. Similar problems threaten Labour's proposals to reduce the number of students expelled from school.

The Social Exclusion Unit's most ambitious recommendation, now accepted as government policy, is that by 2002 there will be a one-third reduction in the numbers of both permanent and fixed-term exclusions.

This is the first of 16 recommendations on exclusions and is completely colour-blind. It is an ambitious target but, by failing to ensure that the existing 'race' inequalities are given equal priority it is inevitable that most effort will be expended on the overall rates of exclusion. The omens for Black students are not good. Historically Black students have not shared equally in the results of education reforms. Although overall rates of attainment have improved for all ethnic groups, for example, students of African Caribbean ethnic background have not improved at as high a rate as their white counterparts (see Figure 8.1). Consequently, the gap between the outcomes of Black and white pupils has actually grown. This pattern of unequal benefit means that a fall in the overall level of exclusion from school is unlikely to be shared equally between students from different ethnic backgrounds. It seems likely that as most attention focuses on the colour-blind headline figure, the existing 'race' inequalities will be left to persist or even worsen. This is because, unless there is deliberate targeted action on black exclusions, it is entirely predictable that Black students will not share equally in any reduction that is achieved. Consequently the over-representation of Black students, relative to their white counterparts, will actually worsen.

This is not to say that the SEU's recommendations on exclusions are entirely colour-blind. Four of the 16 recommendations mention equal opportunities and/or 'race' issues. Hence, exclusions are to be monitored by ethnicity, special inspections of 10 schools per annum will include provision for some that disproportionately exclude minority students. Equal opportunities will be 'adequately incorporated' into teacher education requirements, and finally: 'The DfEE Task Group on raising achievement of ethnic minority pupils will look at what can be done to promote community mentoring in ethnic minority communities' (exclusions recommendation 14, SEU, 1998: 30).

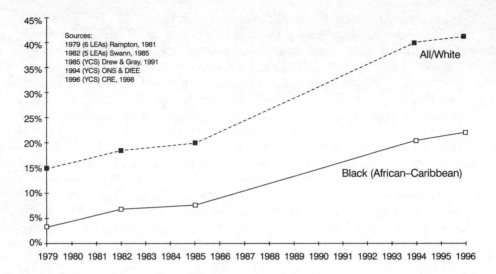

Figure 8.1: *Inequalities of achievement, England (1978–1996): five or more higher grade passes by ethnic origin*

In the body of the main text the SEU report notes the need for mentoring programmes to be 'part of a wider school strategy' that includes 'commitment from senior managers' and good links with 'teachers and parents' (SEU, 1998: 15). These caveats disappear in the recommendations where mentoring seems to be presented as a major, self-contained strategy. Superficially it might be assumed that involving community mentors represents a bold step that challenges the professional educators' exclusive assumption that 'we know best'. However, within the wider context of limited funding, uncertain futures and an over-arching colour-blind target, it is possible that mentoring might actually be taken on as a kind of dumping-ground, a system (outside the mainstream) that shows apparent willing on the part of schools but actually absolves them of responsibility. At worst it might actually pander further to deficit and racist notions that view Black students in particular, and Black communities in general, as beyond the reach of mainstream agencies and professionals. This echoes exactly the kind of deficit theory already evident in Labour's moves to address 'disadvantage' and parenting (see Gillborn, 1998) and further elaborated in the schemes for Education Action Zones (see Hatcher, 1998). A further area where identical processes (of colour-blind policy and racialized outcome) are likely to emerge is the possibility for schools to disapply the National Curriculum for certain students and expand provisions for work-related learning. These proposals have already been consulted on and threaten further regressive effects (Gillborn, 1997).

Naive multiculturalism

In their readiness to name and acknowledge 'race' inequality in education, the current New Labour administration has broken decisively from its Conservative predecessor. Whilst this does represent progress of a sort, it remains inadequate in the face of contemporary racist reality in the British educational system. Although multiculturalism is back on the agenda, it is a *naïve* perspective that deals on a superficial level with questions of difference and entitlement but fails comprehensively to attack deeper issues of inequity and racism. The nature of New Labour's proposals betrays a simplistic and superficial understanding of 'race' and ethnicity. Specifically it is an approach that slips into deficit thinking, views ethnicity as stable and given, and fails to engage with the realities of racism that permeate the education system from national policy through to classroom practice. Fundamentally, it is based on an inadequate and uncritical theory of social justice.

Equity and equality of opportunity

The concept of equality of opportunity has a long and contested history on both sides of the Atlantic (see Apple, 1993; Foster *et al*, 1996; Gipps and Murphy, 1994; Halsey *et al*, 1980; Valli *et al*, 1997). In the United States, in particular, the notion of *equity* has come to prominence in contemporary debate: 'equity has replaced the older concept of equal educational opportunity. Both are related to "egalitarian" concepts of liberty, democracy and freedom from bias' (Grant, 1989: 89). But equity places more emphasis on notions of fairness and justice, even if that requires an unequal distribution of goods and services' (Valli *et al*, 1997: 254). This is an important shift in the terms of debate, as will become clear in the following brief discussion of competing definitions.

Formal equality of access and provision

Writing about the British educational scene, Halsey and his colleagues identified several separate but related understandings of equality of opportunity (Halsey *et al*, 1980). The most limited approach stresses a concern with formal barriers to access and participation. Hence, inequality by this definition would rest on members of one or more social or ethnic groups being denied access to particular schools or examination systems on the basis of their group identity. This is the most conservative definition and is frequently asserted as the *only* viable definition by critics from the right.

Equality of circumstance

Halsey and his colleagues go on to identify a second understanding, which emerged prior to the 1944 Education Act. This perspective is concerned with the inequalities of circumstance that can effectively bar certain groups from participation (especially via poverty) despite the abolition of any formal bar on access. The existence of a separate private education system and the limits on the availability of student 'loans' and other forms of support mean that the contemporary British education system does not satisfy the requirements even of this definition.

Equity of participation (treatment)

Writing in relation to the North American literature, Linda Valli and her colleagues subsume the former two categories, but isolate an understanding (in terms of participation and treatment) that does not receive explicit attention in the British literature. This perspective underlies, but is rarely made explicit in, some British approaches that stress substantive equity of outcomes. Included in this definition are 'the structures and processes that define everyday life in schools' (Valli *et al*, 1997: 254). This includes both the formal and 'hidden' curriculum and would lead schools to 'eliminate tracking, biased testing, and other arrangements' that give structural force to inequalities of 'race', gender and class (Beane and Apple, 1995: 11, in Valli *et al*, 1997: 254).

Equity of outcome

In both the British and US literatures, a final understanding of equity in education concerns the substantive outcomes of education – what has also been called the 'strong' or 'radical' understanding. In Britain this perspective came to prominence in debates concerning selective public education (in the 1960s and 1970s) and was enshrined in the approach of the Rampton and Swann reports on the education of children from minority ethnic backgrounds. According to Valli and her colleagues, this approach: 'refers to the result of educational processes: the equitable distribution of the benefits of schooling. Equitable outcomes of schooling would decrease, if not eliminate, group differences in school achievement, attitudes, dropout rates, college attendance, and employment' (Valli *et al*, 1997: 255).

It is this 'strong' understanding that has been most prominent in critical race research in Britain. Such an approach has the advantage of moving beyond individualistic notions of intent and focusing on concrete questions concerning the educational 'haves' and 'have nots'; 'it rests on collectivist and impersonal notions of justice and equality and is concerned with the structural exclusion of racial groups. It is concerned to look beneath the surface of formal treatment and identify the discriminatory effects of institutional practices' (Dorn, 1985: 21).

New Labour's commitment to 'equality of opportunity' is important, in view of the Conservative's disdain for the notion, but their actions on 'race' and education remain firmly locked into the first and most limited understanding of the term (as concerning access and participation). For example, after a decade of refusals by successive Conservative governments, within a year of its election Labour has granted state funding to Islamic schools: the Islamia primary in London (which first applied for state support in 1986) and the Al Furqan primary in Birmingham (which began moves in 1994). In granting the applications David Blunkett is reported to have emphasized the technical merit of the applications, rather than any ideological shift on the part of the governing party. 'Mr Blunkett said the schools had demonstrated that they will comply with the statutory provisions governing all maintained schools, such as delivering the national curriculum and offering equal access to boys and girls"' (Lepkowska, 1998: 18).

It is interesting that equal opportunities, in terms of gender and access, were mentioned but not, apparently, any of the related issues that the decision raises concerning religious segregation. This is especially surprising in view of the controversy that has, until now, dogged these debates. For example, the last major inquiry into relevant issues, as part of the Swann committee's work, could not agree a unanimous view. The committee argued that: 'The establishment of "separate" schools would fail to tackle many of the underlying concerns of the communities and might exacerbate the very feelings of rejection which they are seeking to overcome' (Swann, 1985: 519). They saw 'a situation in which groups of children are taught exclusively by teachers of the same ethnic group' as undesirable for 'the children, the minority community and society as a whole' (Swann, 1985: 519). Furthermore, a majority of the committee argued that existing anomalies in the funding of certain religious schools in Britain should be reconsidered as part of a review of the relevant sections of the 1944 Education Act (Swann, 1985: 514). Six members of the committee, however, dissented from this position. They argued that 'it is unjust at the present time not to recommend that positive assistance should be given to ethnic minority communities who wish to establish voluntary aided schools in accordance with the 1944 Act' (Swann, 1985: 515).

It is interesting that Labour's decision on this issue has gone almost completely unremarked. My point in raising the issue here is *not* to argue the pros or cons of any particular position in relation to the separate schools debate; rather, I wish simply to note that such a significant change has passed without any explicit commentary by the Government. It may be that the decisions have been made purely on technical grounds of adequacy of teaching, management, curriculum, etc. Alternatively (or additionally) the decisions may represent an attempt to extend formal equality of opportunity (of access and provision) to previously excluded minority communities. In any case, it is highly significant that such precedents have been set without any attempt publicly to debate the implications in terms of social/educational policy, 'race' inequality and ethnic diversity.

The failure to address these wider issues may signal a further element in the Government's present inability to conceive of the multiple and complex interconnections by which issues of racism, ethnic diversity, equality and social exclusion cut across apparently discrete areas of social, economic and educational policy. This can be seen in the Government's refusal to set 'race'-specific targets for the elimination of inequality (say in relation to school exclusion) and in the tendency to view 'race' issues as discrete 'add-ons' of marginal significance. *Excellence in Schools*, for example, began its consideration of ethnic diversity by highlighting the degree of linguistic diversity among the nation's children and repeated the historic emphasis on language – issues typical of earlier assimilationist and integrationist perspectives (see above). The document adopted a clear deficit view that positioned having English as an additional language as a barrier to achievement: 'Children from ethnic minority backgrounds now form a tenth of the pupil population. They bring cultural richness and diversity, but some are particularly at risk of under-achievement. Over half a million do not have English as a first language, and many start school without an adequate grasp of it' (DfEE, 1997: 34).

New Labour has reclaimed some familiar terms, and added some new ones to the lexicon of education policy in Britain: inclusion, social justice, equality of opportunity. Unfortunately, the Government's understanding remains rooted in the least critical and most superficial of perspectives. New Labour may have advanced a somewhat more liberal understanding of equality of access and participation but it cannot credibly claim any interest in equity of treatment or outcome in view of a series of policy proposals (on 'setting by ability', raising attainments, and reducing school exclusions) that refuse to address the reality of the racist structuring of opportunity in British schools.

Equity and education: anti-racism and critical 'race' theory

In this paper I have sought to identify the major contours in the changing landscape of 'race' and education policy in Britain. The view currently is bleak. Despite some superficial changes in policy discourse (once again exalting equality of opportunity and seeking greater inclusivity) New Labour has already shown itself willing to remake and reinforce the historic failures of the British educational system. Despite decades of iniquitous treatment of Black and other minority students, *education policy in Britain remains as incapable and/or unwilling as ever to acknowledge the racism that characterizes the system*.

The inequities historically experienced by Black students are not the result of laziness or a lack of motivation on their part: the evidence suggests they are somewhat more highly motivated than their white peers (Eggleston *et al*, 1986; Smith and Tomlinson, 1989; Mirza, 1997). Their exclusion from the higher reaches of attainment and the most prestigious degree courses is not because they are 'dull' or enter education any less well prepared than their white counterparts. In some parts of the country Black children consistently enter compulsory schooling with higher than average levels of numeracy and literacy (Gillborn and Gipps, 1996). Neither do they endure these inequalities because their families fail to support them in education: on average Black students report greater familial support for education (Drew, 1995). These inequalities, to a significant degree, must be explained by reference to the education system itself; more specifically, to what the education system *does* to and with Black students. The responsibility for changing this situation lies primarily with teachers, headteachers, LEAs, education policy-makers, their numerous advisors, and ultimately with government. It is time that we stopped looking to Black students, their families and communities for the causes of, and answers to, problems rooted in systemic racism.

There are alternatives to the colour-blind rhetoric and racist policy stance that has characterized education in Britain for so long. Earlier I noted the progress made by the anti-racist critique during the 1980s, a progress that has continued (in small pockets) through the dedicated action of communities, practitioners and academics. Despite the setbacks of the late 1980s, anti-racism is far from dead. Some have argued for a more 'critical' and reflective version of anti-racism, tied to other anti-oppressive movements and learning from strategies that work in diverse schools and classrooms (cf Bowser, 1995; Carrim and Gillborn, 1996; Troyna, 1993). The key elements of these approaches are based on a strong understanding of *equity* (rather than a weak version of equality of opportunity) and echo strongly central characteristics in the emerging canon of critical race theory (CRT) in the United States (cf Ladson-Billings, 1998). In an impressive and wide-ranging essay, William Tate has set out some of these defining perspectives:

- CRT recognizes that racism is endemic in US society, deeply ingrained legally, culturally, and even psychologically;
- CRT crosses epistemological boundaries;
- CRT reinterprets civil rights law in light of its limitations, illustrating that laws to remedy racial inequality are often undermined before they can be fully implemented;
- CRT portrays dominant legal claims of neutrality, objectivity, color blindness, and meritocracy as camouflages for the self-interest of powerful entities of society;
- CRT challenges ahistoricism and insists on a contextual/historical examination of the law and a recognition of the experiential knowledge of people of color in analysing the law and society.

(Tate, 1997: 234–35)

Similar perspectives underpin antiracist work on several continents and, whatever umbrella term we choose to work beneath, they provide a solid and critical basis for an approach to policy and practice that might at last challenge the racist structuring of inequality in the British educational system. Tate emphasizes that these elements represent 'a beginning point' (Tate, 1997: 235). Critical race theory, like anti-racism, is a dynamic, complex, uncertain and sometimes contradictory enterprise. These elements provide sensitizing questions and approaches, they are not the rules of some finished and dogmatic ideology. The need for such radical perspectives is evident, from my analysis in this paper of 50 years of 'race' and policy, if education is ever seriously to deliver equity to students regardless of 'race'.

Acknowledgements

This paper has benefited from debate, argument and the patient advice of numerous friends and colleagues, among the most important of whom are Mike Apple, Stephen Ball, Dipannita Basu, Nazir Carrim, Heidi Mirza, Peter Ratcliffe, Fazal Rizvi, Tami Ryan, Sally Tomlinson, Carol Vincent, Geoff Whitty, Deborah Youdell and the late Barry Troyna.

References

Ansell, A E (1997) *New Right, New Racism: Race and reaction in the United States and Britain*, Macmillan, London

Apple, M W (1993) *Official Knowledge*, Routledge, New York

Apple, M W (1997) Introduction, in *Review of Research in Education,* vol 22, ed M W Apple, pp xi-xxi, American Educational Research Association, Washington, DC

Barker, M (1981) *The New Racism: Conservatives and the ideology of the tribe*, Junction Books, London

Beane, J and Apple, M W (1995) The case for democratic schools, in *Democratic Schools*, ed M W Apple and J Beane, pp 1–25, Association for Supervision and Curriculum Development, Alexandria, VA

Bowser, B P (ed) (1995) *Racism and Anti-Racism in World Perspective*, Sage, London

Brandt, G L (1986) *The Realization of Anti-racist Teaching*, Falmer, Lewes

Carrim, N and Gillborn, D (1996) Racialized educational disadvantage, antiracism & difference, Paper presented at the American Educational Research Association annual meeting, New York, April

Commonwealth Immigrants Advisory Council (1964) *Second Report*, Cmd 2458, HMSO, London

CRE/Runnymede Trust (1993) The debate so far, Conference paper 9, Choice, Diversity, Equality: Implications of the Education Bill, A Working Conference, 30 January

CRE (1998) *Education & Training in Britain*, Commission for Racial Equality, London

DfEE (1997) *Excellence in Schools*, Cm 3681, The Stationery Office, London

Dhondy, F (1982) Who's afraid of ghetto schools? in *The Black Explosion in British Schools*, ed F Dondy, B Beese and L Hassan, Race Today Publications, London

Dorn, A (1985) Education and the Race Relations Act, in *Race & Gender: Equal opportunities policies in education*, ed M Arnot, pp 11–23, Pergamon, Oxford

Drew, D (1995) *'Race', Education and Work: the statistics of inequality*, Avebury, Aldershot

Drew, D and Gray, J (1991) The black–white gap in examination results: a statistical critique of a decade's research, *New Community*, **17** (2), pp 159–72

Eggleston, S J, Dunn, D K and Anjali, M (1986) *Education for Some: The educational & vocational experiences of 15–18-year-old members of minority ethnic groups*, Trentham, Stoke-on-Trent

Flew, A (1984) *Education, Race and Revolution*, Centre for Policy Studies, London

Foster, P, Gomm, R and Hammersley, M (1996) *Constructing Educational Inequality*, Falmer, London

Gaine, C (1995) *Still No Problem Here*, Trentham, Stoke-on-Trent

Gillborn, D (1990) *'Race', Ethnicity and Education: Teaching and learning in multi-ethnic schools*, Routledge, London

Gillborn, D (1995) *Racism and Antiracism in Real Schools: Theory, policy, practice,* Open University Press, Buckingham

Gillborn, D (1997) Race and ethnicity in education 14–19, in *Education 14–19: Critical perspectives*, ed S Tomlinson, Athlone, London

Gillborn, D (1998) Racism, selection, poverty and parents: New Labour, old problems?, *Journal of Education Policy*, **13** (6), pp 717–35

Gillborn, D (1999) Race, nation and education: New Labour and the new racism, in *Education Policy and Contemporary Politics*, ed J Demaine, pp 82–102, Macmillan, London

Gillborn, D and Gipps, C (1996) *Recent Research on the Achievements of Ethnic Minority Pupils*, Report for the Office for Standards in Education, HMSO, London

Gillborn, D and Youdell, D (1999) *Rationing Education*, OUP, Buckingham

Gilroy, P (1987) *There Ain't No Black in the Union Jack*, Hutchinson, London

Gilroy, P (1990) The end of anti-racism, *New Community*, **17** (1), pp 71–83

Gipps, C and Murphy, P (1994) *A Fair Test? Assessment, Achievement and Equity*, Open University Press, Buckingham

Grant, C (1989) Equity, equality, teachers and classroom life, in *Equity in Education*, ed W Seceda, pp 89–102, Falmer, Philadelphia

Hallam, S and Toutounji, I (1996) *What Do We Know about the Grouping of Pupils by Ability? A Research Review*, University of London Institute of Education, London

Halsey, A H, Heath, A F and Ridge, J M (1980) *Origins and Destinations: Family, class, and education in modern Britain,* Clarendon Press, Oxford

Hatcher, R (1997) New Labour, school improvement and racial inequality, *Multicultural Teaching*, **15** (3), pp 8–13

Hatcher, R (1998) Social justice and the politics of school effectiveness and improvement, *Race, Ethnicity and Education*, **1** (2), pp 267–89

Labour Party (1997) *New Labour: Because Britain deserves better*, The Labour Party Manifesto, Labour Party, London

Ladson-Billings, G (1998) Just what is critical race theory and what is it doing in a *nice* field like education?, *Qualitative Studies in Education*, **11** (1), pp 7–24

Lepkowska, D (1998) Muslims gain equality of funding, *Times Educational Supplement*, 16 January, p 18

Lynch, J (1986) *Multicultural Education: Principles and practice*, Routledge and Kegan Paul, London

Macdonald, I, Bhavnani, R, Khan, L and John, G (1989) *Murder in the Playground: The Report of the Macdonald Inquiry into racism and racial violence in Manchester schools*, Longsight, London

Major, J (1997) *Britain – The Best Place in the World*, Text of a speech to the Commonwealth Institute, 18 January, Conservative Central Office, London

Massey, I (1991) *More Than Skin Deep*, Hodder and Stoughton, London

Mirza, H S (1997) Black women in education: a collective movement for social change, in *Black British Feminism: A reader,* ed H S Mirza, Routledge, London

Modood, T (1992) *Not Easy Being British: Colour, culture and citizenship*, Runnymede Trust and Trentham Books, Stoke-on-Trent

Modood, T, Banton, M, Cohen, P, Gillborn, D and Shukra, K (1996) The changing context of 'race' in Britain: a symposium, *Patterns of Prejudice*, **30** (1), pp 3–42

Modood, T, Berthoud, R, Lakey, J, Nazroo, J, Smith, P, Virdee, S and Beishan, S (1997) *Ethnic Minorities in Britain: Diversity and disadvantage*, Policy Studies Institute, London

Mullard, C (1982) Multiracial education in Britain: from assimilation to cultural pluralism, in *Race, Migration and Schooling,* ed J Tearney, pp 120–33, Holt, Rinehart and Winston, London

Myers, K (1990) Review of 'Equal Opportunities in the New Era', *Education*, **5**, p 295, October

Ofsted (1996) *Exclusions from Secondary Schools 1995/6*, The Stationery Office, London

Palmer, F (ed) (1986) *Anti-Racism – An assault on education and value*, Sherwood Press, London

Ramdin, R (1987) *The Making of the Black Working-class in Britain*, Westwood House, Aldershot

Rampton, A (1981) *West Indian Children in Our Schools*, Cmnd 8273, HMSO, London

Rattansi, A (1992) Changing the subject? Racism, culture and education, in *'Race', Culture and Difference*, ed J Donald and A Rattansi, pp 11–48, Sage, London

Rose, E J B *et al* (1969) *Colour and Citizenship*, Oxford University Press, Oxford

Social Exclusion Unit (SEU) (1998) *Truancy and School Exclusion Report by the Social Exclusion Unit*, Cm 3957, London

Sivanandan, A (1988) Left, right and Burnage, *New Statesman*, 27 May. Reprinted in *Communities of Resistance: Writings on black struggles for socialism* (1990), ed A Sivanandan, pp 145–52, Verso, London

Slavin, R E (1996) *Education for All*, Lisse, Swets and Zeitlinger, [place]

Smith, D J and Tomlinson, S (1989) *The School Effect: A study of multi-racial comprehensives*, Policy Studies Institute, London

Swann, Lord (1985) *Education for All: Final Report of the Committee of Inquiry into the Education of Children from Ethnic Minority Groups*, Cmnd 9453, HMSO, London

Tate, W F (1997) Critical race theory and education: history, theory, and implications, in *Review of Research in Education, vol 22*, ed M W Apple, pp 195–247, American Educational Research Association, Washington, DC

Thatcher, M (1993) *The Downing Street Years,* HarperCollins, London

Tomlinson, S (1977) Race and education in Britain 1960–77: an overview of the literature, *Sage Race Relations Abstracts*, **2** (4), pp 3–33

Troyna, B (1993) *Racism and Education: Research perspectives*, Open University Press, Buckingham

Troyna, B and Carrington, B (1990) *Education, Racism and Reform*, Routledge, London

Valli, L, Cooper, D and Frankes, L (1997) Professional development schools and equity: a critical analysis of rhetoric and research, in *Review of Research in Education, vol 22*, ed M W Apple, pp 251–304, American Educational Research Association, Washington, DC

Whitty, G (1992) Education, economy and national culture, in *Social and Cultural Forms of Modernity*, ed R Bocock and K Thompson, Polity Press, Oxford

Whitty, G (1997) Creating quasi-markets in education: a review of recent research on parental choice and school autonomy in three countries, in *Review of Research in Education, Vol 22*, ed M W Apple, pp 3–47, American Educational Research Association, Washington, DC

9

Boys and Girls Underachieving: Issues for 14+ Education and Training

Annette Hayton

Introduction

This chapter will consider some of the ways in which participation and achievement in 14+ education and training are linked to gender. As the title suggests, it will consider the performance of both males and females in order to explore more fully the worries about boys' underachievement that have surfaced in recent years. The links between gender and performance have been the subject of much discussion since the early 1970s which marked the beginning of a growing realization that girls' and women's participation and success in education and training was being adversely affected by gender discrimination. However, in recent years the public debate about gender has shifted to the problem of boys' underachievement. Numerous newspaper articles and TV programmes have raised the issue – often using inflammatory titles such as *The Future is Female* (BBC, 1994), *Men Aren't Working* (BBC, 1995), *Perils of Ignoring our Lost Boys* (*TES*, 28 June 1996), *Learning Gender Gap Reveals Redundant Male* (*The Observer*, 4 January 1998) and *Girls really are better than boys* (*The Observer*, 4 January 1998). As we shall see there has indeed been some change in the comparative performance of girls and boys in certain areas. However, further investigation shows that, while gender does have a significant effect on patterns of participation and success, the situation is considerably more complex than it might at first appear. The public debate has tended to equate girls' success with boys' failure and while this oversimplification of the issue may be effective for selling newspapers it is not helpful for those trying to find lasting solutions to serious problems. Although there have been significant improvements in girls' attainment in some areas, there are a number of areas where there is little or no change in the comparative performance of males and females. Also, although gender is important, social class remains the main predictor of educational success, a fact which appears to have been conveniently overlooked in the recent debate about boys' underachievement. Therefore, in order to explore the reasons for differences in participation and attainment we need to consider the ways in which class and gender intersect to influence educational success or failure.

This chapter will begin by considering to what extent the gender differences apparent in 14+ education and training represent significant change in the nature of male and female participation and achievement and how far they follow previously established patterns. As this phase of education also encompasses the transition to work and adult life the chapter also considers some of the factors related to social exclusion in later life, in particular differential participation and reward in the labour market. It then goes on to consider the ways in which young people's opportunities and choices relate to 'masculinity', 'femininity' and class. The chapter concludes by arguing that outdated constructions of class and gender are both intrinsic elements of our education and training system and that attempts to alleviate their negative effects without considering the ways in which they structure the curriculum are bound to fail.

Change and continuity in male and female participation and achievement

The issues regarding male and female performance in education and training are considerably more complex than they appear. There have been some striking changes in participation and achievement in recent years, and indeed in the labour market. However there are also some important, but often overlooked, continuities. This section will discuss some of the areas of change and continuity, and consider the relationship between male and female educational performance and the links with the labour market.

Participation in post-compulsory education and training

The number of young people staying on at school or college after 16 has increased considerably in recent years. In the mid-1980s only 50 per cent of 16 year olds were engaged in full-time education and training, whereas in the 1990s we can see participation rates of around 70 per cent (Hodgson and Spours, 1997). The initial expansion of 16–19 education in the early 1980s was largely a response to youth unemployment and the subsequent reduction in the number of available apprenticeships. In addition, as Arnot *et al* (1998) point out, improved levels of performance by girls at age 16 has resulted in more young women staying on and this is part of the reason for the general increase in participation. At age 16 slightly more young women (72.9 per cent) stay on in full-time education than young men (65.8 per cent) (DfEE, 1998a).

However, when work-based training is taken into account a slight decrease in overall participation rates can be detected (Payne, 1998).

Payne's research also shows that boys who leave school at 16 are more likely than girls to have full-time jobs or to be involved in work-based training. As a result young women at 16 are slightly less likely to be in education, training or full-time employment than young men despite their increased participation in school and college courses.

Opportunities for study at degree level have increased considerably and instead of higher education being an elite system, to which only a minority of the population even aspired, it can now be described as a 'mass' system. In 1985 about 7 per cent of 18-year-olds were studying for a first degree and in 1995 this had risen to around 20 per cent (DfEE, 1995). There has also been a sharp increase in 'mature' students returning to study and the number of women students involved in higher education has increased significantly (Parry, 1997).

Opportunities for girls' success

As we have seen above, girls and women are participating in education and training in far greater numbers then previously. Perhaps one of the most important changes to take place over the last 30 years is the removal of many of the barriers to girls' participation and opportunities for success. One of the most tangible examples of discrimination was the differential allocation of grammar school places through the 11+ system (Deem, 1981). Under this system girls were allocated fewer places at grammar schools than boys regardless of their performance in the examination. The justification for this was that boys matured later and therefore needed more time to develop intellectually and cope with the rigours and constraints of study. The removal of this type of formal barrier to girls' success together with a greater concern for equal treatment of the sexes has given girls the opportunity to achieve at the same level as boys – an opportunity that they appear to have taken.

At this point it is worth remembering that the 11+ policy was built on the underlying assumption that women were naturally less intelligent and intellectually able than men and that therefore equal, or superior, performance was impossible. In addition to highlighting a quantifiable change in policy this example also serves to remind us of the pitfalls that essentialist explanations for differential performance can lead us into when developing policy and considering practice. As Mahony (1998) points out, the belief in male intellectual superiority is still considered self-evident in many sections of society and it seems that 'human nature' is still invoked as an explanation for differential performance in exams as well as differences in behaviour and attitudes towards school. However, as Arnot et al (1998) state, 'Even if biology sets limits to human abilities there is no certainty what these might be, nor whether they are different for men and women.' Certainly, it would seem foolhardy to develop education policy or base curriculum innovation on unproven 'natural' differences between males and females, particularly when, as we shall see below, class remains the most significant predictor of achievement and, of course, when it seems that girls may be doing 'better' than boys.

Changes in attainment at GCSE

The media reports about girls doing better than boys are largely based on results at GCSE and, in more recent years, some changes in attainment at A level. The major change has been an increased proportion of girls achieving five or more A*–C passes at GCSE. Arnot et al (1998) compared the results for boys and girls over the last 20 years and identified three distinct stages. The first stage saw roughly equal proportions of boys and girls achieving five or more passes. This was followed by a period of rapid change when the proportion of boys achieving five or more passes dropped significantly. The third stage began in 1990 when the proportions seem to have stabilized at around 80–83 per cent of boys compared to girls gaining five or more A*–C passes at GCSE. This analysis shows that, although expressions of concern about boys' underachievement are fairly recent, the differential has existed for some years. The provisional results for 1997–98 show a similar pattern. In terms of the overall number of students entered for GCSE 51.5 per cent of all girls gained five or more A*–C passes compared with 41.3 per cent of boys (DfEE, 1998b).

This change in the comparative performance of boys and girls achieving five GCSE A*–C passes coincided with the introduction of the National Curriculum and also the introduction of GCSE, which has led to some speculation that the coursework assessment associated with GCSE favours girls. However, coursework is only one element of the assessment process and girls seem to be doing better in examinations as well (NEAB, 1996). Arnot et al point out that the introduction of GCSE and the National Curriculum has resulted in a significant increase in the number of young people being entered for public examinations in a wider range of subjects. This means that girls are now expected to take Maths and a Science and that more boys are taking English and foreign languages. Although boys are making some improvement in certain subjects, girls are making significant improvement in their performance in Mathematics and Science and this change alone would result in considerable improvement in girls' results overall.

Essentially the difference in the results of those gaining five GCSE A*–C passes means that middle class girls are now doing as well or better than middle class boys. Power et al (1998) point out that this particular change appears to be largely an issue for middle class parents who are concerned that their sons' traditional privilege in higher education and the job market is being threatened as their daughters begin to enter the better paid professions. Power et al (1998) go so far as to suggest that the strength of feeling amongst the middle-classes may well explain the urgency of the current debate. However, as yet this early advantage has not been translated into higher status and better paid jobs in the labour market – for example, women professionals can expect to earn only 80 per cent of their male colleagues' salary (Bonney and Jeffrey, 1998). Given that this group of boys is most likely to have continuous, full-time, well-paid employment and a legacy of power and privilege associated with their class, a significant reduction in their economic privilege in later life seems unlikely.

Boaler (1998: 120) suggests that the difference in performance is a direct result of a more equitable system that allows girls to achieve and therefore rewards 'the group that works hardest and longest'. As Cohen (1998) points out, too much involvement with academic work has long been regarded as slightly suspect for boys but this has not, up to now, adversely affected their career prospects. These have been more dependent on their class, sex and ethnicity than any other factor (Hodkinson and Sparkes, 1997).

Class and gender

However, as Arnot *et al* (1998) point out, it is only in the area of passes at A*–C that significant change has taken place. The differential results shown at lower levels of performance in Figure 9.1 have been constant since the mid-seventies.

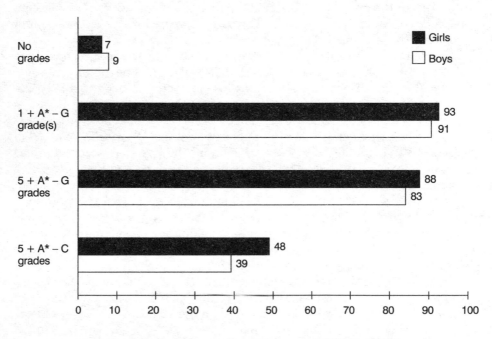

Figure 9.1: *Pupils' overall performance at GCSE in 1995*

Despite changes in girls' performance recent research reaffirms that social class continues to be the most significant indicator of educational success. (Plummer, 1998). As Plummer points outs, 'Although working-class girls do marginally better than working-class boys in public examinations the difference is not enough to reduce class inequalities within gender (or racial) groups.'

Underachievement of working-class boys

Despite Power *et al's* suggestion that middle-class parents may have been largely responsible for fuelling the recent panic about boys' underachievement there is another group of boys which is giving cause for concern. As Chris Woodhead, Chief Inspector for Schools stated in *The Times* (6 March 1996), 'the failure of boys, in particular white working-class boys is one of the most disturbing problems we face within the whole education system'. The underlying concern appears to be that young men will become increasingly alienated from society. As David Hart, General Secretary of the National Association of Headteachers, quoted in the same issue of *The Times*, said, 'too many boys are slipping into long-term unemployment and criminality'. Recent research from NACRO (1998) supports this viewpoint and shows that almost 95 per cent of young men in young offender institutions have been excluded from school or have consistently failed to attend school. In January 1998 Stephen Byers for the DfEE stated that; 'Failure to raise the educational achievement of boys will mean that thousands of young men will face a bleak future in which lack of qualifications and basic skills will mean unemployment and little hope of finding work' (DfEE, 1998c).

These statements require some further analysis for several reasons. Firstly, it is possible to detect a distinct element of fear in the middle-class concern for the plight of these young men. As Skeggs (1997: 134) points out, young working-class men have repeatedly been perceived as a potential threat to the social order in a way that young, working-class women have not. Pearce and Hillman (1998: 3) note how young, working-class men 'are often explicitly dehumanized in press reports and elsewhere: the young man becomes a "ratboy" or a "spiderboy", one of a pack of feral underwolves'. Also, despite the explicit links that are made between unemployment and criminality, the proposed solution is not increased employment but for young men to work hard at school and get better qualifications. In addition, the concentration on white, working-class, male under-achievement in formal education posed against recent female success offers an easy solution to some serious problems. It provides a number of scapegoats in the shape of schools, girls and working mothers as well as the boys themselves. All of these issues serve to distract us from the grinding effects of poverty and long-term unemployment on working-class communities (see Whitty *et al* in this volume). They deny the impact of racism in school and society on the achievement of certain groups, such as Afro-Caribbean boys (Gillborn and Gipps, 1996) and they draw attention away from the problems of young women who are underachieving (Pearce and Hillman, 1998). Most importantly, they do not provide a firm foundation for positive action to deal with their disaffection, non-participation and social exclusion.

Nevertheless, although educational qualifications are not a passport to employment, low levels of educational attainment do act as barriers to many jobs and full participation in modern society. However, the under-achievement of working-class children is a continuing problem and, as we have seen above (Figure 9.1), girls have tended to do slightly better than boys for some time. A great deal of educational research and a number of major policy reforms, for example the introduction of comprehensive schools and GCSE, have been concerned with reducing the effect of class on educational performance. This leads us to ask what has changed if working-class under-achievement, particularly for boys, has remained constant? The major difference is, of course, that these boys cannot expect to underachieve at school and then enter employment at 15 or 16. In the early 1970s young men leaving school with few or no qualifications would have found employment in a factory, or on a building site or in other manual work. Some of them of them would have become apprentices with a particular firm – learning their trade and studying for craft qualifications through day-release courses. Changes in the economy over the last 25 years have resulted in a decline in manufacturing industries and a subse-quent reduction in traditional working-class male areas of employment and work-based training. The predictions for the UK are that these trends will continue with a further decline in manufacturing industries (DfEE, 1998d: 7). The jobs that are available are often part-time positions in the growing service sector and many young men do not consider this type of work appropriate for them.

Subject choice

Although social class has the greatest influence on educational success, gender continues to be the organizing factor in subject choice, both in academic and vocational courses.

GNVQ Advanced

An examination of GNVQ Advanced shows a high degree of gender differ-entiation. Figure 9.2 (opposite) shows the number of entrants to GNVQ Advanced by gender and subject area based on the DfEE provisional figures for 1997/98. The great majority of students take business courses and for that reason this area is not represented on the chart as the large number obscures the differences in other subject areas. Although slightly more boys than girls take business courses, the number of male and female entrants is fairly equal. However, there are marked differences in some of the other areas with nearly 5,000 girls taking Health and Social Care as compared to 325 boys. In Information Technology the overall number of entrants is quite small at about 2,500 but only 12 per cent of the students are girls.

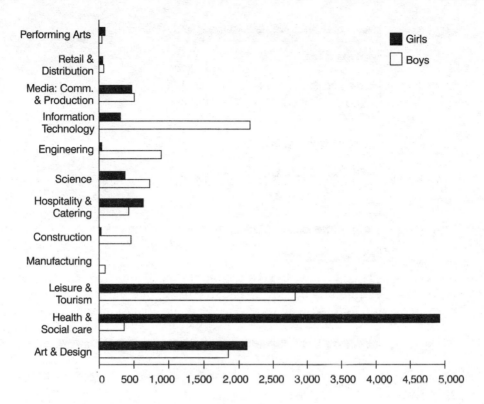

Figure 9.2: *GNVQ Advanced: entrants by subject and gender*
(Based on DfEE, 1998b)

A level

At A level young women and young men have been achieving roughly equal point scores for the last two or three years but they continue to take very different subjects. Young women are in the majority in curriculum areas such as English and Modern Languages whilst young men dominate in Mathematics and Science subjects (see Figure 9.3, page 164). Although more boys are now taking English and Modern Languages, the gender gap in Mathematics and Computer Science has remained the same. In Physics, Technology and Economics it has increased (Arnot *et al,* 1998).

Modern Apprenticeships

Modern Apprenticeships also reflect traditional gender (and race) divisions. Unwin and Wellington reporting on the pilots (1995: 338) stated that: 'The vast majority of apprentices are white males (only 2 per cent responding as non-white). From the responses to the questionnaire it would appear that 88.7 per cent are male and 11.1 per cent are female.'

The 1998 figures indicate some change but the general pattern remains the same (see Figure 9.4, page 165).

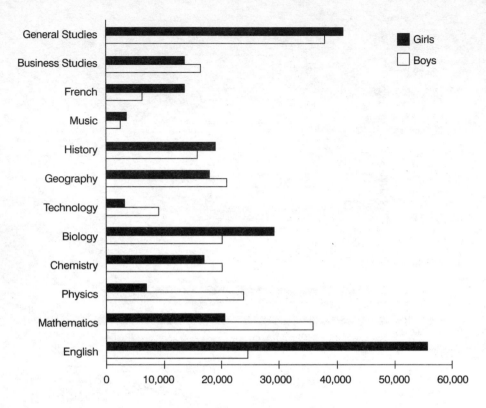

Figure 9.3: *16–18-year-old A level entrants by subject and gender*
(Based on DfEE, 1998b)

As we have seen above there is a continuing division between male and female patterns of participation in education and training based on the subjects and areas that they choose to study. Young women taking the academic route of A levels tend to drop Mathematics and the 'hard' Sciences at the first opportunity – despite their success at GCSE. This implies that their participation has more to do with the element of compulsion in the National Curriculum rather than any lasting solution to girls' disenchantment with Science. Young women taking the vocational routes, such as GNVQ, continue to be found largely in service and caring courses. Boys and young men continue to choose traditional 'male' subjects and careers. In the 'new' subject areas there is some levelling out, as, for example, in GNVQ Business courses, where we see large numbers of young people of both sexes participating. However, in the 'new' subjects at A level there is a large, ongoing gender gap in favour of boys in Computer Studies and an increasing gap in both Technology and Craft, Design and Technology (Arnot *et al*, 1998). In GNVQ Advanced the majority of students taking Information Technology are male.

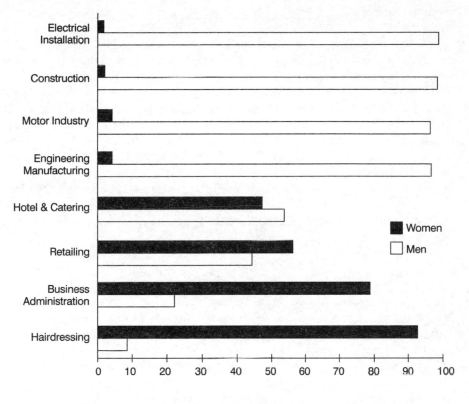

Figure 9.4: *Modern Apprenticeships by sector and gender*

Links to the higher education and the labour market

This situation has some serious implications when considering the link with social exclusion in later life. Boys' non-participation in some subjects and girls' non-participation in others has a significant effect on their higher education options, career opportunities and job prospects. At undergraduate level nearly double the number of men than women take science-related subjects in first degrees but three times as many women take education as a subject than men (HESA, 1996).

Over the last 30 years the number of women in the UK workforce has risen considerably. Between 1971 and 1991 there was an increase of 30 per cent in the number of women in employment (ED, 1992) and, by 1997, women made up 46 per cent of the workforce (DfEE, 1998d). This increase in female employment has resulted in greater economic independence for many women in 1990s Britain. However, the gender differentiation that we have seen in education and training is mirrored by the different areas of work which men and women are engaged in. More than 25 per cent of women work in clerical jobs but only 7 per cent of men; and only 3 per cent of women work in craft occupations compared to 21 per cent of men.

The different types of work that men and women do, which Hakim (1979) described as horizontal segregation, has a significant impact on their earning power. It is one of the reasons for women's relative poverty compared to men and, as such, is a key indicator of social exclusion. Lower achieving boys continue to reject education and training in areas that could prepare them for jobs in the growing service sector and enhance their prospects of finding employment. In contrast, middle-class boys take subjects that give them access to their traditional areas of employment in business and the professions. In addition, they are taking subjects that open up opportunities for employment in highly skilled jobs related to new technology – one of the few expanding sectors of the labour market that commands higher salary levels (DfEE, 1998e). The employment forecasts by gender do not signal any change in this situation in the near future (DfEE, 1998d: 11).

Low pay and low status work

Despite the introduction of Equal Pay legislation in 1974 women still earn less than men. Traditional 'male' areas of work not only command higher pay but also higher status than traditional 'women's' work – although status is, of course, mediated by class as well as gender. Nursing is an excellent example of a 'women's' profession that suffers from low pay and low status. Despite its members being referred to as 'angels' by the tabloid press and despite the long years of training in order to develop a range of technical, social and organizational skills to do the job effectively, nurses are still undervalued and underpaid. A recently published survey by the Royal College of Nursing, *Changing Times* reported in the *Independent* (13 October 1998), states that Staff Nurses need a 17 per cent pay rise in order for them to be paid at the same level as a new teacher.

Nurses' pay has long been an issue for public debate and, at the time of writing, it is being discussed again but in a rather different context – that of low recruitment and retention in the profession. Nurses from as far afield as the Philippines are being flown in to staff the wards while British women are finding jobs in better paid, less demanding areas of the labour market. When questioned as part of the RCN survey, nurses stated that better pay would be the factor most likely to encourage them to stay in the profession. From this it seems clear that well-qualified, economically independent women are no longer prepared to accept low wages when better paid jobs are available. There are also indications that young women's attitudes have changed and that they now expect a greater level of economic independence and also 'equal rights' with men (Wilkinson and Mulgan, 1995). This is indeed a significant change.

However, there is still a large number of working-class girls for whom better-paid employment is not an option. A major factor here is the continued expectation that women should be mainly responsible for the household and related 'caring' activities which has a significant impact on their lives at various stages. Firstly, as Adkins and Leonard (1996) have noted, the compulsory education of working-class girls is often adversely affected by domestic responsibilities. Also, although young men are more likely to be classified as unemployed, many young women are economically inactive in order to meet their domestic and caring responsibilities (Pearce and Hillman, 1998: 39, citing the Labour Force Survey) and their earning potential is severely restricted both in the short and long term.

In terms of household responsibilities women are still mainly responsible for housework and childcare. They continue to undertake 90 per cent of domestic tasks (McCrae, 1991) and are much more likely to leave and enter the labour market in order to meet their caring and domestic commitments. Although the number of women in paid employment has increased significantly they are less likely to have full-time jobs than men. Of the total male labour force 72 per cent have full-time jobs and 10 per cent part-time jobs. The situation for women is quite different with only 50 per cent having full-time jobs and 42 per cent in part-time jobs (DfEE, 1997). Also, as Bonney and Jeffrey (1998) point out, the number of women who remain in the workforce throughout their working life has actually decreased from 15 per cent 30 years ago to 10 per cent today, as women attempt to combine family and career.

We have considered low salaries in the nursing profession, but those confined to other areas of caring work are amongst some of the lowest paid workers in the country. As we have seen, it is mostly young women who take vocational courses in areas such as Health and Social Care which prepare them for these sorts of jobs. Skeggs (1989) has described these as 'domestic apprenticeships' as they not only prepare young women for low paid employment in the labour market but also reinforce the importance of their caring role in the home. In this way their earning potential in the labour market is doubly affected. Bates (1993) describes the painful processes for a group of 'care girls' of coming to terms with working in a home for the elderly. A key element in their eventual acceptance of the work is their growing realization that there are no realistic alternatives open to them. However, an additional factor also noted by Skeggs (1997) appears to be the young women's recognition that their work is important and worthwhile even though it may not be highly valued in our society.

As we have seen there have been several areas of significant change in male and female participation and achievement in education, training and the labour market. Middle-class girls are doing slightly better than middle-class boys at GCSE and more girls and young women are staying on in further and higher education. Women are also found in far greater numbers in the labour market and this has led to a greater degree of economic independence than was usually the case in previous generations. There has also been a change in women's attitudes to work and expectations of adult life in that they now expect more equal relationships. The decline in the manufacturing industry has led to a reduction in the number of jobs traditionally associated with working-class male employment and the expansion of the service sector has increased the number of jobs traditionally associated with women's employment.

However, there are a number of areas where there has been little or no change. Firstly working-class boys and girls are both underachieving in compulsory education. Also young men and women continue to choose different school subjects, different vocational courses and different jobs. Women are still largely responsible for running the household, childcare and care of disabled and elderly members of the family. Despite considerable change in patterns of participation in the labour market men are still more likely to be in full-time employment than women and they also continue to earn more.

Real men and proper women

In a society in which women's work is so undervalued it would not be surprising if young men were to reject such jobs on the grounds of low pay alone. In a recent article on men in childcare in the *TES* (11 September 1998) Chris Randle, co-ordinator of 'Men who Care', was reported as saying, 'Care is still seen as women's work and isn't a viable option for most men. The money is so bad that men would either have to have a vocation or a partner who brought in a second wage.'

However, pay is not the only reason for young men rejecting women's work and 'girls' subjects. Indeed it seems that a number of young men prefer to remain unemployed rather than take jobs in the service sector. When they do take up such employment they are often busily attempting to define gender boundaries within the work as Mac an Ghaill (1994: 73) found when interviewing male students about their part-time jobs: 'Working in a sweet shop might be more girls' work. But in places like video and hi-fi shops, then it's mainly going to be men because they know about these things don't they?'

Similarly girls appear to reject 'masculine' courses and careers which would lead to jobs with higher pay and higher status, despite a number of initiatives designed to encourage them to take up these subjects such as Girls into Science and Technology (GIST) and Women into Science and Technology (WISE) (Whyte *et al,* 1985; Kelly, 1981).

It seems that, despite a number of significant material and cultural changes over the last 30 years, young people still have very traditional ideas about what constitutes an appropriate job or course of study for a 'real man' or a 'proper woman'. Furthermore, these ideas appear to have a profound, often seemingly adverse, effect on their participation in education and training and their subsequent choice of careers.

These sorts of attitudes are often blamed on the 'socialization' of boys and girls into different sex roles, but socialization theory is unable to encompass a number of important factors. Firstly, it cannot explain why socialization is sometimes ineffective, for example, why some men become nursery nurses. Also, changing behaviour and attitudes becomes a very individual matter, where those who do not change in the face of seemingly rational argument become the problem. Many of the initiatives designed to encourage girls to take up science subjects were based on changing girls' attitudes through, for example, modifying curriculum materials and providing positive role models rather than considering whether there might be problems with the curriculum itself (Yates, 1985; Kenway, 1993).

An alternative way of explaining gender differences was developed by Kessler *et al* (1985) who employed the notion of 'hegemonic masculinity' and 'emphasized femininity' to describe 'ideal types' of masculinity and femininity. This approach is useful because, while recognizing the powerful influence of such ideas on individual behaviour, it also allows for individual diversity within the dominant pattern, for example the male nursery nurse or the female engineer. It can also encompass resistance to the dominant pattern and so allow for the possibility of change. Recent research has used this kind of approach to consider the diversity of masculinities and femininities that allow us to explore how class and gender (and ethnicity) interrelate.

Máirtín Mac an Ghaill (1994), in his study of a secondary school, identified four groups of young men developing quite distinct versions of masculinity: the New Entrepreneurs, the Academic Achievers, the Macho Lads and the 'Real Englishmen'. One aspect of boys' behaviour which is often associated with their underachievement is that 'Real boys don't work' (Epstein, 1998). Mac an Ghaill found two groups that explicitly rejected the work ethos of the school, the 'Real Englishmen' and the Macho Lads. He made the link between his Macho Lads, who typify a traditional male working class attitude to education, and the young men Willis (1997) interviewed in the early 1970s. Although, as we have already noted, unlike Willis's lads, the Macho lads are less likely to find jobs:

> Like Willis' Lads, the Macho Lads at Parnell School made a similar association of academic work with an inferior effeminacy, referring to those who conformed as 'dickhead achievers'. Consequently, they overtly rejected much school work as inappropriate for them as men.

(Mac an Ghaill, 1994)

Also, the Macho Lads have continued to retain attitudes which Mac an Ghaill (1994: 71) describes as part of an 'outdated mode of masculinity'. In addition to rejecting academic work the Macho Lads also had highly conventional attitudes towards the division of labour in both the home and the workplace and essentially still believed in the male breadwinner and the full-time housewife. As we have seen, changes in the labour market and the changing attitudes of young women to adult life make adoption of this version of masculinity a high risk strategy less and less likely to lead to any lasting fulfilment either through work or through personal life.

We then have to consider why young people retain these seemingly outdated and self-destructive attitudes. Skeggs (1997) gives this issue some consideration, suggesting that 'Masculinity' and 'Femininity' can be regarded as forms of cultural capital that can be exchanged and traded. For example, 'Macho Lads' may have very little cultural capital other than their 'physical hardness' which, while it is not required by most service sector jobs, does enable them to gain power in their relationships with women. Similarly the working-class young women Skeggs (1997: 9) interviewed had only their feminine cultural capital to trade with, which she describes as:

> only convertible in a diminishing labour market or as unpaid labour in voluntary caring or in the family. When they traded their femininity and appearance on the marriage market they were able to negotiate more power but only in interpersonal terms. . .

If we take into account that a decision about which subjects to take at GCSE, which college course to take or whether to try to get a job is only one aspect of the transition to adult life, then the attitudes of different groups of young men and women begin to make more sense. Wallace (1987) identified three main areas that mark transition to adulthood: success in the labour market, the marriage market and the sexual market. Therefore, participation and success in education and training, and the accumulation of cultural and social capital which accompanies this, has to be weighed against the possible loss of social and cultural capital in other areas of their life. This is not to suggest that this is a conscious process whereby individuals sit down and weigh up the pros and cons of a certain course of action, for example taking GCSE Physics, in a totally rational way. However, for a young man whose chances of academic success appear slim, who, in any case, is unsure about the value of middle-class intellectual work as opposed to practical skills, and whose sexual identity is closely connected to traditional versions of masculinity, even GCSE Physics must appear to be a poor choice, let alone GNVQ Health and Social Care.

The ways in which these tensions manifest themselves vary, depending on complex interactions between class and gender, and indeed race, although this is not dealt with in this chapter. For example, Henwood (1998) noted that the women who enter 'masculine work', such as the engineers she interviewed, are under considerable pressure to emphasize their femininity in various ways as their chosen occupation tends to undermine it. Also, Redman and Mac an Ghaill (1997) detected an interesting change in attitude towards intellectual work amongst middle-class boys on joining the sixth form when they became considerably more positive about academic achievement. Redman and Mac an Ghaill regarded this as part of a key cultural transition into the world of post-compulsory education and the labour market. In this context, intellectual superiority, which they described as 'muscular intellectualness', became an acceptable form of masculinity. Development of this form of masculinity effectively distinguishes this group from other, lower achieving young men and their choice of subjects separates them from young women. In this way, they are accumulating social and cultural capital that will prepare them for entry into high pay, high status employment.

Hodkinson and Sparkes (1997) describe the complexity of the factors involved in young people's decision-making processes (see also Kirton, Chapter 11 in this volume). This includes their feelings and emotions, their own experiences, their ability to access information, their perceptions of the opportunities open to them, their family backgrounds and also their class and gender. They point to 'the futility of policy-making that oversimplifies, or is ignorant of, the social and cultural complexity at which it is directed' (Hodkinson and Sparkes, 1997: 41).

Conclusion

In considering solutions to the underachievement of boys and girls it seems essential that we avoid quick fix solutions that are based on stereotypical ideas about class, race and gender. Certainly the polarization of boys' 'failure' with girls' 'success' does not help us to analyse the problems around gender and social exclusion or, most importantly, to find solutions. As Skelton (1998) has pointed out, a number of initiatives designed to tackle boys' underachievement fall into this trap although they may not consciously set out to undermine girls' success. For example, it has been suggested that schoolwork is too 'feminine' and that this is why boys are disaffected and thus underachieve. This in turn has led to suggestions about how to make schoolwork more appealing to boys, but, if this results in encouraging outdated forms of masculinity, it is a strategy that would be doing boys, particularly working-class boys, a considerable disservice.

In addition, many of the initiatives dealing with boys' underachievement tend to concentrate on developing strategies for improving their perform-ance within the existing system (Bleach, 1998). Obviously teachers confronted with day-to-day problems need the opportunity to discuss concrete strategies for changing practice in the classroom. Indeed, the development of new materials and new forms of teaching and learning are an essential element for promoting change and improving the performance of both boys and girls. However, as we have learnt from the GIST and WISE initiatives mentioned above, a concentration on classroom practice alone can lead us to neglect some of the underlying systemic problems that contribute to gender-related underachievement.

The first step in developing a more inclusive system is a reassessment of some of the basic assumptions that our present system is founded on. Policy innovations that do not make this their first step are likely to cause more problems than they solve. For example, the National Curriculum, although introduced under a Conservative government, was in part an attempt to provide a broad-based, entitlement curriculum for all. This has had some positive effects, for example school students are required to take Mathematics and Science until Year 11 and, as a result, higher achieving girls are getting rather good results at GCSE. However, the National Curriculum subjects studied in secondary school are based on a

19th-century liberal curriculum developed from the traditionally accepted formula for educating upper-class boys (Green, 1995). Consequently the middle-class values embedded in its structure have resulted in widespread disaffection amongst working-class boys and girls.

To some extent the problems of the National Curriculum and the exclusive nature of the post-compulsory system have been recognized by New Labour. In a press release entitled '£800,000 Boost to Motivate Disaffected Teenagers' (DfEE, 1998f) David Blunkett was reported as saying:

> Too many youngsters leave school without a single qualification to their name. Many others effectively drop out a year or two before the school-leaving age. For these teenagers we need to offer something more than the National Curriculum. In the past these youngsters could have learnt a trade and seen the direct link between training and work. We need to rebuild those links.

In addition to outlining specific projects Blunkett also highlights the possibility of disapplying the National Curriculum in certain cases to allow more participation in work-related curriculum initiatives. However, there is no mention in Blunkett's speech of the possible benefits to all young people that a curriculum more closely connected to work and the requirements of adult life might offer. Rather the initiatives concentrate on alleviating the problems of particularly visible groups including disaffected boys: 'The one year projects will develop school–college links; enhance work experience and target work-related learning at the disaffected – especially boys.'

The government has launched a number of initiatives designed to motivate and engage disaffected young people, for example New Start, Fresh Start and New Deal. Although there is considerable justification for some urgent action to tackle some of our most pressing social and educational problems, it is as yet unclear whether the 'New Initiative' approach represents the sum total of New Labour's solutions to social exclusion or whether some of the more systemic problems of education and training will be addressed. At the time of writing the first Education Action Zones have been launched, the post-compulsory qualifications system is under review and we await the review of the National Curriculum. However, if the Government wishes to tackle the problem of gender-related underachievement two distinct organizational features associated with both the National Curriculum and the post-compulsory curriculum and qualifications need to be addressed.

The first is familiar to most practitioners and policymakers involved in 14+ education, and that is the academic/vocational divide which, it has been argued, represents the division between middle-class and working-class education (Finegold et al, 1990). Even John Major's Conservative Government recognized this as an issue and called for 'parity of esteem' between the academic and the vocational in the 1991 White Paper *Education and Training for the 21st Century*. Despite this, the same White Paper announced the introduction of the three-track qualification system of A level, GNVQ and NVQ for post-compulsory education and training. This served to accentuate and compound the differences between the academic and the vocational curriculum and so stifle the development of innovative projects which attempted to cross the divide (Hodgson and Spours, 1997). This situation has arisen precisely because the practical expertise associated with vocational education has been regarded as inferior to intellectual skill, not only by Conservative governments but also by many progressive teachers and educationalists. This grew from a concern to ensure that all children had access to the best general education available and that working-class children should not be fobbed off with practical subjects designed to prepare them for low status jobs. There have been very few policy initiatives which recognize the deficits in the academic curriculum with the notable exception of TVEI, which set out to modernize the curriculum by specifically linking it to the changing demands of the workplace (Young, 1998). Although local schemes were often founded on a narrow interpretation of the initiative, more imaginative schemes resulted in some radical developments that made significant inroads into the academic/vocational divide.

The second, but less theorized and discussed feature of our curriculum and qualifications system, stems from gender divisions which, as we have seen above, have an equally significant effect on participation and achievement. Jane Roland Martin (1985) used the concept of the productive/reproductive dichotomy to describe how the education system has emphasized skills and values related to the public 'productive' sphere, where men have always been dominant, and relegated traditional female capacities to the private sphere. Indeed, as Spender (1981) points out, the 19th-century liberal curriculum was developed when women were still excluded from most areas of formal education and, as a result, they had little influence on its development. Martin argues that female capacities, which she identifies as caring, concern and connection, should be incorporated into the curriculum, not as separate subjects in the way that, for example, home economics was, but as part of all areas of study. If we fail to do so, she argues, these 'nurturing capacities' will retain their lower status and remain the responsibility of women to develop in the private sphere.

Gaskell (1992) makes the comparison between the academic/vocational divide and the productive/reproductive dichotomy noting that: 'The distinction between women's knowledge and men's knowledge has been just as deeply ingrained in the curriculum as the distinction between vocational and liberal knowledge.' She also points to the remarkable similarities between the academic/vocational divide and the productive/reproductive dichotomy in that they both replicate the hierarchies and divisions that occur outside school. They both work on common sense views about class and gender within our culture and they are both socially constructed dichotomies as indeed are the differential values assigned to them.

Although the divisions are never entirely clear cut when we use such typologies, frameworks of this kind can help us to consider some of the underlying structures that make our education and training system socially exclusive rather than socially inclusive. They help us to consider solutions that are based on a reassessment of the purposes and values of our system rather than focusing on the failure of certain groups. However, this approach entails a radical reassessment of the education system including some of the most basic aspects of the curriculum as Jane Kenway (1993: 96) points out when discussing science and technology:

> Not girls', boys' or society's options are enhanced by allowing current versions of maths, science and technology to dominate our perceptions of useful knowledge. Such perceptions not only downgrade the so-called 'soft' subjects, they also steer students away from the values such subjects – at best – embody and the human questions that they encourage students to ask . . . Clearly students of both sexes need an inclusive and expansive curriculum.

It does seem evident that young people attempting to make sense of a complex, rapidly changing world deserve what Michael Young describes as a 'Curriculum of the Future' (Young, 1998) rather than one based on the values and purposes of a previous era. Whether New Labour will meet this challenge or rely on high profile 'New' initiatives is yet to be seen.

References

Adkins, L and Leonard, D (1996) *The Family of Young People, Their Education and Post-16 Careers*, ESRC end of Award Report ROOO221179

Arnot, M *et al* (1998) *Recent Research on Gender and Educational Performance,* Ofsted, The Stationery Office, London

Bates, I (1993) A Job which is 'Right for Me'? in *Youth and Inequality* (1993) ed I Bates and G Riseborough, University Press, Buckingham

BBC (1994) *Panorama: The Future is Female*, 24 October

BBC (1995) *Panorama: Men Aren't Working*, 16 October

Bleach, K (1998) *Raising Boys' Achievement in Schools,* Trentham Books, London

Boaler, J (1998) Mathematical equity – underachieving boys or sacrificial girls? *International Journal of Inclusive Education*, **2** (2), pp 119–34

Bonney, N and Jeffrey, G (1998) *The Truth Behind the Full Monty*, Careers Guidance Today, **6** (4), Winter

Cohen, M (1998) 'A habit of healthy idleness': boys' underachievement in historical perspective, in *Failing Boys: Issues in gender and achievement,* ed D Epstein, J Elwood, V Hey and J Maw, Open University Press, Buckingham

Deem, R (1981) State Policy and Ideology in the Education of Women, 1944–1980, *British Journal of Sociology of Education*, **2** (2), pp 131–43

Department of Education/Employment Department/Welsh Office (1991) *Education and Training for the 21st Century*, White Paper, HMSO, London

DfEE (1995) *Participation in Education and Training by 16–18-year-olds in England: 1984/5 to 1994/5*, Statistical Bulletin Department for Education and Employment, The Stationery Office, London

DfEE (1997) *Youth Cohort Study: The activities and experiences of 16-year-olds: England and Wales: 1996,* Statistical Bulletin 8/97, Department for Education and Employment, London

DfEE (1998a) *Participation in Education and Training by 16–18-year-olds in England: 1987 to 1997*, Statistical Bulletin 335/98, Department for Education and Employment, The Stationery Office, London

DfEE (1998b) *GCSE/GNVQ and GCE A/AS/Advanced GNVQ Results for Young People in England, 1997/98 (provisional)*, Statistical First Release 557/98, Department for Education and Employment, London

DfEE (1998c) Byers outlines co-ordinated action to tackle boys' underachievement, Press release, 5 January, Department for Education and Employment, London

DfEE (1998d) *Labour Market and Skills Trends 1998/1999,* Department for Education and Employment, London

DfEE (1998e) *Increasing Demand for Technical Graduates,* Skills and Enterprise Executive Issue 3/98, Department for Education and Employment, London

DfEE (1998f) £800,000 boost to motivate disaffected teenagers, Press release, 1 July, Department for Education and Employment, London

ED (1992) *Labour Market Skills and Trends 1992/1993*, Employment Department, London

Epstein, D (1998) Real boys don't work: 'underachievement', schooling and gender relations, in *Failing Boys: Issues in gender and achievement*, ed D Epstein, J Elwood, V Hey and J Maw, Open University Press, Buckingham

Finegold, D *et al* (1990) *A British Baccalauréate: Overcoming divisions between education and training,* Institute for Public Policy Research, London

Gaskell, J (1992) *Gender Matters from School to Work,* Open University Press, Buckingham

Gillborn, D and Gipps, C (1996) *Recent Research on the Achievement of Ethnic Minority Pupils,* Ofsted Reviews of Research, HMSO, London

Green, A (1995) Technical education and state formation in nineteenth-century England and France, *History of Education,* **24** (2), pp 123–39

Hakim, C (1979) Occupational segregation: a comparative study, Research Paper 9, Department of Employment, London

Henwood, F (1998) Engineering difference: discourses on gender, sexuality and work in a college of technology, *Gender and Education*, **10** (1), pp 35–49

HESA (1996) *Qualifications Obtained by and Examination Results of Higher Education Students in England and in the UK for the Academic Year 1994/95,* Higher Education Statistics Agency

Hodgson, A and Spours, K (1997) *Dearing and Beyond: 14–19 qualifications, frameworks and systems*, Kogan Page, London

Hodkinson, P and Sparkes, A (1997) Careership: a sociological theory of career decision making, *British Journal of Sociology of Education*, **18** (1), pp 29–44

175

Kelly, A (ed) (1981) *The Missing Half: Girls and science education*, Manchester University Press, Manchester

Kenway, J (1993) 'Non-traditional' pathways: are they the way to the future? in *Gender Matters in Education Administration and Policy*, ed J Blackmore and J Kenway, Falmer Press, London

Kessler, S *et al* (1985) Gender relations in secondary schooling, in *Gender and the Politics of Schooling* (1987) ed M Arnot and G Weiner, Hutchinson, London

Mac an Ghaill, M (1994) *The Making of Men: Masculinities, sexualities and schooling*, Open University Press, Buckingham

McCrae, S (1991) *Flexible Working Time and Family Life*, Policy Studies Institute, London

Mahony, P (1998) Girls will be girls and boys will be first, in *Failing Boys: Issues in gender and achievement,* ed D Epstein, J Elwood, V Hey and J Maw, Open University Press, Buckingham

Martin, J R (1985) *Reclaiming a Conversation: The ideal of the educated woman,* Yale University Press, New Haven, CT

NACRO (1998) *Wasted Lives,* National Association for the Care and Rehabilitation of Offenders

NEAB (1996) *Gender differences in the GCSE*, NEAB Standard, Summer

Parry, G (1997) Patterns of participation in higher education in England: a statistical summary, *Higher Education Quarterly*, **51** (1), pp 6–28

Payne, J (1998) *Routes at Sixteen: Trends and choices in nineties research*, Report No 55, DfEE Research Briefs

Pearce, N and Hillman, J (1998) *Wasted Youth: Raising achievement and tackling social exclusion,* Institute for Public Policy Research, London

Plummer, G (1998) Forget gender, class is still the real divide, *Times Educational Supplement*, 23 January

Power, S *et al* (1998) Schoolboys and schoolwork: gender identification and academic achievement, *International Journal of Inclusive Education*, **2** (2), pp 135–53

Redman, P and Mac an Ghaill, M (1997) Educating Peter: the making of a history man, in *Border Patrols: Policing the boundaries of heterosexuality*, ed D L Steinberg, D Epstein and R Johnson, Cassell, London

Skeggs, B (1989) Gender reproduction in further education, *British Journal of Sociology of Education*, **9** (2), pp 131–49

Skeggs, B (1997) *Formations of Class and Gender*: *Becoming respectable,* Sage, London

Skelton, C (1998) Feminism and research into masculinities and schooling, *Gender and Education*, **10** (2), pp 217–27

Spender, D (1981) Education: the patriarchal paradigm and the response to feminism, in *Gender and the Politics of Schooling* (1987), ed M Arnot and G Weiner, Hutchinson, London

Unwin, L and Wellington, J (1995) Reconstructing the work-based route: lessons from the Modern Apprenticeship, in *The Vocational Aspect of Education*, **47** (4), pp 337–52

Wallace, C (1987) From girls and boys to women and men: the social reproduction of gender, in *Gender and the Politics of Schooling*, ed M Arnot and
G Weiner, Hutchinson, London

Whyte, *et al* (eds) (1985) *Girl Friendly Schooling*, Methuen, London

Wilkinson, H and Mulgan, G (1995) *Freedom's Children: Work, relationships and politics for 18–34-year-olds in Britain today*, Demos, London

Willis, P (1977) *Learning to Labour: How working-class kids get working-
class jobs*, Saxon House, Aldershot

Yates, L (1985) Is Girl Friendly Schooling What Girls Need?, in *Girl
Friendly Schooling*, ed J Whyte, R Deem, L Kant and M Cruickshank,
Methuen, London

Young, M F D (1998) *The Curriculum of the Future: From the new sociology
of education to a critical theory of learning*, Falmer, London

10

Special Needs, Inclusion and Social Exclusion

Jenny Corbett

Introduction

This chapter will examine the ways in which the area of special education has addressed issues of inclusion and social exclusion. These have become polarized into ideological positions based upon either the medical model or the social model of disability. The politics of special education exemplifies the prevailing tensions that exist between a market economy of education and inclusive values relating to justice and equity. Many of the dilemmas that relate to discriminatory practices regarding ethnicity, gender and social class are relevant to disabled learners. Where the difference is significant, however, is in the contentious assessment procedures surrounding the diagnosis and prognosis of various disabilities. Other learners are generally seen as distinctly male or female, white or black, wealthy or poor. These factors are more readily discernible in most aspects of equal opportunities policy-making but disability remains a fluid and contested concept. This is one of the reasons why special education must be recognized as an intensely political arena, although for many years it was assumed to be largely apolitical, based on notions of care and compassion. It is an integral part of the education system, influenced by market forces and inextricably bound up with those issues that affect education as a whole.

This chapter will begin by indicating the extent to which current special education theorizing addresses disaffection, non-participation and social exclusion. It will then illustrate ways in which schools and colleges are trying to confront these challenges and discuss the nature of those obstacles which market forces create and which threaten inclusive values. Whilst the central debates will be around the 14–19 age range, illustrative examples will include the primary and higher education sectors. Social exclusion does not begin or end at set points but is often a life-long process of experiencing alienation and frustration and, therefore, it needs to be addressed in the early stages of education as well as being recognized as a justification for the extension of lifelong learning opportunities.

Special Education theorizing and social exclusion

There has been a gradual but distinctive shift of emphasis over recent years which has moved special education theorists away from what is termed a medical model into an allegiance with a social model of disability. This has also meant a move away from the traditional dominance of psychological theorizing towards a more sociological and curriculum-focused way of assessing situations. The medical model assumed an 'in-child deficit', wherein the problems that children were experiencing in school and in the classroom were directly attributed to their disabilities and were not seen as a response to external factors. The social model recognizes the negative impact of discrimination, prejudice and inequity. Social exclusion has become a significant issue in relation to pupils with special educational needs who are excluded from mainstream provision in increasing numbers.

In a recent analysis of the discourse of inclusion, Slee (1998) suggests that inclusion is interpreted in widely different ways. It can just refer to technical issues such as resourcing, managing, social grouping and instructional design. Slee presents the practicalities of inclusive practices as a form of cosmetic surgery that fails to excise the deep culture of exclusion. Taking the example of ADHD (Attention Deficit Hyperactivity Disorder), he questions the value to the excluded pupils themselves of the specialist treatment they receive. He suggests instead that the immediate beneficiaries of exclusion and chemical treatment are the other students, the teachers and parents who are all relieved of a difficult problem. This is an example of special education as policing, presented within a medical model of drug treatment. It is an irony that a market-driven school culture has promoted a return to medical models of disability, particularly in relation to labels like ADHD, dyslexia and Asperger's syndrome, all of which have recently become more readily diagnosed as constituting specific forms of special educational need.

Slee's perspective is valuable, as he looks from an Australian perspective at policy-making in the UK. He reflects that:

> Particular forms of schooling promote greater levels of exclusion. The current surge in suspension and exclusion in the UK accompanies the press for selection, back to basics, market competition, league tables, inspection and national standardised testing. Within this educational policy context, conservative special educational theory has a glove-like relationship with the hand of exclusive schooling.
>
> (Slee, 1998: 134)

Slee calls for a radical reform in special educational theory in which theorists are prepared to confront the politics of exclusion and will refuse to be complicit in the excluding process.

Special needs and social exclusion zones

Whilst Slee recognizes the effect of competition in and between schools as a facet of exclusion, it is important also to acknowledge the negative impact of poverty, unemployment and overall social exclusion on school performance. It is no coincidence that schools in the most socially deprived areas of inner cities tend to have the highest levels of children deemed to have special educational needs.

In the recent report on truancy and school exclusion, the Social Exclusion Unit (1998a) confirmed that grounds for exclusion from school varied widely between different schools, some relating to issues as minor as the wearing of correct school uniform. They also noted wide variations between LEAs, recording that the school exclusion rate in Hammersmith and Fulham was four times that of Newham and more than six times that of Oxfordshire. The report suggested that a positive approach to avoiding high rates of school exclusion was to create unambiguous rules in the school, with a clear hierarchy of sanctions that are applied consistently. Parents, staff and governors needed to demonstrate solidarity and to support agreed policies.

In February 1998, a case came to the Central Criminal Court in London which shocked the general public in that it involved alleged sexual abuse by 10-year-old children in a primary school setting. I made a close study of this case at the time as it was especially focused around the special educational needs of the accused and the alleged victim. My major concern was to evaluate the extent to which a child, who was presented as displaying emotional and behavioural difficulties, could cope in the alien environment of a courtroom. Consequently, the key observations emerging from this research recorded the ways in which the woman judge acted as a discourse conduit to enable the child concerned to express her feelings and perceptions in what was a frightening and bizarre experience for her (Corbett, 1998). Other aspects of this study illustrated the overwhelming obstacles that some children and their families have to confront when schooling is linked to social exclusion and poverty.

The number of exclusions from the primary school which these children attended was unusually high even in a borough with a high exclusion rate. The very features that the Social Exclusion Unit report indicates are fundamental to fostering an orderly school community were absent here.

There had been a high turnover of staff, including headteachers, which led to inconsistency and a lack of shared sanctions. Tensions between some parents, staff and governors meant that there were not agreed procedures on policy relating to behaviour and there had been instances where parents had challenged staff on their decisions relating to discipline. The school had gained a reputation as being out-of-control, with children running riot and going on and off the premises at will. When this case came to the attention of the popular press, the school and the surrounding estate was presented in some tabloids as indicative of all that was wrong with urban state education in Britain in the late 1990s. Not only were the children presented as potential criminals but also their teachers were seen as weak and ineffective and their parents as irresponsible. Within the coverage by tabloid newspapers, there was an equation of special educational needs with social exclusion and degeneracy. The inference was redolent of the eugenics movement earlier in the century in suggesting that this was an underclass that bred mad or bad children who would go on to become a social menace, draining the public purse.

If we are to grasp the uncomfortable side of social exclusion and its relationship with the labelling of children as having special educational needs, we need to confront deep-rooted prejudice against people with perceived learning disabilities or disturbed behaviour. The tabloids provide a more powerful and accurate indicator of public attitudes than do the plethora of academic texts on inclusion and exclusion. There is no sensitivity towards political correctness; rather, the bigotry and fear of many ill-informed readers are fuelled by sensationalizing and simplifying what are complex and intractable social issues. What is significant for the children concerned is that, unless they are highly resilient, they are likely to absorb these negative images of themselves and take on the roles of passive victim or social outsider.

An inclusive curriculum and school culture

One of the major challenges for a school in an area which is characterized by social exclusion is to adopt a culture, pedagogy and curriculum which is truly inclusive of all learners. Mortimore (1998) has recently noted that the dramatic rise in school exclusions is directly related to market forces and reflects the inequities within such a system. In secondary schools, there are four boys excluded for every one girl and in primary schools, fourteen boys for every one girl. There are seven Afro-Caribbean boys to every one white boy and six statemented pupils to every one non-statemented pupil. There is a real dilemma for those secondary schools least favoured by parents being forced to take disproportionate numbers of the most challenging pupils. This calls for exceptional skills from headteachers and for a cohesive commitment from staff to confront and overcome the debilitating effects of a competitive, unequal market economy. It is easier for teachers to work with selected groups if they have to achieve specific attainment targets, yet there are strong directives from the government that they wish to promote inclusive education within the mainstream wherever possible (Morris, 1998).

Prime Minister Tony Blair recognizes the relationship between social exclusion and learning disabilities in saying:

> Our crusade to drive up standards in education is all part of the attack on social exclusion. There is no worse form of exclusion than being unable to read and write. That is why there can be no backing down from the tough targets we have

set to raise standards of literacy and numeracy in schools. Poverty of ambition in education and an acceptance of second best have damaged the country for too long.

(Blair, 1998: 26)

Effective schools are thus equated with high achieving schools, which succeed with the intake they have. Including all learners in the culture of a school requires that teachers be prepared to listen with respect to views which might be outside their own experience and to recognize that there are multiple intelligences, not just those which are accorded high academic and social status (Corbett, 1998b). There are tensions between recognizing individual needs and promoting inclusive values. It may be seen to be within the very nature of what constitutes inclusivity that it promotes community rather than individualized values by establishing goals of social responsibility, active citizenship, solidarity and co-operation. Yet there remains an impetus to balance a commitment to overall high achievement with individual needs and pedagogic realism that is better approached through individual target setting and a form of 'connective pedagogy'. The teacher connects firstly with the individual and then connects them with the wider community of classroom, school, recreation and housing (Corbett and Norwich, 1998, 1999). Addressing this 'connective pedagogy' has to involve an awareness of the baseline from which learners start and the nature of the community of which the school is a part.

Two examples of inner-city comprehensive schools will be used to demonstrate how it is possible to address disaffection, non-participation and social exclusion. Both these schools are located in social exclusion zones according to current government criteria. They have high numbers of children defined as having special educational needs yet both manage to keep low rates of exclusion and both have developed a rise in popularity among local parents such that their schools have become over-subscribed. I shall examine the processes by which they achieved this success, using the following sub-headings: confronting the context; high expectations; pride in the school and public relations; staff development; curriculum and pedagogy; relationship with the local community.

Confronting the context

In School A, the average reading age on entry is nine years and many pupils are reading well below this. Sixty per cent of pupils are on free school meals, high proportions have a combination of behavioural difficulties and learning disabilities and the school is in the 5 per cent of the most disadvantaged in the country. In 1975, when it opened, 95 per cent of its intake were black Afro-Caribbean, whereas now it has 40 per cent white pupils. School B has 44 per cent Bangladeshi pupils, 22 per cent refugees and a total English as an additional language intake of 81 per cent. Of its total school community, 36 per cent have statements of special educational needs and the lowest achieving group in the school consists of white working-class boys and girls. Both of these schools reflect disproportionately high intakes of the hard-to-teach groups to which Mortimore refers, which creates a distinct challenge for academic standards.

High expectations

School A fosters high expectations in pupils through a process of providing positive role models and through mentoring. In a school where 60 per cent of pupils are from various ethnicities, including Chinese, Vietnamese, Asian and Afro-Caribbean, 23 per cent of the staff are black. This is a remarkably high proportion for the average secondary school and is instantly impressive on visiting the school. The black headteacher who has been there for many years is a most positive role model in himself, demonstrating to the pupils that black people can achieve positions of authority and status. He takes care to recruit good quality black teachers to serve as positive role models for the pupils. The mentoring scheme, which has existed for four years, links successful employees working in big city firms with pupils in the school. This provides a focal point and gives added motivation to a sample of pupils in years 9 to 13, deliberately selected as a mix of gender, ethnicity and academic capability. There was a small-scale research study linked to the school that indicated that those pupils who had been mentored achieved a higher GCSE outcome than those who had not. Part of its recognition of cultural diversity is that GCSE Cantonese is offered to pupils.

School B focuses upon the quality of teaching and learning, recognizing that only 4 per cent of its pupil intake is at the higher level of the ability range. They run an Open Learning Centre that is open for students from Monday to Friday after school and on Saturdays. It is supported by a Learning Resources Manager, an Information Technology Manager and the teachers who work in it are paid overtime to do this. Part of their response to raising levels of achievement has been to provide this additional support and to recognize specific individual and cultural needs. Bengali is taught to Advanced level and Bengali pupils come at 16+ from other local schools to participate in this opportunity. It has often been the case that pupils of 14 or 15 join the school unable to even read or write in their own language. Part of the approach to raise achievements has been to value community links and extend notions of progression.

Pride in the school and public relations

School A has a most attractive entrance hall with exceptionally well-presented paintings on the walls, all done by pupils. This immediately conveys a sense of pride in the appearance of the school as does the policy of the headteacher of using a sample of 15- and 16-year-olds to show visitors around their school, rather than being the guide himself. I was very impressed with the way in which the pupils spoke of their school with evident affection. This seemed to be completely genuine as did the easy, respectful manner in which teachers talked to the pupils throughout my visit. There was a celebration of difference in wall displays showing maps of where all the pupils came from in the world and in celebrating the achievements of black women and the history of black civil rights through a study of Malcolm X.

In School B, there has been a tremendous effort to counter racial tensions by working to foster a cohesive school community. A drama group was brought in to help pupils work through some of the issues related to their experiences of racist attacks encountered on their journey to school. In both instances, the difficulties which some of their pupils are coping with are confronted and worked through rather than ignored as being outside the responsibility of the school setting.

Staff development

Staff development is a crucial element of both schools' programmes for raising levels of achievement. Both headteachers recognize that working in their schools calls for exceptional commitment and energy and they reward their staff accordingly. In School A there is a budget of £20,000 for teacher training among the 60 staff and the school regularly runs staff-based INSET. In School B staff are well supported at a clerical level, with lunchtime supervision and with less meetings than usual to attend. They receive extra pay for their additional duties. Both headteachers have established the stable levels of staffing which are so instrumental to success in inclusive schools and they have attracted committed people who they then nurture. As the head of School B emphasized, it is very important to attract the right people.

Curriculum and pedagogy

In School A there are many departments which have consistently produced their own teaching materials specifically designed to meet the needs of their intake. They have recently started considering buying more course books and are beginning to balance the use of their own and published materials. They have always taught in mixed-ability groups but will be setting by ability in Year 8 Science and Mathematics from now onwards because of the difficulty of teaching children who are unable to read alongside others who have higher literacy skills. The teachers have been finding the new assessment targets frustrating as all their effort can go into those pupils who are able to get through the SATs, leaving behind those that cannot. They are trying to concentrate on the Action Points, helping pupils to see what it is they need to do to achieve the next level.

As part of their approach to pedagogy, School B uses black mentors with the credibility to demonstrate that they have moved from a low base to high standing through a process of self-help, showing to the pupils that they can succeed despite disadvantage. The school has also appointed a senior teacher responsible for Community Development, who is working initially with parents. This appointment indicates the importance that both schools place on the role of the wider community in the overall learning experience. It is a pedagogy of community values and community pride.

Relationship with the local community

School A brings the local community groups in, with Saturday and Sunday schools for Chinese and Vietnamese, Afro-Caribbean and Turkish groups. School B has a Somali Chair of Governors and has hired a community consultant to get the views of the local community. On Saturdays and Sundays, School B is used by the Bengali community. It has arranged coffee mornings in the community rather than bringing people in. In an effort to reduce racial tensions, local police have been asked to be out on the streets to protect children coming to and from school, just as they would police the streets for a football game. The school has planned a residential weekend for Bangladeshi mothers. Staff have been trained in conflict resolution and spend time working with groups of, for example, Somali and Bengali pupils, to dissipate potential difficulties before they escalate. Both schools have avoided high levels of exclusion, although it is used as a short-term option.

Both schools recognize and confront challenges within their local communities: drug dealing; racial conflicts; poor housing; shifting populations. They have both managed to offer improved facilities in recent years, funded by various enterprises and sponsorship: in School A, a new music centre and an excellent sports arena; and in School B a new community wing and sports hall. Both schools are now over-subscribed and seen by local parents, including those white parents who were initially hostile towards what they saw as 'black' schools, as both high achieving and maintaining good standards of discipline.

What a detailed examination of sample secondary schools, like this, can offer is a realization that promoting an inclusive school culture requires effort and a sustained value system that can withstand prevailing and often destructive trends. It does not happen by magic.

Participation in further education

In the further education sector the issue of participation is closely bound up with the restraints imposed by a market economy. Colleges are used to developing strategies to counter disaffection among their students, having for many years coped with those who came reluctantly on day-release or who were attending as an alternative to the dole. Reflecting on disaffection in further education, a decade ago, I suggested that a realization of the real limitations behind the rhetoric of freedom of choice can promote disaffection. This applies to both students and staff in post-compulsory education. External factors can severely impede scope to exercise choice in decision-making (Corbett, 1990: 4).

This disaffection bred by frustration may be seen to have escalated during the last few years, as uncertainty and change became endemic to the sector. For staff, drastic cuts in funding, non-financially viable colleges going bankrupt and many employees being asked to take pay cuts in order to keep their jobs have eroded their sense of loyalty and commitment. For students, changes in funding procedures have reduced the flexible range of options that offered a wider scope for participation.

This inflexibility has particularly influenced the way in which colleges are able to respond to prospective students whose disabilities or learning difficulties make considerable demands on their financial and staffing resources. The Further and Higher Education Act 1992 introduced reforms regarding the organization and funding of further education, which have had particular implications for the assessment of students with special educational needs. This assessment is taking place at two levels, with the LEA deciding whether a disabled student should attend their local college or go away from home to a specialist residential college (a far more expensive option). The local college identifies support needs to gain funding from the Further Education Funding Council (FEFC). As Johnstone (1995) says, 'The FEFC clearly anticipates that colleges will continue to assess students and relate any demands for additional resources to the clarity of their assessment practices. This has a number of implications for students who are socially disaffected, rather than demonstrating distinct physical and/or sensory disabilities' (p 28). Guidelines from the FEFC on how to calculate additional support are highly complicated and can be widely interpreted by different colleges.

Tresham (1998) gives the following example of how this assessment operates in practice and demonstrates the reliance on external funding:

Student A
He wishes to enrol on a BTEC National Course in Sports Science. He is hearing impaired and has been attending a special boarding school for the deaf. His first contact with the college is through the visiting teacher for the deaf who makes an appointment with the Learning Support Co-ordinator at the college. The interview lasts for an hour, during which time his support needs are discussed. In order to access the curriculum he will need a note-taker in all his theory classes (15 hours per week). He is also dyslexic and will need one-to-one support in the Learning Centre for at least one hour per week. He will also need a laptop computer. The cost of his support is calculated on an hourly basis with different hourly rates charged for the note-taker and the dyslexic support. The depreciation on the laptop computer is also added. An extra cost is added for the pre-entry interview and reviews once a term with the Learning Support Co-ordinator. This student also needs an hour per week support from the specialist teacher of the deaf. The total cost of student A's support is in excess of £13,500 so he is put into Band 7, for which the college receives 900 units. Each unit is worth £16.20 so

this one student is worth £14,580 to the college. It may appear to be a large sum of money but he will almost certainly cost the college more than that.

(Tresham, 1998: 29)

Whereas, in the recent past, disabled students came into further education on a much more ad hoc basis, often reliant upon the goodwill and level of commitment of individual college principals, the FEFC procedures now ensure than each element of their additional requirements is costed. This has the advantage of being a standardized procedure and, therefore, fairer to all students in general. However, it can mean that some particularly diffi-cult cases are judged to be unsuitable for inclusion. In her recent research, Hallahan (1998) noted that some students whose behaviour was unpre-dictable, potentially dangerous and anti-social, whether it be because of mental ill-health or learning disabilities, tended to be either excluded early in their college experience or refused entry at the initial assessment stage. As in any market culture, where funding is limited and accountability may demand a realistic level of safety for the majority rather than compassion for the few, individual needs are balanced against outcomes and overall performance indicators.

Participation and inclusion in higher education

In the introduction to this chapter I suggested that the issue which distin-guished disability from other areas of equal opportunities is that of assess-ment procedures and diagnosis leading to the allocation of resources. This is particularly the case in higher education, where students have to participate in a lengthy assessment process prior to their entitlement to a Disabled Student's Allowance (DSA). In a recent research study (Corbett and Parker, 1998), I found that the development of more focused and elaborate methods of assessment could lead to fewer students being entitled to the degree of support which might help them fully participate in the higher education learning experience. In the case study new university, there was an Access Centre being established, with funding from the HEFC. This was a resource base where students could try out technological equipment and be assessed for dyslexia. Because resources, including staffing support, were dependent upon the DSA, the small team of learning support staff found themselves having to turn away students who wanted their help but who did not have a label which entitled them to funding. As with the statementing procedures in the school sector, those with certain labels tended to be entitled to the DSA and those with unspecified learning difficulties had to cope with minimal support. Where new universities are encouraging the widening of access to non-traditional learners, it seems imperative that learning support systems be developed alongside this initiative. As it stands at present, certain groups of students (eg those with physical and sensory disabilities or with dyslexia) tend to receive a disproportionate share of the available support.

In her analysis of the impact of the Dearing, Kennedy and Fryer Committees, Webb (1998) suggests that the access agenda has been reconceptualized in terms of lifelong learning, equity and fairness. She reflects that:

> as long as diversity in the system ensures that the market value of educational experiences varies, competition will increase for access to the most sought after qualifications, and the principle of institutional autonomy will permit some institutions to operate lifelong learning within the spirit of selectivity, while others look more to the principles of equity.
>
> (Webb, 1998: 8)

This is already developing in different universities, where some see their mission to encourage local, mature students while others select from wide geographical areas. In relation to special educational needs, it has meant that certain inner-city new universities have already been labelled as catering for students needing additional support. One learning support co-ordinator told me that his university had received phone enquiries asking 'Are you the dyslexic university?' as the reputation which his Access Centre had gained for its high levels of support had made this aspect a prominent public perception. How many universities, in the competitive market economy, wish to gain a reputation for their support for students with special educational needs? As Webb suggests, many will choose to interpret lifelong learning as equating with selectivity rather than with equity, as this fits the market model.

Concluding reflections

I began this chapter by suggesting that special education is an intensely political issue, influenced by market forces and integrally linked with education as a whole. Taking the three key themes of disaffection, non-participation and social exclusion, I shall reflect on how they are illustrated within special educational provision.

Disaffection and the experience of social exclusion can begin very early, as the primary school case study example illustrated. Ten-year-olds had already become out of control and rejecting of what school had to offer. In this school, the LEA and the series of headteachers tried to address the impact on the pupils of living in a social exclusion zone and to redress the balance where they could. The challenge that this imposed was considerable, as school is only a small part of the total experience of these children. It is appropriate to refer to disaffected communities rather than just disaffected individual pupils. These are communities where people lose hope and self-respect, where they then find it very difficult to motivate their children. In the two detailed examples of what comprehensive schools can develop as a means of addressing community disaffection, strategies were shown which located the school very firmly within its particular community. The learning support programmes were not just about individual education plans but were about community needs, taking the school systems into the local area, where they could influence policing, family support networks and cultural pride. Both examples showed the need to be pro-active. Inclusion is not just about policy documents but it has to be acted upon consistently and courageously, for it is a political activity that demonstrates value systems.

Non-participation is a current concern in further and higher education. Learning support systems can help colleges and universities to include a wider range of learners than in the recent past. However, some colleges and universities are taking higher proportions of certain students than others. For example, many colleges are reluctant to take on students with a reputation for difficult and disruptive behaviour. Those colleges that do take these students may then risk losing the more motivated learners who will opt for alternative choices: the market works against the inclusion of disaffected learners in the post-compulsory stage. In higher education, students who can prove that they have dyslexia can gain access to resources that can significantly advantage them in relation to other students who have general difficulties with their work. It has become a growing trend that acquiring a label in higher education is an asset, not a stigma. This is another sign of the market economy that disability has to be pathologized in the out-dated medical model format if it is to be recognized as meriting additional resources. A social model of disability is politically popular but a high-risk within a bargaining culture.

Slee suggested that the conservative special education theorizing was insufficiently supportive of inclusion. In the current emphasis on competition and testing, inclusive values are continually threatened and it is difficult for practitioners or theorists to confront so systematic a market ideology. Perhaps one of the most positive aspects to emerge from the examples discussed in this chapter is that there are some brave headteachers who are using their market astuteness to support inclusion. Both examples described in detail were of failing schools turned round by business-minded headteachers who were able to combine an awareness of the market with a deep commitment to the community and the pupils. Their attitude and responsiveness was based on respect. This seems to me to be at the heart of inclusive practices. Respect, more than anything else, can help to heal the debilitating effects of social exclusion.

References

Blair, T (1998) In Britain today, millions are still trapped in a cash economy; vulnerable, extorted, prey to loan sharks. In Britain today, that is not acceptable, Leader comment, *The Observer*, 31 May, p 26

Corbett, J (1990) *Uneasy Transitions: Disaffection in post-compulsory education and training*, Falmer Press, Basingstoke

Corbett, J (1998a) 'Voice' in emancipatory research: imaginative listening, in *Articulating With Difficulty: Research voices in inclusive education*, ed L Barton and P Clough, Paul Chapman, London

Corbett, J (1998b) Inclusive education and school culture, *International Journal of Inclusive Education*, **2** (4), pp 301–16

Corbett, J and Norwich, B (1998) The contribution of special education to our understanding of values, schooling and the curriculum, *Curriculum Studies*, **6** (1), pp 85–96

Corbett, J and Norwich, B (1999) Pedagogy and learners with special educational needs, in *Pedagogy and its Impact on Learning*, ed P Mortimore, Paul Chapman, London

Corbett, J and Parker, V (1998) When does an initiative become a commitment? Establishing a secure service for disabled students in a case study of a British university, Third International Conference on Higher Education and Disability, University of Innsbruck, 13–16 July

Hallahan, C (1998) Inclusive further education in a market economy, PhD thesis, University of East London

Johnstone, D (1995) *Further Opportunities: Learning difficulties and disabilities in further education*, Cassell, London

Morris, E (1998) In . . . and out of the mainstream, *Guardian Education,* 9 June, p 4

Mortimore, P (1998) The current position of education in relation to social exclusion, Paper in seminar *The Educational Implications of Social Exclusion/Inclusion in Intercultural Urban Areas*, Institute of Education, University of London, 22–26 June

Slee, R (1998) The Politics of Theorizing Special Education, in *Theorizing Special Education*, ed C Clark, A Dyson and A Millward, Routledge, London

Social Exclusion Unit (1998) *Truancy and School Exclusion*, Report presented to Parliament, May

Tresham, A (1998) Learning support in colleges of further education: how effective is it and what effect does it have on retention and achievement?, MA thesis, University of London, Institute of Education

Webb, S (1998) What makes a fair system?, *Education Today and Tomorrow*, **50** (1), pp 6–8

11

Lessons from Access Education

Alison Kirton

Introduction

This chapter briefly traces the historical development of Access education[1] with its diverse schemes and routes to offer programmes of study to those 'who might be excluded, disadvantaged, delayed or otherwise deterred by a need to qualify for entry in more conventional ways' (Parry, 1996: 3).

Such education was traditionally aimed at mature adults and provided progression into higher education. However, at the end of the 1980s schemes were developed to provide Access education for 16–19-year-olds, influenced both by the success of Access education for mature adults and frustrated by the Government's persistent refusal to reform A levels.

Dependence on A levels as an entry requirement resulted in large numbers of young people being excluded from higher education. One such Access scheme, the Polytechnic Link Course (which became HE Link Course in 1992) located in a sixth form college in a North London borough provides the focus of this chapter. I undertook a small scale, case study, researching one cohort, 12 non-traditional A level students, by interviewing them at key points in their transition from college to higher education.

It is impossible to do full justice to the historical development of Access education here, however the policy cycle model developed by Bowe *et al* (Bowe and Ball with Gold, 1992) provides a useful analytic framework for organizing an understanding of some of the key issues in the development of Access education. Bowe and colleagues take a post-structuralist approach in which policy making is regarded as a cyclical process with policies being initiated in any of the primary contexts: practice, influence and text production. The authors use this approach to consider how the Education Reform Act, in particular, the National Curriculum, was 're-created' by teachers in schools according to institutional realities or the specific micro-politics of schools. I will be using it to locate three episodes of Access education in order to trace how such policies started as small 'pockets of activity' (Parry, 1996). They were then expropriated by the central state in the context of influence, and recontextualized as possible partial solutions to social and economic problems.

The post-structuralist approach to policy making is an attempt to move away from traditional policy analysis that tends to regard policy as initiated by central government, defined by legislation and something that 'gets done' to people by a chain of implementers. On the contrary, a more de-centred reading of the history of Access education shows that local, diverse and practice-led policies can also be re-created or recontextualized by the central state according to the macro-politics of power. Additionally this model demonstrates that policy making is conflictual, contradictory and often contingent.

Episode One: 1973–1982, pockets of activity

In histories of Access education the first official policy is often taken to be 1978, when the Department of Education and Science invited seven LEAs to set up pilot Access courses (Access studies) targeted, though not exclusively, at getting adults from ethnic minorities into the teaching profession. This took place against a 'bigger picture' of concern by the Labour Government about economic recession, unemployment and race relations.

Did policy on access originate here, in high places within and through the state? Rather the evidence seems to suggest that Access education policy had its roots in the context of practice. That it was 'a self-created collective movement from below . . . designed to transform a whole social system' (Parry, 1996). He describes 'pockets of activity' in the 1970s and into the 1980s that were mainly local, usually small, formally separate and often very different forms of Access activity. Historically there have been several schemes for allowing mature entrants into higher education: London University and those in the Joint Matriculation Board, for example, allowed entry by examination or assessment; pioneering courses in the 1970s were offered by Nelson and Colne College as alternatives to O and A levels, developed by the Open College Federation of the North West to accredit the prior learning of adults; 'Second Chance to Learn' courses, provided by the Workers Education Association; and also courses such as those at City Literary Institute in London specifically aimed at women returners. Additionally, links for Social Work and BEd courses for ethnic minorities were pioneered by the Polytechnic of North London and the City and East London College. All these activities were evidence of a robust commitment by teachers, polytechnic lecturers and admission tutors to notions of empowerment and social justice. Their pedagogic approach was usually informal and interactive, drawing on and affirming students' own experience (Green and Percy, 1991).

It is clear that Access education was initiated, in the context of practice, by teachers in further education colleges, adult education and polytechnics. The concept was then expropriated by the Department for Education and

Science as a possible partial solution to pressures on government at the time.

The Labour Government of the day was under pressure to respond to a White Paper from the Home Office,' The West Indian Community' (Home Office, 1977). This policy White Paper was itself a reaction to the anger and alienation of black young people on the streets of the major cities (John, 1981). Rimington (1992) describes the political and social conditions which came together to forge the first Access courses at City and East London College.

Civil order and a workable multi-racial society required there to be successful black role models and mentors for the next generation to identify with and emulate. The chimera of economic growth meant, in addition, tapping sources of unfilled academic talent and potential from all classes, races and from both sexes (Rimington, 1992: 23).

A more cynical view regards the policy as an attempt 'to diffuse disenchantment and disaffection in many alienated communities by creating a black middle-class in an effort to control communities from the inside' (quoted by Benn and Burton, 1995: 446, referencing Benn and Fieldhouse, 1991; Kearney and Diamond, 1990; John, 1981). It is also possible that the DES had a further political motive in supporting Access education since this would allow them to 'keep a significant presence in adult education and training in the face of the colonizing strategies of the Manpower Services Commission' (Lieven, 1989: 162). The MSC had been set up in 1974 by the Heath Government and was answerable to the Secretary of State for Employment. It was an effective autonomous organization with power to intervene in the educational system in ways that were not open to the Secretary of State for Education. Chitty (1991: 18) describes this power 'with its freedom of manoeuvre, it was in a good position to exploit the inertia and complacency of DES civil servants who placed the youth service, further education and adult education very low on their list of priorities'.

The four year DES pilot project included careful monitoring and evaluation. These assessments indicated sufficient evidence for Access education to be expanded further. At least two out of three students had succeeded at the preparatory stage and, of these, two-thirds were likely to complete their degrees and diplomas satisfactorily. Millins found that of 1,830 Access students 51 per cent were of Caribbean origin, 5 per cent of Asian origin, 37 per cent were white British and most students were working class (Millins, 1984). In the early 1980s higher education was elitist and exclusive with only 12.5 per cent of the 18–19 cohort participating (Benn and Fieldhouse, 1991). Despite the expansion recommended by the Robbins Report in 1963, the relative chances of working-class children entering higher education had not improved significantly (Egerton and Halsey, 1993).

Episode Two: 1983–1989

Derision

Research findings in 1984 as part of the Millins Report indicated that ex-Access students achieved significantly better completion and degree results than standard A level students in higher education. Despite this evidence, concerns were reported about the lowering of academic standards and the quality of courses, 'Arrangements of this kind can result in the formation of relationships and understandings that lead to students from Access courses being accepted for degree courses even if they lack the ability to reach degree standard' (DES, 1985: 70, Lindop Committee Report).

Subsequent research comparing the results of traditional and non-traditional students has shown such concerns raised by the Lindop Report to be largely unjustified (Bourner and Hamed, 1987).

The second attack on standards was more specific and centred on the Polytechnic of North London. Allegations of political bias and lack of academic rigour were made in relation to two Social Science degree courses operating 'direct entry' access policies. Her Majesty's Inspectorate upheld the allegations, calling into question the abilities of Access students and procedures for ensuring the standards for awards. However these attacks on standards had the unintended consequence of transforming these 'pockets of activity' into something more like a self-conscious Access movement. In 1986 a national organization, the Forum for Access Studies, was born to represent and promote Access education.

Regulation

The shift from equality concerns to quality control led to a national system for the accreditation of Access courses. The Council for National Academic Awards and the Committee of Vice Chancellors and Principals established a committee called the Access Courses Recognition Group whose main role was to license validating agencies to approve courses and award kitemarks. While there was a welcome for a national framework from Access educators as recognition of their work, there was also considerable disquiet, 'there was the fear that what some regarded as core principles and processes, positive action, integrated curricula, collaborative working and enhanced progression, might be displaced or diluted in the quest for wider acceptability' (Parry and Percy, 1995: 5). Some practitioners felt that despite the drawbacks of the national framework, it was developed 'with a lightness of touch, devolution and flexibility in the spirit of Access philosophy' (Rimington, 1992: 28).

However, Access courses that were kitemarked and validated, packaged and legitimated seemed to be replacing the original concept of Access education with its emphasis on a diversity of schemes and routes.

Normalization

The main aim of the national framework had been for Access courses to gain acceptability and currency in the higher education system as a whole. Yet the whole system was changing. The once aloof Universities, suffering a severe decline in the numbers of traditional A level entrants, began to consider mature students from non-traditional backgrounds. By the late eighties Access education was more centrally on the agenda not only of the universities but also of the Conservative government and multi-national companies. An important new pressure was the UK's international competitiveness in global markets related to the supply of highly qualified manpower particularly under-recruitment in Science and Technology courses in higher education. British Petroleum commissioned a report (Smithers and Robinson, 1989) on how such shortages could be best tackled. Radical changes were also taking place in the secondary school curriculum that led the Committee of Vice Chancellors and Principals and the Standing Conference on University Entrance, to request that Universities review their entrance policies.

Despite the continuing reluctance of some universities to respond positively to non-traditional entrants, by 1987 Access courses were officially recognized as the third route into higher education (DES, 1987), the other two being traditional A levels and vocational qualifications.

The policy cycle: recontextualization

The status of Access education had changed. Originally it was conceived as a minority provision strongly grounded in notions of social justice and empowerment by teachers in response to their students. By the late eighties it had come to be regarded as part of the solution to improving Britain's economic performance and dealing with a demographic trough. In terms of the policy cycle analytic framework, power had thus moved from the context of practice to the context of influence, the more conventional focus of text production. The concept of Access education had been decontextualized from its original location and recontextualized into a new assemblage of meanings and practices. It had become one of the major policy issues on influential agendas. By 1989 there were approximately 400 Access courses in 50 LEAs with 6,000 students in further education colleges, adult and community education centres and open college federations (figures quoted in Smithers and Robinson, 1989).

Episode Three: 1988–1994

New pockets of activity

In the late 1980s teachers in schools and colleges took advantage of the new climate of concern about poor staying-on rates, a decline in the

16–19 cohort and Britain's poor economic performance. They developed alternative schemes and routes to higher education and training for 16–19-year-olds. Teachers were both encouraged by the success of Access education and frustrated by the Government's refusal to reform A levels after ignoring the recommendations of reports such as Higginson (1988). Examples of these new 'pockets of activity' were: the Recording Achievement and Higher Education Project based in the Wigan LEA; the North Worcestershire Higher Education partnership; the Two Towns Project run by Keele University and Staffordshire Polytechnic; links between some ILEA schools and Sussex University; and British Petroleum's 'Aiming for a college education'. All these schemes aimed to develop links between schools and further and higher education by providing alternative routes and methods of accrediting learning, to target excluded or disadvantaged groups within the 16–19 age range.

The policy cycle: education and training markets

Many of these schemes have been overtaken by legislative changes in the context of influence. Successive Conservative governments since 1979 have introduced, consistently, if not coherently, educational policies aimed at re-structuring education along market lines. The Education Reform Act 1988 devolved the funding of education from the Local Education Authorities to the schools and further education colleges. In 1992 further education colleges and sixth form colleges became independent of local authority control and a new funding council was established. Consistent with other changes in educational policy, these newly incorporated colleges were 'a market hybrid in which local market competition is combined with strong central control from the FEFC with a mission to promote the rapid growth of the sector at reduced unit cost' (Betts, 1996).

This indicates a new modality of state control, consistent with research findings by Whitty, Power and Halpin (1998) in their international study of devolution and choice in education in five countries. They suggest:

> Despite the rhetoric about 'rolling back' or 'hollowing out' the state, certain aspects of state intervention have been maintained – indeed strengthened. The strong, evaluative state is a minimalist one in many respects, but a more powerful and authoritarian one in others.
>
> (Whitty, Power and Halpin, 1998: 46)

In higher education similar forces were at work, a single funding body was established and the formal distinctions between polytechnics and universities disappeared. Funding arrangements rewarded those institutions that could expand their numbers most cost effectively. Numerically this was the beginning of a mass system, 'British higher education has become a mass system in its public structures, but remains an elite one in its private instincts. . . The current age participation index in British higher education is 32 per cent, which suggests that the system is more than half way to becoming a universal system' (Scott, 1995: 2).

The marketization of education and the move to a mass system of higher education raise many interesting questions about the future of Access education.

Policy effects

Has Access education achieved the various aims set out by its advocates? Unfortunately until very recently reliable national statistics have not been collected systematically. We know that the numbers of mature entrants to first degrees doubled between 1980 and 1990 from 24,300 to 49,300 and by 1990 they constituted a third of all first degree students in England and Wales (DES/DFE 1988–1992). It is, however, a pity that the contribution of Access education to this increased participation rate by mature students cannot be accurately estimated.

Wakefield's (1993) research of 27 Access courses in 11 institutions, found a smaller proportion of women students than Millins (1984), although they are still the largest group overall. She attributes this to the emergence of 'second wave' courses in mathematics, science, business studies, engineering, computing and law, where the proportion of males to females was three to one. There was also a shift away from the participation of ethnic minority students with a fall of 50 per cent over previous figures. This she attributes to expansion outside the urban areas of the original 'pockets of activity'. In order for Access courses to succeed in attracting working-class students she recommended, 'If Access courses are to expand, the social class profile of students, as well as their gender and ethnicity, should be monitored and different groups targeted to prevent provision from beginning to mirror the existing social class inequalities in higher education' (Wakefield, 1993: 228). If the participation of ethnic minorities in Access courses has decreased since 1984 this has not been reflected in their participation in higher education. Modood (1993) refutes the long-standing claim of under-representation of ethnic minorities. He provides a complex picture with the over-representation of some groups and the under-representation of others. He shows that ethnic minority students are concentrated in the new universities in inner city areas. He recommends targeting poorly motivated white working-class populations through Access measures justified because virtually all working-class minority groups achieve better examination results than their white working-class peers.

While Access courses have undoubtedly made an important contribution the fact remains that while absolute access to higher education has increased for all, the middle class has maintained its relative advantage especially in their domination of the most prestigious institutions (Egerton and Halsey, 1993). It appears that the move to a mass system has merely resulted in more sophisticated forms of hierarchy with the terms 'old' and 'new' universities re-signifying the old divisions. Most of the 'old' universities continue to recruit traditional students on the basis of a combination of social origins and academic performance (Smith *et al*, 1993). Whilst there are greater numbers of non-traditional students in higher education, there is little evidence that this has transformed their social characters by making them more responsive in their curriculum offers and pedagogical approaches.

Policy in the context of practice: the HE link course

In 1988 Humanities teachers at Northside College, set up the HE Link Course. They had several motives and aims. They wished to provide Access opportunities for non-traditional students. They held a strong commitment to keeping local, mainly working class students within the educational system. The college, which had replaced the sixth forms in its partner schools, was extremely popular and over-subscribed. In the local economies of schooling, students from these partner schools with poor GCSE results, could easily lose out to better qualified A level students from elsewhere. This situation required a policy to provide distinct forms of learning support making it possible for such students to do A levels.

At this time polytechnics wanted students to matriculate. This was prior to massive expansion and the introduction of markets into higher education in 1992 which heralded a more flexible approach to admissions. The teachers decided to employ an A level framework rather than a more flexible structure usual in Access courses. This allowed students to matriculate and A levels were qualifications with currency in the labour market if they decided against the higher education option. A further aim was to empower students through development of the skills necessary to become both autonomous and collaborative learners. Students were recruited for the HE Link by tutors and admissions staff as having the potential for study in higher education but having under-achieved in their secondary schools for reasons of 'educational or social disadvantage'. Students were to choose two A level subjects in Humanities and Social Science and were to receive two support sessions of an hour and a half per week, one double staffed. This support programme was negotiated to meet the needs of students and the academic timetable. On successful completion and two E grades in their A levels, students were assured of a place in one of two polytechnics (a third was added to the scheme). These were chosen by teachers at Northside because they had contacts in the selected departments, known for their good pastoral systems and Access education traditions. While students might apply to other institutions, this two E grade offer was designed as an 'insurance' for students embarking on a two-year course.

Introducing the cohort

My study tracks 'the career trajectories' of twelve students, the 1990/ 1992 Cohort of the HE Link course. The term 'career trajectory' in studies of the transition to work has been critiqued by (Hodkinson and Sparkes, 1997) since they consider the term implies that such careers are determined, set and predictable. Drawing on Bourdieu's (Bourdieu and Passeron, 1977) concept of habitus,[2] they present a new model of career decision making called 'careership.' The first feature of the model refers to pragmatically rational decision making located in the habitus of the person making the decision. Secondly interactions with others in the 'field' are related to the unequal resources that different 'players' possess; and thirdly the model considers the location of decisions within the partly unpredictable pattern of turning points and routines that make up the life course. Their use of the concept of habitus is useful in bringing together structure and agency, seeing these students not as completely socially determined but as having certain choices within limits or constraints. This theorization helps to capture the conflict, contradiction and *adhoc*ery in human courses of action. Also useful is their framework of 'turning points' and 'routines' (Hodkinson and Sparkes, 1997) to analyse the transitions of this cohort from school to college and then into training, work or higher education. In my use of these approaches I want to plot the social and educational biographies and 'careership' of these five young men and seven young women to suggest their experiences are interesting and complex. It is difficult to do full justice to this here so as much factual detail as possible has been included in Table 11.1 and 11.2.

However, I have extracted from the study five or six key experiences or 20 turning points which may be useful to teachers, educationalists and policy makers in indicating the processes involved in changing learner identities and including the excluded. Table 11.1 shows that only three students were unambiguously working class using the Hope/Goldthorpe categories.[3] This raises the question: were these students truly disadvantaged? Was this yet another policy, like the assisted places scheme (Edwards, Fitz and Whitty, 1989) aimed at working-class pupils but highjacked by the service class? However, the complex interactions of students' social and educational experiences, gender and ethnicity indicate patterns of disadvantage. Two examples serve to illustrate this. Tim's parents and Lisa's mother are service class. Tim was an adopted child. He described himself as black British and his parents were white British. Lisa was a single mother at seventeen who worked part-time at a local Community Centre to support herself and her daughter through college and higher education. Both had identified with the working-class culture, shared by other members of this cohort, where it was considered 'uncool' to work hard and achieve academically. All the students attended inner city comprehensives in Northside or surrounding boroughs. All had under-achieved at school, only five of them had the requisite number of GCSEs to enrol for A levels at Northside College (see Table 11.2). Even these students felt that they would require extra support to succeed. Northside's secondary schools have always had a poor profile in terms of examination results and have persistently been near the bottom of the national examination league tables.[4] As a proxy indicator of

Table 11.1: *Social biographies of the cohort*

Name	Gender	Parental occupations	Self-described ethnicity	Religion
Ade	F	Businessman Caterer and night nurse	Black African	Pentecostal Christian
Danny	M	Psychiatric nurse Unemployed nurse	Black British	None
Denise	F	Postroom worker Housewife	Black British	Worldwide Church of God
Eleni	F	Insurance agent Secretary/interpreter	Greek British	None
Kit	F	Unemployed electrician; Machinist	Afro-Caribbean	Seventh-Day Adventist
Lisa	F	Van driver FE lecturer	White British	None
Lola	F	Minicab business Lift maintenance	Black African	Seventh-Day Adventist
Mark	M	Shop owner Therapist	Anglo French	None
Max	M	Retired seamstress	Black British	Christian
Seth	M	Health visitor	Black African	Seventh-Day Adventist
Tim	M	Senior civil servant Registrar in HE	Black British	None
Zelda	F	Primary teacher	Black British	Mildly religious

social and economic disadvantage the Local Education Authority uses the number of pupils eligible for free school meals.[5] Poverty is rendered somewhat invisible by the borough's affluent image. In reality, deprivation and poverty exist alongside extreme wealth and privilege. Additionally, strikes, high teacher turnover and amalgamations also badly affected the secondary schooling of this cohort.

Turning points

For this cohort deciding to apply to Northside College was a 'turning point' (Hodkinson *et al,* 1996). 'Such turning points occur when an individual has to 'take stock, to re-evaluate, revise, re-scc and re-judge' (Strauss, 1962). This decision to stay on post 16 despite under-achieving educationally resulted from several factors but mainly the realization that there were no appropriate jobs in the local labour market as well as a recognition that they needed to get themselves some qualifications. Their choice of Northside was

Table 11.2: *Career trajectories of the HE Link Course*

Name	GCSEs at school A–C	GCSEs at North-side	A level results	HEFE or work	Degree/ Certificate result	Employment
Ade	5	2	Sociology E Psychology E	Polytechnic Law	2:2 Law	Trainee accountant
Danny	5	1	English C Sociology C	Polytechnic English – transferred to Law	2:1 Law	Clerk in solicitor's office
Denise	4	1	Business Studies E English E	NNEB course in FE	NNEB	Nursery nurse
Eleni	O	3	Media Studies D Photography E	Art & Design (left in 1st year); Media Studies	NNEB	Nursery nurse
Kit	O	4	Sociology D English D	University Sociology	2:2	Professional gospel singer
Lisa	2	1	Art D Politics D Sociology C	Polytechnic Psycho-social Studies	2:1	Account handler in advertising agency
Lola	1	3	Sociology E English D	Resit A levels in FE – got 2 Bs	2:2 Broadcast Journalism	Temp and Media work
Mark	O	4	Media Studies C Politics N	Professional footballer	n/a	Professional footballer
Max	3	2	Politics U Psychology N	Work in supermarket and DJ	n/a	Various p/t work
Seth	6	1	Media Studies E Art E	Resit A levels in FE	to complete 1999 Media Studies	Member of a rap band
Tim	3	3	Politics E Geography E	Polytechnic, Town Planning	2:2	Works in a planning office
Zelda	4	1	Media Studies C English D	Year out to work on a newspaper; then University, Media Studies	2:1	P/t temp work in Media/TV

'pragmatically rational' (Hodkinson *et al*, 1996). For some it came on the recommendation of 'significant others' like friends or brothers and sisters who had attended and liked it. For others they heard 'it had a good reputation', 'exam results were good', 'you were treated like an adult'.

Seven of the students spent an extra year before embarking on the HE Link Course doing GCSEs. They were guided by the staff into doing interesting and relevant one-year GCSEs like Media Studies, Community Studies, Law, Theatre Studies, Psychology, rather than resits of their school subjects. This was also a 'turning point' in which they gained confidence and began to see themselves as potential A level students. Their 'learner identities' began to change significantly. Tim describes this transformation after getting two B grades and a C for Mathematics:

> I didn't think I was entitled to you know ... but it really made me think about it ... what work is and what it can achieve ... after passing more GCSEs. That really made me believe in myself ... that I could pass exams so ... that's why I decided to do my A levels. I knew I could do something ... I could work here.

This GCSE year was also a year in which teachers and tutors could identify potential A level students who would benefit from the HE Link. In career terms this opportunity was crucial. Students appreciated the opportunity to have a 'second go' or 'a fresh start'. These courses were well resourced and taught and students could achieve good grades. This opportunity was clearly more fruitful than making inappropriate, early, vocational choices because of the label 'non-academic'.

Other 'turning points'

Student biographies indicate other 'turning points', pregnancy for Lisa, being thrown out of home for Max, illness, particularly sickle cell anaemia, for Lola and Max, moving from Nigeria to London for Ade, parental divorce for Mark. These indicate that post 16, indeed all careers, are educational, occupational and domestic. Interestingly Lisa stressed that having Jade, her daughter, made her even more determined to succeed:

> There's no decision there. You don't think about how difficult it's going to be, you just do it. So having a child was never really a hindrance, because I grew up doing it. I always had her and it gave me the push, because I thought if I don't do something then I'm going to have no money and I'm going to have no lifestyle.

This is clearly at odds with the pathologization of young single mothers as feckless and on route to social exclusion.

Redistributing cultural capital

Students realized as they embarked on a two-year course that to avoid humiliating failure at the end of it they were going to need as much support as they could get. Danny described the HE Link Course, 'it was a kind of ... insurance blanket ... a sure-fire way of getting into HE which of course was my objective.' Part of this insurance blanket was to provide students with some of the cultural capital, particularly the confidence, they needed to succeed educationally which they did not get at home. Firstly, being on the course gave them the 'right' to this support, 'It's really good to have a set time when you can bug them (the teachers) as much as you want and they are actually being paid to be bugged . . . rather than just doing it in their lunch hour' (Lisa). Several students mentioned just how important this support from tutors was and that they would not have succeeded without it, 'The teacher who's running the Link Course is quite supportive to you for personal problems as well as with problems with your work and they are always pushing and willing for you to do well which is good for some people who don't have that outside college' (Kit).

Kit refers here to the interaction between familial habitus and institutional habitus (Reay, 1998a). The institution successfully made up for knowledge and dispositions not present at home but necessary to unlock the code of succeeding at A level and applying to higher education. Despite the robust support from working-class parents for their children to do well in the educational system, students repeatedly explained that their parents had no real idea what was involved and seemed to have a fear of engaging in the process. This possibly stems from their own negative educational experiences and for the ethnic minority parents even if they possessed cultural capital it was in the wrong currency (Reay, 1998a; Gerwitz, Ball, Bowe, 1994).

The college culture

Applying to higher education was a 'nightmare' for most students without the support from parents who understood the system. Reay (1998b) describes the pitfalls for working-class students making choices about higher education: 'They are having to negotiate increasingly complex, differentiated educational fields in which they have widely disparate access to the range of resources necessary to de-code the field.' To support students in this process a Higher Education Conference was held with representatives from universities running workshops to describe and explain their degree offers. Former successful students from different ethnic and social class backgrounds were invited back to give 'real' accounts of life in higher education. These conferences were very successful in challenging notions that it was 'uncool' to go onto higher education. John Barton, the careers adviser attached to the HE Link course was also available to answer questions and give advice about progression routes. Students were given help with applications and mock interviews. They attended lectures at Northside University to provide a taste of higher education. John Barton's knowledge of the institutions of higher education and progression routes was impressive. He had a very positive relationship with students:

> I think basically we are trying to help them realize what is possible for them and help them to aspire higher. That always seems to me to be the ethos of the place. Together with the fact that we offer as much encouragement and support along the way as we can; which is not the characteristic of other educational institutions I've worked in.
>
> (John Barton)

The institutional habitus of Northside made it 'cool' for everyone to go on to higher education. This was a function of the truly comprehensive nature of the place and the social class mix helped to create this culture: 'There was a core of middle-class students for whom it was an expectation, and that all sort of rubbed off on everyone else. And that all added to the positive atmosphere from the institution' (John Barton).

The discourses of disadvantage

Student data indicates some criticisms of the course. Firstly what I have called 'the discourses of disadvantage'. Discourses frame what can be said and thought and establish discursive limitations; policies like this should offer possibilities for 'thinking otherwise'. The HE Link illustrates such constraints and possibilities. Both staff and students were uneasy with the discourses of 'disadvantage'. Such discourses were the only ways available of talking and thinking about students' positioning in a system that had disadvantaged them. Attempts to establish alternative equal opportunities or social justice discourses floundered against the stronger discourses in the world outside the college. This highlights a very real problem for policies which target 'disadvantaged' students. Students are immediately labelled as different. In recognizing their 'difference' and their needs and providing some kind of positive discrimination in terms of resources the policy may in fact disadvantage them further. One student in particular felt very stigmatized by the course:

> I always have this feeling that especially in lessons that there is a stigma attached to the Link course. I think that some people have told me that they feel inferior . . .when they go into a class . . . they are on the Link and they know that the majority of students in that class aren't and they are doing three A levels . . . and I think they feel inferior . . . and I think the teachers make them feel like that. I think there is a stigma attached and I think that the teachers who teach on the Link are fully aware of that.

> (Danny)

He felt that this was a legacy from secondary school where any pupil requiring extra help or support had been regarded as 'thick or dumb'. Changing this culture was difficult. However, not all the students felt stigmatized and some students indicated that their peers were jealous of the support and encouragement and felt it should be available to all students. Lisa parodied the teachers' unease:

> And also when the teachers explain to others what the Link is, it is really funny because they have to be careful with their choice of words . . . they can't say it's all these deprived kids . . . and they need an extra push so they've got to say it's people that need a bit of extra help because they've got problems at home . . . you know they don't know what to say. That's funny.

> (Lisa)

Inflexible links

The second main criticism was the limited nature of the HE links. Many of the students had been attracted to the course because it offered an insurance offer of two E grades at three institutions in higher education. However, when they actually came to decide on a degree course those in the scheme were not what they wanted. However the success of the HE Link course resulted in careers staff setting up a University Network Scheme for all students in the college applying to HE. The Network Scheme[6] was an important first-order effect of the HE Link policy.

Origins and destinations

It is impossible within the space here to complete the student trajectories after college in detail. Their 'careership' tended to be characterized by stops, starts, disruptions, interruptions, years repeated, career changes and incomplete modules. However, by the summer of 1997 seven out of the 12 students had successfully completed degrees and two had completed their NNEB courses. Students' experiences of higher education indicate that they were unable to put to good use the skills of collaborative learning which were acquired on the HE Link course. The structures and culture of higher education worked against this, suggesting that these institutions had not become responsive to the needs of non-traditional A level students in terms of curriculum and pedagogy. The level of support provided at Northside was sorely missed as Lisa's mother indicates:

> I think there is a conflict with taking more and more people in universities, it means that the actual amount of support decreases. If she hadn't had me, I don't know what she would say. Because it was a problem for her the first year at university because she came from Northside College, where she had a lot of adults interested, and she did really appreciate the tutors and suddenly there was nothing. She didn't even go in the library for the first year, she said she was too scared.

In terms of employment only three of the graduates had graduate employment, though none of the cohort was unemployed.

Conclusion: lessons for 'the third way'

What lessons does this history of Access education have for current discourses and practices concerned to develop a 'third way' approach to educational policy? This 'third way' approach claims to reject the free market model favoured by the 'new right' and the over-centralized state control of the 'old left'. It attempts to take some of the values of the 'old left' like social justice, community and solidarity and rework them to meet the requirements of a new global, post-modern world. However, it was the values of the 'old left' that informed some of the early Access initiatives, 'a self-created collective movement from below. . . designed to transform a whole social system' (Parry, 1996). As I have described, since the 1970s, the Access education movement has expanded and suffered from derision, regulation and control. A great deal has been lost in the process. Much of the earlier flexibility and diversity of outcomes has gone and commitments to equity and empowerment have been watered down. Higher education has not been transformed from below by the presence of a new type of student. Massification has occurred but an increase in numbers does not ensure a radical change in ethos and pedagogy. In its private instincts higher education is still elitist, and applying Labour's commitment to 'high quality education for the many rather than excellence for the few', in higher education will require real commitment rather than clever rhetoric. Firstly, if in the absence of resources for all, targeting must also take place, then as Wakefield (1993) and Modood (1993) indicate, careful statistical monitoring must take place to determine exactly who are the excluded groups and how they can be encouraged to take advantage of Access education. Secondly, though the recent changes to 16–19 qualifications are welcome, it is necessary for both A levels and vocational qualifications, or combinations of both, to be acceptable to admissions tutors in all institutions to ensure entry for a wider range of students and to break down middle-class domination of the most prestigious institutions. This could be ensured through funding mechanisms. Thirdly, possibly the biggest threat to the participation in higher education of such groups is the institutionalization of student loans and the culture of self-finance that could deter working-class students.

At a more focused level what are we are to learn from the 'careership' of the cohort in my study? They benefited from attending a well-resourced institution with good learning support mechanisms and a dedicated, committed staff. The truly comprehensive nature of the college created an institutional habitus of academic success and the normalization of progression onto higher education. Without policies like the HE Link course a number of students, written off in their secondary schools as non-academic, would not have progressed on to higher and further education.

However, in 1996 the HE Link course was discontinued. After Northside College was removed from local authority control, new funding arrangements were complex and budget cuts occurred making the double staffing and extra support difficult to sustain. So this route to higher education no longer exists. It could be argued that massification has rendered it redundant but it was the learning support and the redistribution of cultural capital that was as vital to students' success as the assured places in higher education. Their experiences also add weight to the rejection by Hodkinson and Sparkes (1995) of new-right market models that are being incorporated into New Labour's 'third way':

> The new individualist market paradigm for education and training is, at best, a dangerous rhetorical illusion. Successful policy, which is genuinely aimed at raising education and training standards for all and/or empowering even the most disadvantaged young people, must be built on a better understanding of real social processes and contexts, in all their confusing complexity.

Notes

1. The term Access education is used throughout this chapter. It is derived from Parry (1996) and is used because it is flexible and broad enough to cover the diversity and complexity of schemes and to signify wider aims than purely progression to higher education.
2. Habitus is a concept which usefully brings together the ways in which individual subjective beliefs, dispositions and bodily ways of being as well as the social structure influence human action.
3. The Hope/Goldthorpe classification uses 36 categories of occupations which it combines into seven groups and three broad classes – Service Class, Intermediate Class and Working Class.
4. The number of Northside 16-year-olds gaining more than five A*–C grades in GCSE examinations in 1995 was 22.8 per cent compared to 26.3 per cent for Inner London and 39 per cent nationally (Source, Northside School Examination Results).
5. In 1996 the average for Northside Secondary Schools was 49.6 per cent compared to Inner London average of 49.6 per cent and a Greater London average of 33.1 per cent (Form 7 1996 Secondary School total).
6. It was established in 1992 so that all Northside College students who applied to higher education could benefit from links made with institutions that had undertaken to consider their applications very carefully.

References

Benn, R and Burton, R (1995) Access and targeting: an exploration of a contradiction, *International Journal of Lifelong Education*, **14** (6), pp 444–58

Benn, R and Fieldhouse, R (1991) Adult education to the rescue in Thatcherite Britain, in *Adult Education in Crisis Situations*, ed F Poggeler and K Yaron, Magnes, Jerusalem

Betts, D (1996) The formation of a national sector of incorporated colleges, in *Beyond the FEFC Model*, ed K Spours and N Lucas, Working Paper 19, Post-16 Education Centre, University of London Institute of Education

Bourdieu, P and Passeron, J C (1977) *Reproduction in Education, Society and Culture,* Sage, London

Bourner, T and Hamed, M (1987) *Entry Qualifications and Degree Performance*, CNNA Development Services publication

Bowe, R and Ball, S with Gold, A (1992) *Reforming Education and Changing Schools: Case studies in policy sociology*, Routledge, London

Chitty, C (1991) *Post-16 Education: Studies in access and achievement*, Kogan Page, London

Department of Education and Science (DES) (1978) Special courses in preparation for entry to higher education, *Letter to Chief Education Officers*, 2 August

DES (1985) Academic Validation in Public Sector Higher Education: The Report of the Committee of Enquiry into the Academic Validation of Degree Courses in Public Sector Higher Education (Lindop Report), HMSO, London

DES (1987) *Higher Education: Meeting the Challenge*, HMSO, London

DES/DFE *Statistical Bulletins*, 1988–1992, HMSO, London

Edwards, E, Fitz, J and Whitty, G (1989) *The State and Private Education: An evaluation of the assisted places scheme*, The Falmer Press, London

Egerton, M and Halsey, A H (1993) *Oxford Review of Education*, **19** (2), pp 183–96

Gerwitz, S, Ball, S and Bowe, R (1994) Parents, privilege and the education market-place, *Research Papers in Education*, **9** (1), pp 3–29

Green, M and Percy, P (1991) Gender and access, in *Post-16 Education: Studies in access and achievement*, ed C Chitty, London Education Studies, Kogan Page, London

Higginson Committee (1988) *Advancing A Levels*, HMSO, London

Hodkinson, P and Sparkes, C (1995) Markets and vouchers: the inadequacy of individualist policies for vocational education and training in England and Wales, *Journal of Educational Policy*, **10**, pp 189–207

Hodkinson, P and Sparkes, A C (1997) Careership: a sociological theory of career decision making, *British Journal of Sociology of Education*, **18** (1), pp 29–44

Hodkinson, P, Sparkes, A C and Hodkinson, H (1996) *Triumphs and Tears: Young people, markets and the transition from school to work*, David Fulton Publishers, London

Home Office (1997) *The West Indian Community*, The Stationery Office, London

John, G (1981) *In the Service of Black Youth: A study of the political culture of youth and community work with black people in English cities*, NAYC Publications, Leicester

Kearney, A and Diamond, J (1990) Access courses: a new orthodoxy?, *Journal of Further and Higher Education*, **14** (1), pp 128–38

Lieven, M (1989) Access courses after ten years: a review, *Higher Education Quarterly*, **43** (2), pp 161–74, Spring

Millins, P K C (1984) *Access Studies to Higher Education: September 1979–December 1983*, A report, Roehampton Institute, Centre For Access Studies to Higher Education

Modood, T (1993) The number of ethnic minority students in British higher education: some grounds for optimism, *Oxford Review of Education*, **19** (2), pp 167–82

Parry, G (1996) Access education in England and Wales 1973–1994: from second chance to third wave, *Journal of Access Studies*, **11** (1), pp 10–33

Parry, G and Percy, K (1995) Licensed partnership: state, region and institution in the regulation of Access education in England 1987–1992, *Higher Education,* **29** (1–18)

Reay, D (1998a) *Class Work: Mothers' involvement in their children's primary schooling*, UCL Press, London

Reay, D (1998b) 'Always knowing and never being sure': familial and institutional habituses and higher education choice, *Journal of Educational Policy* (forthcoming)

Rimington, M (1992) Access courses at City and East London College, in *Beyond Qualifications: Alternatives routes to higher and further education*, Unified Post-16 Curriculum Series, vol 2, pp 23–31, Institute of Education, London

Scott, P (1995) *The Meanings of Mass Higher Education*, SRHE and Open University Press, Buckingham

Smith, D, Scott, P and McKay, L (1993) Mission impossible? Access and the dash for growth in British higher education, *Higher education Quarterly*, **47** (4), pp 316–33

Smithers, A and Robinson, P (1989) *Increasing Participation in Higher Education*, School of Education, BP Educational Service, University of Manchester

Strauss, A (1962) Transformations of identity, in *Human Behaviour and Social Processes: An interactionist approach,* ed A M Rose, Routledge and Kegan Paul, London

Wakefield, N (1993) Beyond educating Rita: mature students and Access courses, *Oxford Review of Education*, **19** (2), pp 217–30

The West Indian Community (1977), Home Office, London

Whitty, G, Power, S and Halpin, D (1998) *Devolution and Choice in Education: The school, the state and the market*, Open University Press, Buckingham

12

Some Reflections on the Concepts of Social Exclusion and Inclusion: Beyond the Third Way

Michael Young

Introduction

Overcoming social exclusion has become a major policy goal for the New Labour government; its high profile is evident in the decision to establish a Social Exclusion Unit in 10 Downing Street. The new focus can be seen as having at least two important political objectives. First, it clearly differentiates the government's policies from those of the Conservative Party who are still unable to free themselves from being identified with the Thatcherite view that those at the bottom of society are there as a result of their own individual inadequacies. Second, a focus on social inclusion equally clearly differentiates New Labour politics from old. It is, Giddens (1998) suggests, a way of updating or modernizing the commitment to reducing inequality that has at the centre of Labour ideals since the party was founded.

This chapter welcomes the new focus on social exclusion in that it highlights the predicament of a section of society that is both objectively poor and, in political terms, given its relatively small size and propensity not to vote, in danger of being forgotten. Furthermore, it follows Giddens's analysis in linking social exclusion closely to poverty and the conditions facing people in the inner cities without jobs or qualifications.[1] However, it is one thing to highlight the problem but quite another to diagnose its causes and propose effective remedies. I shall argue that, if solutions to the problem of social exclusion focus only on an identifiable 'excluded' group, they are doomed to failure just as countless compensatory education policies for the disadvantaged have failed in the past. In developing this argument, I shall begin by examining how Anthony Giddens, often seen as New Labour's leading intellectual analyses social exclusion in his recent book *The Third Way* (Giddens, 1998). I shall go on to point to discrepancies between what he proposes and what is emerging as government policy. In reconceptualizing the problem of social inequality in terms of social exclusion, Giddens seeks a way of dealing with it that avoids the conservatism of Old Labour and the inadequacies of market-based alternatives.

On the other hand, the priority given to overcoming social exclusion by the government appears more to do with holding together its various electoral constituencies. Second, I shall examine some of the limitations of Giddens's own analysis and its inherent ambiguities that allow the contradictions of government policy 'off the hook'. Finally, I propose a different approach that draws on one of Giddens's own ideas – the concept of reflexive modernization (Giddens, 1994; Beck, Giddens and Lash, 1994). In his earlier work, Giddens argued that modern societies are 'risk producing' as well as wealth producing. The concept of reflexive modernization directs us to the processes inherent in modernization that produce what Giddens refers to as 'manufactured risks'. His examples point particularly to the environmental problems generated by the application of modern science and technology. I shall extend the idea of modern societies being 'risk producing' to suggest that social exclusion can itself be seen as a 'manufactured risk'. In the final section of the chapter, I shall, in relation to the educational manifestations of social exclusion, suggest an alternative approach that would involve (a) reconceptualizing the internal organization of schools and their relationships with their environment and (b) linking the real experiences and predicaments of those who are excluded to the conditions that produced their exclusion. This is a very different 'Third Way' from that espoused by the present government and one with significantly different implications from the approach developed by Giddens in his recent book of that title.

Social exclusion and Giddens's Third Way politics

Giddens sees social inclusion as at the core of a 'Third Way' politics; he argues that it should be a major focus of what he refers to the 'social investment state'. He suggests that giving priority to overcoming social exclusion can be seen as a way of modernizing the redistributive approach to inequality traditionally adopted by Labour. At the same time, a focus on overcoming social exclusion is clearly differentiated from meritocratic approaches to inequality that he associates with neo-liberal policies based on markets. Meritocracy represents a clear challenge, at least in principle, to any system based on inherited privilege. It is understandable, therefore, that it has always been attractive to some on the Left as a system in which people are rewarded for their capabilities. However, as Giddens points out, any attempt to make meritocracy *the* principle for the distribution of wealth in society is doomed intellectually and politically. It would not only produce an increasingly disaffected underclass, but is itself contradictory; the more privileged groups in society would inevitably seek to confer advantages on their own children, thus undermining the principle of meritocracy. Furthermore, as the 1997 General Election demonstrated, a political party which even hints that it might endorse the kind of 'winner takes all' politics that is the logic of a meritocracy would be an electoral disaster.

The Labour Party's traditional approach to reducing inequalities was in principle, if not often in practice, redistributive. The Party's goal in the past was to minimize general social and economic inequalities through the tax system. It was also committed, though not unambiguously, to reducing the more specific forms of educational inequality by arguing for the abolition of the various mechanisms that were available to the more privileged sections of society to confer advantages on their children. Selective grammar schools within the state system and fee-paying private schools are the classic examples. For Giddens and New Labour, such a redistributive approach has been rendered out of date by the political consequences of the economic changes of recent decades. When two-thirds of the working population were employed as manual workers in industry on relatively low wages, redistributing the wealth of society from the minority to the majority made electoral sense and was what the Labour Party was founded to achieve. However, with the proportion of manual workers falling to less than one in five, a growing section of society is likely to see redistribution as something from which it would not benefit, at least not directly. The political rationale for the dropping by New Labour of its redistributive approach is that it is difficult to see where the electoral support for it would lie, even at the level of general principle, when 'the poor' are a minority rather than a majority. However, regardless of whether one accepts this rather instrumental view of politics, there are pragmatic reasons why Giddens's concept of a Third Way for social democracy has to be taken seriously.

Despite the claims for meritocracy from the Tory Right and the long term opposition within the Labour Party both to grammar schools in the state system and the privileges of the public schools, over 150 grammar schools still remain and the proportion of children sent to fee-paying schools has shown little sign of falling. Furthermore, not only, as research for the Dearing Report on Higher Education showed, has the *proportion* of students from working-class families entering university shifted little since the Second World War, but the gaps in attainment between the successful and failing schools are increasing not decreasing (Pearce and Hillman, 1998). This pattern of polarization is repeated, as Whitty *et al* (Chapter 4) show in housing and health care. In other words the problem, whether it is described as inequality or social exclusion, remains and is, if anything, growing despite existing policies of both Right and Left. A Third Way politics that focuses directly on the problem of social exclusion, in all its manifestations, at least offers an alternative approach. The key question, on which Giddens and government policy makers seem in less than total agreement, is what is meant by social exclusion. For Giddens it refers to people being excluded from 'civil and political rights. . . (as a reality). . . (from) opportunities. . . (and from) involvement in public space'. The crucial *opportunities* from which people are excluded in our society remain, for Giddens, work and education. It is from these, together with adequate health services and an infrastructure of public amenities including transport, that a growing section of those who live in the inner cities, and to a lesser extent elsewhere, are excluded.

Giddens describes the process of social exclusion as a mechanism for the detachment of certain groups from the mainstream of society. However, he makes an important additional point that appears to be missing from government policy statements. He sees exclusion as a *dual* process. At the top, the wealthy exclude themselves voluntarily from state-provided services – what has in the USA been called 'the revolt of the elite'. At the bottom, an excluded section of society fails to benefit from any services, public or private. Giddens recognizes that these two processes of exclusion are interdependent. For example, the falling quality of public services in the inner cities is a direct outcome of the withdrawal of support for them by growing numbers of relatively better off people. The logic of seeing social exclusion as a dual process, as Giddens explicitly recognizes, is that any programme for social *inclusion* must also be a dual process. Strategies have to be developed for including 'the top' as well as 'the bottom' of society within the mainstream of public provision. It follows, he argues, that public provision, including welfare, cannot be just a safety net targeted at the poor, as in the USA. Yet many of the government's policies – for example, the New Deal, Lifelong Learning and the University for Industry – are in serious danger of taking on exactly that character with, as Giddens points out, inevitably divisive outcomes. Furthermore, the Downing Street Social Exclusion Unit appears to be focusing on mapping only 'exclusion at the bottom' (IOE, 1999). There is no evidence from the documents produced by the Unit that it has even recognized, let alone is addressing the dual nature of social exclusion.

Exclusion 'at the top' and 'at the bottom' are interdependent in quite specific ways. Families with high enough incomes to afford alternatives avoid the state secondary schools in most inner London boroughs precisely because many of the pupils in such schools are from families who would, on any criteria, be classified as being among the excluded. In boroughs where better off families continue to use LEA secondary schools, they use the other mechanism available to them – moving into the catchment area of the best schools. Both processes are, as Giddens says, also self-reproducing – an echo of Sir Keith Joseph's 'cycle of deprivation' argument in the 1970s, although he seemed to forget the related 'cycle of wealth'. It is in not following up this argument about the interdependence of the two processes of exclusion that the ambiguity in Giddens's analysis appears. He states that 'any strategies which break poverty cycles should be pursued'. However, he fails to link examples of 'poverty cycles' to 'wealth cycles' in the way that would appear to follow from his argument about their interdependence. While noting that, 'investment in education is an imperative of government today, as a key basis. . . of. . . the 'redistribution of possibilities', Giddens recognizes that the education system largely reflects wider economic inequalities *which have to be tackled at source* (my italics). However, what 'tackling at source' might involve is not discussed and we are still left with the gap between 'possibilities' and their realization. Arguably, the problem of Old Labour – a focus on symptoms (inequality) not causes (the organization of the economy) is repeated in the new language of 'possibilities'. Without a theory of how exclusion is produced, policies, as was the case with Old Labour, can become a series of well intentioned but piecemeal reforms. Giddens's specific proposals illustrate this point well. He argues that:

- people should be involved in the labour force and not just dead-end jobs;
- the needs of those who cannot work should be provided for;
- policies for inclusion should 'stretch well beyond work';
- community-focused approaches to the eradication of poverty should be developed which permit more democratic participation;
- economic resources should be used to support local initiatives.

There is little to disagree with in these proposals, although they are hardly new. At a general level, the government would no doubt endorse them as principles and claim that they are reflected in current policies, albeit within the limits of available resources. The difficulty with them as principles is the almost intractable problems that they hide. First, they fail to make clear the magnitude of the resources that would be needed if social exclusion in the inner cities really was to be tackled. In other words, we are taken back to the issue of redistribution. The government would doubtless argue that it is not politically feasible to generate the kind of resources needed through the tax system. This leaves unanswered questions about the alternatives that could make Giddens's proposals realizable in practice. Second, Giddens's emphasis on the importance of community building and 'the cultivation of social capital' is a vital new ingredient in any policy for tackling social exclusion that was neglected in many previous policies that attempted to overcome social disadvantage. However, Giddens does not seem to realize the very great difficulties involved in putting such ideas into practice in areas where social capital is so obviously lacking (see Garmarnikow and Green, Chapter 3).

Social exclusion and Giddens's Third Way: some theoretical problems

There are number of theoretical problems with Third Way politics, as espoused by New Labour and as articulated by Giddens. First, in rejecting Old Labour's redistributive approach of 'tax and spend', and replacing it with one based on 'limiting both taxes and public spending', it fails to address the need for a new approach to wealth creation that might be the basis of an alternative approach to resourcing inclusion. It is, as it were, a new approach to social policy without a new approach to political economy. The implications of such a one-sided analysis are that it neglects the economic changes that would be necessary if new employment opportunities are to be created. The problem is illustrated in a practical way by the emphasis on employability in recent government education policy and the almost total neglect of demand-side factors that might generate employment

(Keep, 1998). New jobs, at least in inner London, tend to occur either in sectors such as security services and fast food restaurants which employ casualized low wage labour that does not need qualifications or in sectors such as financial services where the jobs are out of reach of the unemployed even if they achieve basic qualifications.

Secondly, Giddens fails to follow through a number of the key issues that it raises. These are, first, the interdependence of exclusion 'at the top' and at the bottom' referred to earlier. He describes social exclusion as a 'dual mechanism of detachment' but does not explain how 'detachment at the top' is related to 'detachment at the bottom'. Giddens recognizes the differences between the two processes but does not explore their policy implications. Whereas 'exclusion at the top' occurs as a result of voluntary choices on the part of the well-off who decide to opt out of public services, 'exclusion at the bottom' is forced on people by circumstances outside their control. New Labour's Third Way has rejected increasing taxes, the traditional method of limiting 'exclusion at the top' and resourcing the removal of exclusion at the bottom – the approach of relatively high-tax systems such as those found in the Nordic countries. It is striking that the most inclusive societies of Europe are those Nordic countries where private provision for health and education has the least significant role. With regard to solving the problem of 'exclusion at the bottom', government strategy is to make small amounts of additional resources available through policies such as the Education Action Zones (Power and Whitty, 1999). The strategy appears to rely largely on a combination of voluntary business support and the ability to help the excluded help themselves even though circumstances leave them with few choices. Self-help projects may enable a few families to find ways of leaving deprived inner city areas; it is inconceivable that they could be a basis for the massive transformation of those areas that is necessary. In lending support to the government's educational priorities for 'redistributing possibilities' Giddens poses the rhetorical question 'Who could gainsay that a well-educated population is desirable for any society?' However, he begs what may be the crucial question, as to what it means for a population to be well educated for the next century?

My conclusion is that Giddens's analysis is valuable in pointing to the interdependence of the two processes of exclusion and of the cumulative effects of inadequate education, housing, health and lack of more general social amenities. However, in not explaining the mechanism linking the two processes of exclusion, he provides little more than an outline of a strategy for overcoming them. The result is not a challenge to the piecemeal and one-dimensional nature of government policies that often seem a largely rhetorical attempt to show that they are doing something. This is not to imply that it would be easy to develop a really effective way of tackling exclusion that was at the same time politically feasible. The social problems associated with exclusion are endemic to modern societies and there are severe constraints on the political options which social-democratic governments feel able to take up. For example, however much one might argue for a substantial redistribution of wealth through the tax system, this is unlikely to be practical politics in the foreseeable future. This means that in any strategy for overcoming social exclusion there will be a discrepancy between the resources available and the resources needed. Furthermore, even with a really substantial redistribution of 'economic' capital, the lack of 'social' capital (see Gamarnikow and Green, Chapter 3) in excluded areas would have to be addressed. That said, however, it seems worth trying to separate, at least in theory, a sociological analysis of the problem of exclusion from a political analysis of the feasibility of different options for dealing with it. Giddens's analysis, as the subtitle of his book, *The Renewal of Social Democracy* indicates, is primarily concerned with the political issues facing social democratic parties in the light of the massive social and economic changes of the past decades. He is less directly concerned with how those same social changes might themselves have created the problem of social exclusion. It is in attempting to tackle this question that I now draw on one of Giddens's own ideas: the concept of reflexive modernization which he, with Scott Lash and Ulrich Beck (Beck, Giddens and Lash, 1994) developed both as an explanation of the process of industrialization and as a description of contemporary society.

Social exclusion and different concepts of modernization

Different attempts to explain the origins of social problems reflect the range of theoretical traditions in the social sciences and the very different world views in which they are embedded. The first attempt I shall refer to is what has been called *classical modernization*. From this perspective, social problems (both of the inner city and the environment more generally) are transitional issues for an old order turning into something new. Social problems are the necessary price of modernization and the enormous benefits associated with it that have resulted from the application of science and technology to human affairs. A current example of this approach is the government's response to uncomfortable research findings on the use of genetically modified crops. In so far as *classical modernization* offers a strategy for dealing with social problems, it is what Bowles and Gintis (1976) referred to many years ago as 'band-aid remedies' – or efforts to ameliorate the worst outcomes of modernization. This combination of seeing social problems as 'a necessary price of the benefits of modernization' and the provision of 'band-aid remedies' can be found in the policies of virtually all western governments of both Right and Left, although the balance of the combination has varied widely. The problem for *classical modernization* is that many of the 'problems' – those associated with inner cities are a good example – appear to be endemic and anything but transitional.

A second approach, which takes various forms all of which can be described as *Marxist,* argues that it is not modernization itself but the *capitalist form* that modernization has taken in all industrialized countries of the West that has led to problems such as social exclusion. Developed more as a critique of existing society than as a basis for a positive strategy for dealing with social problems, the only solution proposed by Marxists has been political – the overthrow of capitalism. However, the environmental, political and economic disaster of Eastern Europe, and the relative success of capitalist societies in alleviating the worst excesses of modernization, has destroyed the credibility of Marxist approaches for all but a few.

A third approach is to shift the explanation of social problems from the capitalist form of modernization to the whole modernizing project itself. Such critiques of modernization take a number of forms, of which I shall mention two. One is the group of ideas associated with 'post-modernism' that rejects any concept of general social progress or improvement based upon the application of science or other forms of expertise. However, in undermining the grounds for applying expert knowledge to human affairs, post modernism can only stand on the sidelines in relation to a social problem such as exclusion. It is perhaps not surprising, therefore, with the growth of popularity of post modernism in some intellectual circles, that public confidence in intellectuals is at such a low ebb. Another example of a critique of modernization is represented by the Green Movement. Green politics have been important in highlighting the unintended consequences of modernization that most governments would much prefer to ignore. However, when they move from critique to policy, as is indicated in the difficulties of the recently formed Green/Left coalition in Germany, Green politicians tend to focus on symptoms and not causes and neglect the extent to which modernization invariably brings with it both benefits and penalties. As a result, Green politics becomes little more than a 'politics of protest'.

Reflexive modernization theory represents yet another approach to the social problems generated by modernization. It argues that one outcome of the growth in the productive power of modern societies has been the growth of risks – economic, technological and ecological. These 'risks', as Giddens points out, can be distinguished from the 'risks' that beset pre-modern societies that for the most part had natural origins. For Giddens, the 'risks' of modernization are 'manufactured'; they are the systematic, albeit unintentional outcome of the process of modernization itself. Ulrich Beck (Beck, 1992) makes the useful distinction between two modes of thought which he associates with classical and reflexive modernization – *reflection* and *reflexivity*. Whereas reflection is the existing basis for increases in scientific knowledge, reflexivity, for Beck, involves: 'the self confrontation with the effects of risk society and its autonomous modernization processes which are blind and deaf to their own effects and threats'.

What are the implications of this distinction for the problem of social exclusion? Here I shall be concerned primarily with its economic and educational manifestations, although the implications of the analysis are much wider. Viewing social exclusion as a 'manufactured risk' of modern societies directs our attention away from the attributes of those who are excluded and from targeting programmes for them; it proposes that social exclusion should be seen as the direct outcome of certain modernizing trends.

Global competition between international companies and between national economies is increasing and businesses (and in some cases whole sectors of national economies) are being forced to improve the quality of their products and in some cases reduce their prices if they want to survive. To achieve these goals, more dedicated, more skilled and more knowledge-able workers are needed. This means that there are fewer and fewer jobs for those lacking such skills and knowledge and the economic basis is laid for the social exclusion from work of those without qualifications.

In parallel with these changes in work, and as a result of similar pressures, governments have become increasingly concerned with the accountability and quality of public services. In education, this trend is expressed in league tables and the emphasis placed by government on standards and target setting. Schools and colleges get measured and ranked according to the attainments reached by their students. For a considerable proportion of those in the 'middle quartiles' of each cohort, these changes have led to real gains; many get qualifications and growing numbers enter higher education who would not have reached anywhere near such a level in the recent past. The 'price' of this progress, however, is the growing marginalization of the educational failures. Whereas in the past those leaving school with no or few qualifications amounted to two out of three in each cohort, they now represent only around 10 per cent. The unqualified are thus becoming, in terms of access to employment or further education, an *excluded* group. In other words, educational exclusion, in the objective sense of a particular group being denied opportunities and in the subjective sense of their being marginal to mainstream society, can be seen as a product of the way that schools have become more 'modern' – in the sense of being more oriented to the specific goal of raising attainment. This process of exclusion is often portrayed by politicians and by Ofsted as a sign of the failure of particular schools and particular groups of pupils, which of course in a direct sense it is. However, this diagnosis gives a misleading message. First, it implies that the problem of educational exclusion can be dealt with as an educational problem when this is only how it is manifested in the schools. Second, in so far as educational strategies are suggested, these tend to be an extension of the modernizing methods that have 'created' the excluded group in the first place. For Ulrich Beck, reflexivity means: 'self confrontation with the effects of risk society *that cannot be dealt with and assimilated within the system of industrial society*' (my italics) and challenges both these notions. First, the focus on school strategies for overcoming exclusion neglects the extent to which schools and the social exclusion that they give rise to reflect the wider process of modernization; it thus deflects attention from causes to symptoms (see Mortimore and Whitty, Chapter 5). Second, a reflexive approach rejects the view that the problem of social exclusion, as 'an effect of risk society', can be dealt with by schools responding to the pressures they are under to raise attainment.

This emphasis on attainment in government policy has, despite raising the educational standards of the population as a whole, exaggerated the marginality of the 'failing group'. The increasing emphasis on measured outcomes makes schools concentrate more and more on examination results (and grades). This leads them to give more attention to those likely to achieve higher grades – especially those just below the Grade C level – and neglect those with lower grades or no grades at all, thus introducing a polarization between 'included' and 'excluded' students. This exclusion is not the result of a greater focus on standards of attainment *per se*, but of the approach to standards and raising attainment based on external measures and rankings. The more attention that is given, particularly by schools in disadvantaged areas, to improving their position in national league tables, the less time teachers have for developing new approaches to teaching and learning that might lead to real improvements in attainment by slower learners.

This approach to raising educational standards based on external monitoring, measurement and ranking that has been adopted by recent governments is an example of what elsewhere (1998) I have referred to as *technocratic modernization*. Reflexive modernization questions such an approach and asserts that the uncritical application of quantitative procedures to human affairs should be challenged, not by rejecting them but by counterposing them with new ways of making schools and colleges accountable that involve both their staff and the communities which they serve. John Stewart refers to this as enhancing 'the process of public learning' (Stewart, 1996). This is not an argument against league tables, tests or examinations. It does, however, point to their limitations in enhancing the educational role of schools and colleges. In Beck's (Beck, 1992) terms they represent a *reflective* rather than a *reflexive* approach to accountability and effectiveness and therefore they are likely, on their own, to generate as many problems as they solve. A *reflexive* approach would begin by considering how some existing approaches to making schools more accountable might be involved in producing the exclusion of certain groups of students. It points to an alternative that shares the goal of higher standards of attainment but not the means and would involve the staff of schools rethinking the internal organization and relationships of schools and the external links of schools with their environment. What this might mean and how it might contribute to the problem of exclusion are the issues to which I now turn.

Both the internal and external changes in schools suggested by a reflexive critique of modernization challenges the form of educational specialization: this refers to the process of concentrating highly valued activities such as learning into institutions such as schools with clearly defined and limited goals. The trend of ever greater *specialization* of different activities has been a dominant feature of the modernization of all societies over the last 150 years. In their efforts to achieve their goals, schools and colleges have taken on many of the characteristics of other bureaucracies – top-down and hierarchical management, rigid divisions of labour, clear boundaries between different activities and the insulation of the activities of schools from those outside. Like modern science, schools were, at least in theory, freed from nepotism and protected by their structure and recruitment methods from incompetence. However, as with all bureaucracies, their original goal became displaced and keeping the activities for which they were responsible *under their control* became the priority. In its extreme form this trend allows for the protection of vested interests; in its more benign form found in many schools and colleges, it can restrict information flows to a one-way process from headteacher to heads of department and down to classroom teachers and finally to students.

Bureaucratic models are increasingly under scrutiny in the business organizations where they originated. In the changing circumstances of late capitalism, leading-edge businesses are finding that they need the 'knowledge in the heads' of even their most junior employees (Morgan, 1988; Zuboff, 1988). Similarly, classroom teachers and pupils have access to many aspects of the learning process in schools that are not made available to headteachers or governors within existing hierarchical structures. The issue of the learning difficulties of those likely to become excluded is a case in point. Schools need to be given the opportunity to exploit the 'knowledge about learning' of classroom teachers and the pupils themselves which they have 'hidden' within their own boundaries. To make this possible government would have to place more trust in schools to take responsibility for raising standards, and step back from introducing more external measures and controls. The latter can only in the end exaggerate the problem by giving greater attention to recording and identifying incidences of exclusion rather than to the re-examination of the processes that might have led to it.

The second aspect of specialization over the whole period of the growth of mass schooling has been for educational policies to focus on the learning that goes on in schools and colleges. As higher proportions of each cohort gain qualifications, this trend exaggerates not only the marginality of those without qualifications but makes it less likely that the learning potential latent in contexts other than schools and colleges is realized (Young, 1998, 1999). One consequence of this 'schooling of learning', which has been widely commented on by employers, is affecting both school successes and school failures. In schools and colleges students learn, with varying degrees of success, how to pass examinations; however, they do not learn how to transfer their capacity to learn into contexts where learning is not the core activity. The 'included', or school successes, at least have the intellectual resources to overcome this lack of capacity to learn and to cope in workplaces that may offer limited opportunities for learning; the excluded or school failures lack even those resources and can be seen as doubly excluded. The importance of this new demand on those who leave schools (and colleges) whether as successes or failures gives a clue to a fresh approach to the problem of exclusion that is partially grasped in the recently fashionable idea of lifelong learning. Much of the new talk about lifelong learning is of course rhetorical. However, it does have a kernel of truth in it which has relevance to the problem of social exclusion.

Learning and the production of knowledge have always been at the heart of how societies reproduce themselves, particularly during the process of modernization. In the past these processes have only explicitly involved a relatively small section of the society – entrepreneurs and those concerned with research and development. The remainder of the population was left to undertake various types of routine work. As opportunities for these forms of routine work became less, the form of reproduction that was geared to selecting a small section of the society with the capacity to innovate also produced an excluded group who found it difficult to gain employment. In other words the recent and more technological phase of modernization and the selection processes that are intrinsic to it produced the two types of exclusion described by Giddens – 'exclusion at the top' and 'exclusion at the bottom'. This divisive form of specialization is beginning to be challenged by the demands of global competition which require the majority, not the minority of the population to be involved in learning and the production of knowledge. Such an alternative, which elsewhere I have conceptualized as connective specialization (Young, 1998), would involve new kinds of links between the processes of learning and knowledge production in schools, colleges and universities and learning in workplaces and communities. This is not an argument for community service or extended periods of work experience, although both can have an educational role (Griffiths and Guile, 1999). It is an argument for a new curriculum that extends the learning goals of schools and colleges from a largely internal focus on the attainment of their students in examinations to a broader educational role that links learning in school with learning in society as a whole. Such new curriculum goals and the relationships to work-based learning that they imply could provide schools and colleges with a framework for enabling students to develop into lifelong learners. At the same time such a curriculum with its links to the world outside school would make schools less likely to produce an excluded group, disaffected from the curriculum with its and any kind of learning. The new links, however, would have to be two way and would depend on changes in the attitudes of employers to their own employees and to the schools and colleges from which they recruit new staff. In other words overcoming social exclusion is as much an economic and political as an educational issue.

Conclusion

In the final section of this chapter I argued that reflexive modernization offers an approach to the problem of social exclusion, not by targeting directly the excluded groups but by beginning (in the case of educational exclusion) where the exclusion begins: namely within the schools and in their relationships to the outside world. This approach, which draws on Beck and Giddens's concept of reflexive modernization, I have referred to as *connective specialization*; it involves new relationships between schools and employers and between school-based and work-based learning. It agrees with Third Way politics that the pleas for redistribution that were a feature of Old Labour are unrealistic and self defeating. On the other hand, the Third Way approach to overcoming social exclusion, as is indicated by Power and Whitty's analysis of Education Action Zones (Power and Whitty, 1999), seems unlikely to have much impact and is certainly unable to address the growing social inequalities.

Reflexive modernization does not suggest any quick or easy solution to social exclusion; the patterns of thinking and practice, as well as the interests that are involved in creating it, are deeply embedded. Its claim to offer the basis of a more effective strategy rests on a number of its implications. First, it reminds us that, like other 'risks' of modernization, exclusion is something that is socially produced and therefore not out of our control. Second, it builds on Giddens's idea that social exclusion is a dual process and that 'exclusion at the top' and 'exclusion at the bottom' are interdependent. Competitive modern economies will require those 'at the top' as well as those 'at the bottom' to have an interest in improving the quality of public services; this involves overcoming both forms of exclusion – 'at the top' and 'at the bottom'. Finally, in shifting the focus on social exclusion from its symptoms to its origins, and in locating those origins in the process of modernization, it warns against any strategy that focuses only on education. The Prime Minister's claim in the recent Green Paper *The Learning Age* (DfEE, 1998) that 'education is the best economic policy that we have' is more likely to reflect what he thinks the government has control over than a new confidence that educational policies can act against rather than reflect economic inequalities.

The approach to overcoming social exclusion that I have suggested shifts the debate from what to do about the victims of modernization to the broader issue of modernization itself and the form it takes. It goes beyond improvements in education to the need for *new relationships between* education and the rest of society, in particular, but not only the world of work. Company competitiveness strategies, therefore, are as important as school strategies for raising attainment. This is not an argument for a return to the forms of economic intervention of the 1960s and 1970s. It is, however, a recognition that ownership and incentives do matter and the current way that we regulate private enterprise is not the only alternative to old-style State intervention. The political implications of these conclusions take us far beyond anything currently contemplated by New Labour and suggest that Giddens's Third Way is at best a first step in his goal of renewing social democracy.

Acknowledgements

I am very grateful for comments by Toni Griffiths, David Guile and Geoff Whitty on earlier drafts of this chapter.

Notes

1. Social exclusion can, as is demonstrated in other chapters in this book, be used more broadly to encompass the variety of ways in which modern societies exclude particular groups.

References

Beck, U (1992) *The Risk Society,* Sage, London

Beck, U, Giddens, A and Lash, S (1994) *Reflexive Modernization,* Polity Press, Cambridge

Bowles, S and Gintis, H (1976) *Schooling in Capitalist America,* Basic Books, New York

DfEE (1998) *The Learning Age: A renaissance for a new Britain,* Cm 3790, Department for Education and Employment, London

Giddens, A (1994) *Beyond Left and Right,* Polity Press, Cambridge

Giddens, A (1998) *The Third Way: The renewal of social democracy,* Polity Press, Cambridge

Griffiths, T and Guile, D (1999) Pedagogy and learning in work-based contexts, in *Pedagogy and its Impact on Learning,* ed P Mortimer, Sage, London

IOE (1999) *Response to Consultation by the Downing Street Social Exclusion Unit on the Participation of 16–19-year-olds in Education, Training and Employment,* Institute of Education, University of London

Keep, E (1998) Changes in the economy and the labour market: We are all knowledge workers now, in *Work and Education,* Report of Post-16 Network Conference, Post-16 Education Centre, Institute of Education, University of London

Morgan, G (1988) *Images of Organization,* Sage, London

Pearce, N and Hillman, J (1998) *Wasted Youth: Raising achievement and tackling social exclusion,* Institute of Public Policy Research, London

Power, S and Whitty, G (1999) *New Labour's Education Policy: First, Second or Third Way?* Paper presented to the 8th Quasi-Market Seminar, University of Bath, 6–7 January

Stewart, J (1996) Thinking collectively in the public domain, *Soundings,* (4), Lawrence and Wishart, London

Young, M F D (1998) *The Curriculum of the Future: From the new sociology of education to a critical theory of learning,* Falmer, London

Young, M F D (1999) *Knowledge, Learning and the Curriculum of the Future,* Institute of Education, University of London

Zuboff, S (1988) *In the Age of the Smart Machine,* Heinemann, London

Index